HUME'S PROBLEM: INDUCTION AND THE JUSTIFICATION OF BELIEF

COLIN HOWSON offers a solution to one of the central, unsolved problems of Western philosophy, the problem of induction. In the mid-eighteenth century David Hume argued that successful prediction tells us nothing about the truth of the predicting theory. No matter how many experimental tests a hypothesis passes, nothing can be legitimately inferred about its truth or probable truth. But physical theory routinely predicts the values of observable magnitudes to many places of decimals and within very small ranges of error. The chance of this sort of predictive success without a true theory seems so remote that the possibility should be dismissed. This suggests that Hume's argument must be wrong; but there is still no consensus on where exactly the flaw in the argument lies. Howson argues that there is no flaw, and examines the implications of this disturbing conclusion for the relation between science and its empirical base.

Hume's Problem

Induction and the Justification of Belief

COLIN HOWSON

CLARENDON PRESS · OXFORD

2000

OXFORD

UNIVERSITY PRESS

Great Clarendon Street, Oxford OX2 6DP

Oxford University Press is a department of the University of Oxford.
It furthers the University's objective of excellence in research, scholarship,
and education by publishing worldwide in

Oxford New York

Athens Auckland Bangkok Bogotá Buenos Aires Calcutta
Cape Town Chennai Dar es Salaam Delhi Florence Hong Kong Istanbul
Karachi Kuala Lumpur Madrid Melbourne Mexico City Mumbai
Nairobi Paris São Paulo Shanghai Singapore Taipei Tokyo Toronto Warsaw

with associated companies in Berlin Ibadan

Oxford is a registered trade mark of Oxford University Press
in the UK and in certain other countries

Published in the United States
by Oxford University Press Inc., New York

British Library Cataloguing in Publication Data

Data available

Library of Congress Cataloging in Publication Data

Howson, Colin.
Induction and the justification of belief: Hume's problem / Colin Howson.
p. cm.
Includes bibliographical references and index.
1. Induction (Logic). 2. Science—Philosophy. 3. Hume, David,
1711–1776—Contributions in logical induction. I. Title.
BC91 .H69 2000 161—dc21 00–056652
ISBN 0–19–825037–1 (alk. paper)

1 3 5 7 9 10 8 6 4 2

Typeset by Hope Services (Abingdon) Ltd.
Printed in Great Britain
on acid-free paper by
T.J. International Ltd.
Padstow, Cornwall

None but a fool or madman will ever pretend to dispute the authority of experience.

(David Hume)

The greatest, and perhaps the only, use of philosophy of pure reason is thus purely negative, since it serves not as an organon for the extension of knowledge, but as a discipline for determining knowledge's limits; and, instead of discovering truth, has only the modest merit of preventing error.

(Immanuel Kant)

The laws of probability are laws of consistency, an extension to partial beliefs of formal logic, the logic of consistency.

(F. P. Ramsey)

ACKNOWLEDGEMENTS

To Tom Baldwin, Richard Bradley, Craig Callender, David Corfield, Philippe Mongin, Margie Morrison, Demetris Portides, Jon Williamson, all the students taking the Philosophy of Science option in the LSE 1997–8, and two anonymous referees: many thanks for their kind help. I am also very grateful to Charlotte Jenkins for her patience and able assistance in seeing this book through the press. I would also like to acknowledge the patient support of Peter Momtchiloff, a constant source of encouragement and help.

My greatest debt of all is to Peter Urbach, whose ideas on these issues over a period of twenty-five years, which included co-authorship of a book on the Bayesian theory, have become so inextricably linked with my own that I can no longer tell which are which, except that his are probably the better ones.

CONTENTS

Introduction

Half-way through the eighteenth century the Scottish[1] philosopher David Hume published a philosophical argument that was, metaphorically, dynamite. Its famous conclusion, that there is no justification for regarding what has been observed to happen in the past as any sort of reliable guide to the future, subverted the prevailing methodology of observation and experiment on the back of which rode the new mathematical sciences that seemed at the time Hume wrote to have attained an extraordinary degree of success, and have gone on doing so. Yet no uncontroversially definitive answer has ever been forthcoming to Hume, and most people have followed his own example of behaving as though nothing had happened. I find this extraordinary, and I believe it is time to face up to the unpalatable possibility revealed by Hume that all our hard-won factual knowledge is not secured by any process of demonstrably sound reasoning (and I mean sound reasoning in general, not merely deductive) to an empirical base, and see whether that is true and, if so, what follows from it.

In the course of the investigation we shall be obliged to consider the respective claims of all the major 'isms' of contemporary philosophy of science: reliabilism, realism, falsificationism, naturalism, and Bayesianism. We shall also encounter the Anthropic Principle, significance tests, and miracles. Evaluating Hume's argument can therefore be made into a stimulating way of acquainting students with a wider class of philosophical issues, at the same time challenging them with a classic open problem which can be simply stated but not simply solved, if it can be solved at all. This book grew out of a course of lectures in philosophy of science employing just such an approach. The first chapter sketches the intellectual background to Hume's argument, presents that argument and then looks at some of the quicker attempts to rebut it. The subsequent chapters examine the more sophisticated replies, touching as they proceed on each of the 'isms' listed above.

[1] Not English, as Glymour states (1992: 108).

My primary purpose in writing this book is not pedagogic, however. It is to support a claim that, despite its seeming absurdity,
Hume's argument is actually correct. I shall present the argument,
in Chapter 1, in a way that I think best reveals its quite extraordinary power, a power which, I believe, is still too little appreciated.
The argument is deservedly one of the great classics of philosophy:
Hume, no mean wielder of crushing arguments, produced in this
one possibly the most crushing of them all. And not only crushing,
but apparently attended by the gravest consequences for our standards of justified belief. But just as the force of Hume's argument is
usually underestimated, so the devastation it is supposed to bring in
its wake is usually exaggerated, and my supplementary thesis is that
there is none the less a positive solution to Hume's problem. Indeed,
I will argue the apparently paradoxical claim that there are nevertheless demonstrably sound inductive inferences! The resolution of
the paradox is that inductive inference arises as a necessary feature
of consistent reasoning, *given* the sorts of initial plausibility assumptions scientists habitually make. We are already familiar with and
accept the idea that deductive soundness is a property of inferences
and not their conclusions; I believe that the correct analysis of
Hume's problem, and Hume's own view of inductive reasoning,
forces us to view inductive soundness in the same way, a property
of inferences rather than of what we conclude from them. This may
not sound the sort of conclusion to warrant fanfares, but in mitiga-
tion two things can be said. First, Hume's argument gives us no reason to suppose that relying on our scientific knowledge is in any
way misguided; it does not tell us we are *wrong* to do so. It merely
says that the attempt to show that there is any sound inductive reasoning to that knowledge from observation alone will fail. But it
may well be that we are fully justified, *in terms of its truth or near-
ness to the truth*, in relying on it.

Secondly, I believe that Hume genuinely has solved the problem of
induction. He solved it by showing, in general terms, that a sound
inductive inference must possess, in addition to whatever observational or experimental data is specified, at least one independent
assumption (an inductive assumption) that in effect weights some of
the possibilities consistent with that evidence more than others. I
take this to be a great *logical* discovery, comparable to that of deductive inference itself, and with consequences of as much practical as
theoretical importance. For the problem of induction, considered as

the problem of characterizing soundness for inductive inferences, has recently become hot (so to speak). People are now for the first time in their chequered, too-frequently-bloody, history allocating substantial intellectual and material resources to the design of intelligent machinery, and in particular machinery that will learn from data. At present these systems fall into two main types, neural networks and rule-based systems. Functionally, in terms of mapping inputs to outputs, they are less dissimilar than they appear, since any input–output map generated by the one can be mimicked by the other. What is clear is that some logical basis for learning will certainly have to be built into any successful system. Hume's problem implicitly posed two hundred and fifty years ago the question of how, if at all, *logic* enters into inductive inference. Quite a lot of this book will be devoted to arguing that we now possess that logic, and that it can be identified with so-called Bayesian probability.

This claim has been denied by two of this century's most influential writers on scientific methodology, K. R. Popper and R. A. Fisher. Popper, to take a notable example, is well known for claiming that the 'logic of discovery'[2] is only ever deductive logic, applied in the design of tests to falsify hypotheses. In a remarkable coincidence of ideas, expressed in uncannily similar language, the great statistician R. A. Fisher at about the same time urged the same view. Both these thinkers emphatically rejected the view, prevalent between the beginning of the eighteenth century and the end of the nineteenth, that the evaluation of hypotheses in the light of evidence is in terms of probability. Popper's rejection was motivated by a desire to avoid what he thought to be a corollary of it, that knowledge is *inductively* based, Fisher's by what he saw as an inevitable subjectivism. Both were mistaken. In fact, though it is often called the subjective Bayesian theory, it is not actually a subjectivistic

---

[2] 'Logik der Forschung' is the original title of Popper's most influential work. It was inspired by some informal comments of the historian Lord Acton, which were developed by Popper into a systematic methodological system. It is worth quoting Acton: 'It is they [scientists] who hold the secret of the mysterious property of the mind by which error ministers to truth, and truth slowly but irrevocably prevails. Theirs is the logic of discovery, the demonstration of the advance of knowledge . . . Remember Darwin taking note only of those passages that raised difficulties in his way; the French philosopher complaining that his work stood still, because he found no contradicting facts; Baer, who thinks error treated thoroughly nearly as remunerative as truth, by the discovery of new objections; for . . . it is by considering objections that we often learn' (1960: 35).

theory at all. On the contrary, its rules, those of mathematical probability, are wholly objective and indeed interpreted as conditions of consistency. Nor can they justify induction, as we shall see.

But the Baconian ideal of a secure pathway from experience to truth dies hard, and the idea that there might be a logic of induction which does not justify induction has yet to be recognized, even by Bayesians. Here I should make a disclaimer. Though they may sound novel, the ideas in this book are really just elaborations of those of other people, and two in particular: Hume and Ramsey. The first part of the book endorses what I take to be Hume's argument that inductive conclusions are only soundly inferred from inductive premisses, and applies it, equally destructively I believe, to more modern attempts to justify induction. The second re-develops Ramsey's argument that reasoning from evidence is probabilistic reasoning and as such is nothing but the application of logical principles of consistency. My main purpose in writing this book is to show how the work of these two people amounts to the best possible solution of the problem of induction: there is a genuine logic of induction which exhibits inductive reasoning as logically quite sound given suitable premisses, but does not justify those premisses.

Some who have read only this far might, however, feel that they have already read enough. Surely it can't really be being suggested that current scientific knowledge lacks all foundation? Or that obedience to a set of rules that do not guarantee, or even make probable, truth as an end-product is anything other than art for art's sake, which cannot possibly explain why science has been so extraordinarily successful as compared with other goal-oriented human endeavours. It is one thing to argue this sort of thing as an academic exercise, quite another to take it seriously. Modern science is a vast, intricately interlocking system which has successfully predicted quite unexpected new facts—electromagnetic waves propagating at the speed of light, the velocity-dependence of mass, spin, the existence of antiparticles, etc.—uniting in the process what had formerly seemed quite disconnected domains and simultaneously underwriting the advanced technology required to inspect them. It would clearly be quite impossible for it to make the incredibly precise predictions it does make and for the theories on which it is based not to possess at least a very substantial core of truth. QED.

That simple argument is called the No-Miracles argument. It is very convincing and probably the best argument for believing in the truth of science. It has also been enormously influential. *And it is wrong.* I hope that the sceptical reader's appetite is now sufficiently whetted to continue a little further.

Hume's Argument

Introduction

It is a commonplace that our scientific knowledge far exceeds the observational basis on which it is grounded. It seems equally commonplace that a good part of it is securely grounded on careful observation. The inferential process by which observation, suitably controlled, is regarded as conferring an affidavit of reliability on what in a strict logical sense extends beyond it philosophers have traditionally called *induction*. Note: this is not to be confused with the mathematicians' principle of induction, which is simply a true statement about things called well-ordered sets.[1] Induction in the philosophers' sense has nothing to do with mathematics, but with the process of reasoning that leads people to conclude that observational data obtained in suitably rigorous ways confirm some general hypothesis. For example,

consider the natural scientist who wishes to establish a universal law, for example, one relating to the conductivity of copper. . . . How does [he] proceed? He attaches a piece of copper wire to a live electric terminal and uses the ammeter to measure the flow of current through the wire. Having observed that copper wire is a good conductor of electricity he is disposed to conclude right away that all pieces of copper are good conductors of electricity. If he is cautious, he will seek to establish that the copper wire is pure copper; that the observed effect is not due to an undetected alloy. He will undoubtedly go on to show that the maximal flow of current through a copper wire is a function of the wire's diameter and of its temperature. (Macnamara 1991: 28)

---

[1] Where the set is the non-negative whole, or 'natural', numbers, the principle in its best-known form is called the *Principle of Mathematical Induction* (it says that if 0 has a property Q and if an arbitrary n's having Q implies that n + 1 has Q, then every natural number has Q).

What exactly are the further enquiries he has to conduct to justifiably alleviate his caution and draw the desired conclusion—that is, at what point the induction is deemed soundly enough based—is not specified. It is, after all, only an example of the sort of reasoning that goes on all the time in research laboratories. What seems clear enough is that enough suitably designed observations *are* taken to establish robust law-like generalizations and, conversely, that generalizations acquire that status only by being experimentally established by such a procedure.

Francis Bacon and the Logic of Induction

If the standard of experimental proof sounds obvious today, it was novel enough to the intelligentsia of the early seventeenth century when it was advanced, in a powerful and influential manifesto, the *Novum Organum* (1620), by the lawyer-philosopher, James I's Lord Chancellor, Francis Bacon (1561–1626). As the Kneales point out (1962: 309), the title *Novum Organum* is an implicit snub to Aristotle; the logic expounded in Aristotle's great work, the *Organon*, Bacon famously dismissed as quite useless for deciding what are the sound inferences from observation. In other words, Aristotle's logic was not a logic of *induction*,[2] and this Bacon set out to provide. And Bacon the lawyer had a professional advantage. He could see the analogy between skilful questioning in courts of law and the careful posing of experimental questions: 'For the subtlety of experiments is far greater than that of sense itself . . . ; such experiments, I mean, as are skilfully and artificially devised for the express purpose of determining the point in question' (*Works*, iv. 26); and at a time when torture was a legitimate forensic device he likened experiment to torturing nature to reveal her secrets: 'For like as a man's disposition is never well known or proved till he be crossed, nor Proteus ever

---

[2] What Bacon was dismissing was the logic of the syllogism. This logic is actually valid as far as it goes, but the conclusions sanctioned by it contain no more factual content than the premisses jointly do. To this extent deductive inferences cannot 'discover' facts not already implicit in what is premissed. Such a feature is now recognized to be a necessary condition of the correctness of any deductive inference, but it is clearly of no use to anyone who, like Bacon, wishes to conclude generalizations from premisses about particular instances. Aristotle did recognize that there was a problem there to be solved, but did not contribute to a solution beyond some perfunctory remarks.

changed shapes till he was straitened and held fast, so nature exhibits herself more clearly under the trials and vexations of art than when left to herself' (*De Dignitate*, quoted in Montuschi 2001; Montuschi's very interesting paper shows how Bacon's views on scientific method make implicit reference to the inquisitorial procedures of Roman law rather than to the adversarial processes of common law).

Such parallels undoubtedly inspired Bacon's 'third way' between the still-dominant philosophical apriorism deriving from Aristotle and the unstructured empiricism of the alchemists and others:[3] that of systematic, carefully designed observation, designed to elicit the hidden causal springs underlying the appearances. He was, in Hacking's words, 'the first and almost last philosopher of experiments' (1984: 159). Bacon proposed an equally novel criterion for a sound principle of induction and thereby for a principle of good experimental design: if the hypothesis ('axiom') is 'larger and wider' than the existing factual basis, in the sense of making a prediction beyond it, then an experiment verifying the chancy prediction 'confirms its wideness and largeness by indicating new particulars, as a kind of collateral security' (*Novum Organum*, I. 106). The intuitive justification for this type of induction is that such an investigation is likely to reveal the falsity of a hypothesis if it is false; for there are very many ways the prediction could have failed and only one—if it is precise—in which it could have succeeded. This idea has become the foundation of a good deal of work in modern approaches to induction, and appears in different guises in modern theories of inductive inference: it is canonized in statistics as the principle of minimizing a Type II error, and in the Bayesian theory it is important in determining the so-called Bayes factor. We shall explore its fortunes in later chapters.

Bacon's contemporary, Galileo, was of course already actually employing the method of well-designed experiments with brilliant success (at any rate in devising them if not actually performing them), and the great scientific revolution generally regarded as commencing with the publication of Copernicus's *De Revolutionibus* (1543) and ending with Newton's *Principia* was already under way by

---

[3] In view of the fact that Bacon expressed nothing but contempt for the mere unsystematic amassing of data ('puerile'), it is astonishing that he should stand accused of promulgating just this view by Popper, who took great pains to contrast his own 'severity' approach to what he wrongly alleged was Bacon's (Popper 1959: 278–9). Peter Urbach's discussion (1987) sets the record straight, as well as providing an excellent exposition of Bacon's philosophy.

the time Bacon wrote his great methodological treatise. But there has been an almost universal perception of Bacon as its spiritual leader and chief propagandist. Most revolutions acquire a defining manifesto, then or later. Later commentators have seen as the manifesto of this one the *Novum Organum*. The early members of the Royal Society certainly did, and Sprat's *History* of the Society (1667) cites Bacon's work as 'the best . . . that can be produced for the defence of Experimental Philosophy; and the best directions, that are needful to promote it'. Cowley contributed an Ode to that History which declared that '*Bacon*, like *Moses*, led us forth at last, | The barren wilderness he passed, | etc.'; for Voltaire the *Novum Organum* was the scaffolding on which the 'New Philosophy' was erected (*Lettres Philosophiques*, XI); and so on.

Bacon's programme, which he felt he only partially achieved in the *Novum Organum*, was to write down a complete set of rules, which could be implemented mechanically (this was a fundamental consideration), by which nature could be made to reveal her secrets.[4] Much criticized as scientifically useless in the nineteenth and twentieth centuries, and never seriously employed, the *Novum Organum* was nevertheless the forerunner of a long line of attempts to specify a working *logic* for inductive arguments.[5] Some pursued Bacon's own particular type of programme: Mill's Methods of Agreement and Disagreement (1891) were a fairly direct nineteenth-century descendant of Bacon's ideas. Some didn't: the use of probability theory, initially developed in the late seventeenth century to be the foundation of inductive inferences, was a radically different approach (we shall review it later). The objective gradually became seen to be not so much *performative*, the production of prescriptions (after all, anyone could do this), but *explanatory*, in much the sense in which the so-called meta-theorems of modern formal logic are explanatory, of the *soundness*—or otherwise—of such prescriptions. In short, what was lacking was a set of prescriptions *accompanied by* a convincing explanation of why they should be regarded as sound.

---

[4] In a tribute less to the particulars of Bacon's recommendations than to their spirit a computer program constructed to perform inductions from data has been named BACON (Langley *et al.*, 1987). BACON, a curve-fitting program, actually 'discovered' Kepler's third law from Tycho's data.

[5] A survey of views of inductive reasoning up to Hume's time is in Milton 1987.

Unfortunately progress in this direction failed to match that of the contemporary science itself, a success which, ironically, the development of an inductive logic was supposed to facilitate. People went on cheerfully interrogating nature, weighing the answers and forming judicious conclusions with outstanding success even if no one seemed to be able to offer a convincing explanation why. What was wrong? For a start there was always perceived to be something not quite right, if not seriously defective, with every candidate system for such an explanation. Worse was the fact that not only were philosophers unable to do the decent thing and uncontroversially sanctify inductive practice (though not for want of trying); they were not even able to counter an apparently absurd argument put forward two and a half centuries ago by the philosopher David Hume, that *there is no good reason to suppose that inductive practice should have been successful at all.* Thus the initial problem of how to justify induction—'the problem of induction'—difficult enough in itself as it began to turn out, became modulated into the far more serious *Hume's Problem*, the problem of reconciling the continuing failure to rebut Hume's argument with the undoubted fact that induction not only seemed to work but to work surpassingly well. The Cambridge philosopher C. D. Broad's famous aphorism that induction is 'the glory of science and the scandal of philosophy' was both a tribute to Hume and a token of the exasperation that Broad felt at the stubborn resistance of Hume's argument to refutation (1952: 143).

And so that argument has stood since it was first presented, a philosophical classic, not really believed but withstanding all attempts to overturn it. The continuing failure suggests that it might actually be correct. I believe that, for all its apparent absurdity, it is. In the following pages I shall explain why I think it is, look at the attempts to counter it, explain why they don't work, and then see what can be salvaged from the wreck.

The Argument

Hume's argument was presented first in his great philosophical work (written while he was still in his twenties), the *Treatise of Human Nature*, and then more pithily a decade later in the *Treatise*'s abridgement, *An Enquiry into Human Understanding*. It is very simple. Hume commences by pointing out that such no inference from the observed to the as-yet unobserved is deductive:

> That there are no demonstrative arguments in this case seems evident; since it implies no contradiction that the course of nature may change. (*Enquiry*, section 4, part 2, p.35.)[6]

Nor can such an inference be justified, without circularity, as a 'probable argument', based on but not entailed by observational data. For in the light of what considerations would such an argument be probable? That inferences 'of the same type' (I put 'of the same type' in quotes because it will turn out to be surprisingly ambiguous) have been successful in the past will not work, without circularity, for that evidence is itself merely a record of what has happened in the past, and any conclusion based on it would therefore presuppose the validity of inferences from past to future, the question at issue. So what could such an inference rest on? Since 'the course of nature may change', indeed proceed from here in a virtually uncountable number of different ways, the inference that the future will proceed or even probably proceed in any one of them must beg the question. Since also, as we shall see later, each of these extrapolates the data under some true description of those data, and therefore according to that description 'resembles' the past in that way, we can conclude with Hume—his *circularity thesis*—that

all inferences from experience suppose, as their foundation, that the future will resemble the past

—in some way or other.

The argument can be put in a manner possibly more familiar to modern ears. Let P be the conjunction of all factual statements known to be true. Suppose that the inference from P to a statement Q describing some event not known to be true is not deductive (establishing that this is so where P stands for 'past' and Q for 'future' is the first part of Hume's argument). It follows immediately from the definition of deductive validity[7] that in some subset W of all the possible worlds in which, like ours, P is true and Q is false. The

---

[6] Throughout, most of the references will be to the *Enquiry* rather than to the *Treatise* because Hume's statements of his position are clearest there; the brevity and sharpness of the *Enquiry* were specifically designed to make the public impact for Hume's views that the *Treatise* failed to do: 'falling', in Hume's famous words, 'dead-born from the Press'.

[7] An inference is defined to be deductively valid if there is no possible world or structure in which the premises are true and the conclusion false.

second part of Hume's argument can be imagined as arising from trying to answer the question: what further information could be
appealed to which would make it more likely that our world is not in
W? Well, the only world we know is this one, so the information must
presumably be about some aspect of this world. But the only
information we have about this world that is known to be true is
already in P. In other words, there is no further information. All we
know is that in our world Q may be true or it may be false: nothing
more. Hence any principle claiming to justify the inference from P to
the truth *or even the probable truth* of Q must beg the question:

> It is evident that Adam, with all his science, would never have been able to
> demonstrate that the course of nature must continue uniformly the same
> . . . Nay, I will go farther, and assert that he could not so much as prove by
> any probable arguments that the future must be conformable to the past.
> (Hume 1740)

It is the 'going farther' that is the original, and if correct quite devastating, part of Hume's argument. That there is no deductive link
between statements about past and future had been known since
antiquity. Where Hume goes beyond the traditional sceptical position is in arguing the link cannot in principle justified even as a 'probable inference'.

A frequently-voiced objection to any such claim is that Hume's
argument is no more than an appeal to some familiar facts about
deductive logic, namely: (i) P′ does not deductively entail Q; (ii) the
weakest assertion which when conjoined with P′ will yield Q as a
deductive consequence is the conditional 'If P′ then Q' (we are assuming here that P′ can be represented as a long finite statement); (iii) any
deductively sound link between P′ and Q can be achieved only by
appending an additional premise which will itself deductively imply
'If P′ then Q'; (iv) since the truth of that conditional is exactly what
requires justification, any sound 'inference from experience' will necessarily beg the question. Understood in this way Hume's own argument clearly begs the question, that the only authentic justification of
'inferences from experience' must be deductive in character and could
not be some type of sound non-deductive inference: for example, a
probabilistic one. Thus, when Hume concludes that not only is it

> evident that Adam would never have been able to *demonstrate* that the
> course of nature must continue uniformly the same

but also

that he could not so much as prove by any *probable* arguments that the future must be conformable to the past. (italics added)

it would seem that he is simply exceeding his logical mandate. Stove, one of the most forceful advocates of this view (a group which includes Mackie (1980) and van Cleve (1984)), points out that since for Hume 'probable reasoning' means merely 'reasoning concerning matters of fact and existence', he could not consider the possibility that there might be sound *authentically probabilistic* arguments from past to future, and more generally from the observed to the unobserved. At any rate, whether he could or whether he couldn't, he didn't: 'Reasonable but probabilistic inferences, then, have not been excluded by Hume's argument, for the simple reason that Hume did not consider this possibility' (Mackie 1980: 15).

But there are decisive historical and textual objections to this view. Hume certainly knew of the contemporary mathematical theory of probability, and its rudiments, and knew that there was already a keen interest in trying to use it as a logical basis for inductive arguments, according to the programme of the manifesto-like part V of James Bernoulli's seminal *Ars Conjectandi* (1715), which Hume is known to have read. Bernoulli had written there that 'the art of conjecturing is the art of measuring as exactly as possible the probabilities of things', using for this purpose the mathematical theory he had developed in the earlier parts of his treatise. Bernoulli's own attempt to use it in the context of a problem of statistical inference was not thought to be wholly successful, and how to improve on it was a live issue in eighteenth-century European mathematics and philosophy, probably comparable to any of the famous twelve problems that Hilbert set mathematicians in the early years of the twentieth century; indeed, it was the problem that Bayes attempted to solve about the time that Hume was working on the *Treatise*. Hume was almost certainly aware of these developments, even if he had no knowledge of Bayes's own work.

Not only does the intellectual context in which Hume wrote make it a more than reasonable presumption that arguments from the formal theory of probability *were* included in Hume's 'probable arguments'; the presumption is borne out by the *Treatise* itself. Hume discusses explicitly what is achieved by a mathematical *definition* of probability, which in the contemporary theory, the so-called doctrine of chances, was as the proportion of chances favouring an event's occurrence:

Should it be said, that though . . . it is impossible to determine with *certainty* on which side the event will fall, yet we can pronounce with certainty, that it is more likely and probable it will be on that side where there is a superior number of chances, than where there is an inferior: should this be said, I would ask, what is here meant by *likelihood* and *probability*? The likelihood and probability of chances is a superior number of equal chances; and consequently, when we say it is likely the event will fall on the side which is superior, rather than on the inferior, we do no more than affirm, that where there is a superior number of chances there is actually a superior, and where there is an inferior there is an inferior, which are identical propositions, and of no consequence.

Indeed,

The question is, by what means a superior number of equal chances operates upon the mind, and produces belief and assent, since it appears that it is *neither by arguments derived from demonstration, nor from probability*. (1739: I.iii.xi; my italics)

We can flesh out the argument thus: mathematical, indeed any, definitions say nothing about matters of fact ('It is indeed evident, that we can never, by the comparison of mere ideas, make any discovery which can be of consequence in this affair' (ibid.)). In order for them to do so special assumptions are required. Not only will these beg the question of their truth in general, but in view of the fact that 'the course of nature may change', and in very different ways, any extrapolation sanctioned by a probabilistic argument will beg the question of why that particular way should be regarded as a probable one. In fact, Hume's circularity thesis applies to arguments from mathematical probability as much as it does to any sort of non-deductive 'probable inference', and we shall see later how inductive arguments constructed within the mathematical theory of probability fully corroborate it.

If I am correct, Hume's argument does not presuppose that the only form of justification is deductive: his argument is the very simple and effective one that any evidence that we take to indicate that our world is likely to be among those in which some general assertion is true requires some additional assumption to the effect that it is indeed evidence. The argument is so effective just *because* it makes no assumption about what exactly constitutes valid reasoning—deductive, probabilistic, or whatever. Entirely simple and informal, Hume's argument is one of the most robust, if not the most robust, in the history of philosophy.[8] David Miller (1994, ch. 6) has compared its impact with that of Gödel's great limitative results this century in logic, that put paid to Hilbert's Programme for so-called absolute proofs of consistency for mathematics. According to Miller, Hume's argument has the same devastating force *vis-à-vis* Bacon's programme for founding the sciences inductively on experiment that Gödel's had on Hilbert's. But the consequences for the theory of knowledge of Hume's work seem on the face of it considerably worse than the impact of Gödel's results on mathematics, where the practical effects appear to be very few, if any. If Hume is correct, then it seems to follow that we have no grounds for believing that science is any more reliable than soothsaying as a predictor of the future behaviour of the systems it studies. Coming on the heels of the greatest scientific revolution the world had yet seen, whose laws, according to the greatest actor in that revolution, Sir Isaac Newton, are in all cases no less than *deduced* from the phenomena, such a conclusion seems incredible. And indeed we do not see people assailed by Humean doubt, while science, based apparently on the sorts of inferences from observation Hume's argument flatly declares without any validity, continues to flourish in defiance of him. People have understandably preferred on the whole to regard the success of inductive practice as an intuitive reductio of Hume's argument, and have sought either to refute it directly, or indirectly by constructing systems of inductive reasoning that are proof against it. What follow now are some of the quicker attempts to dismiss it or evade its force. In subsequent chapters we shall consider the more sophisticated responses.

Some Quick Responses

I list eight.[9] There are more but these are the best-known of the quick ones. (i)–(iii) attempt to show in different ways that Hume's argument does not rule out the possibility of our having a justified belief that our hypotheses are reliable predictors of the future. A more sustained defence along these lines will be presented in the next chapter.

---

[8] It is also a wonderful example of what Kreisel called 'informal rigour' (1969), achieving its goal despite not appealing to the sort of technical apparatus a symbolism-conscious later age regarded as being—well, *de rigueur*.

[9] This list overlaps a similar one given in Earman *et al.* 1992: section 2.6

(i) Contrary to what Hume argues, we do have provably reliable hypotheses, in science. We prove their reliability by following this recipe: *Instantiate the appropriate experimental conditions and see what happens*. We know that what will happen, of course, is that the predicted effects will be observed and that any modern follower of David Hume prepared to put their money where their mouth is will quickly go bankrupt. QED.

Answer. Hume is questioning whether we really do know that. Despite its rhetorical force the objection merely asserts without argument the claim that Hume is attacking. Collect all the reports of such observations carried out according to the recipe. Call them O. Now simply repeat Hume's reasoning: in O we always have a statement about what *has* happened, and it is inferences from these which Hume claims are unjustified.

(ii) The fact that tests on these hypotheses have in the past always confirmed their predictions tell us that these hypotheses are reliable: that is just what the word 'reliable' means.

Answer. No it isn't. 'Reliable' means that the tests will continue to have the outcomes predicted. Hume is arguing that we have no reason to believe this.

(iii) A variant of (ii), due to Strawson. This is a nice example of 'ordinary language' philosophy. Strawson claims that it is 'analytic', that is, true by definition, that induction is reasonable:

It is an analytic proposition that it is reasonable to have a degree of belief in a statement which is proportional to the strength of the evidence in its favour; and it is an analytic proposition, though not a proposition of mathematics, that, other things being equal, the evidence for a generalisation is strong in proportion as the number of favourable instances, and the variety of circumstances in which they have been found, is great. So to ask whether it is reasonable to place reliance on inductive procedures is like asking whether it is reasonable to proportion the degree of one's convictions to the strength of the evidence. Doing this is what 'being reasonable' *means* in such a context. (Strawson 1952: ch. 9; italics in original)

Answer. This completely misses the point. Saying that *by definition* 'being reasonable' includes in its meaning an acceptance of inductive reasoning implies nothing at all about the non-linguistic world, and in particular nothing about its tendency to verify (or not) predictions based on such 'good reasons'. Broad's comment is apt:

It is fashionable at present in some quarters to insist that the question: 'How, if at all, can induction be justified?' is in some sense a meaningless or improper one, which can be asked only under a misapprehension and therefore needs no answer. I take this opportunity of saying that I have seen no argument which seems to me to establish this contention. (1952: p. ix)

Quite so. Let us move on.

(iv) This is a slightly more sophisticated version of Strawson's argument due to Goodman. It is that Hume mistakes the nature of a justification of inductive inferences (Goodman 1946: 62–5): inferences are justified by whether or not they conform with accepted canons as expressed in the judgements people actually make after the process of making mutual adjustments between proposed rules and accepted inferences has settled to a stable conclusion (p. 64; Rawls famously described such a procedure as the approach to 'reflective equilibrium'). This, claims Goodman, is just as true of inductive inference as it is [allegedly] of deductive: 'Principles of deductive inference are justified by their conformity with accepted deductive practice. Their validity depends upon accordance with the particular deductive inferences we actually make and sanction. If a rule yields unacceptable inferences, we drop it as invalid . . . All this applies equally well to induction' (ibid.).

Answer. Goodman is mistaken about deductive logic. A rule of deductive inference is not judged valid according to the standard of whether or not it conforms with practice; it is *defined* to be valid ('sound' in logicians' jargon) if no counterexample exists, and it is *judged* valid if it can be shown that this condition is satisfied. In other words, deductive rules are justified only if it can be shown that they satisfy appropriate semantic criteria. Pursuing the (now accurate) analogy, inductive rules should be judged valid only if it can be shown that they meet their appropriate semantic criteria. What are these? Suppose we take 'reliably indicating the truth or probable truth of a specified hypothesis' (this seems a plausible candidate): Hume's argument shows, or seems to show, that no noncircular demonstration can be provided. In the next chapter we shall assess a defence of the claim that circularity is not a vitiator of justification. I shall postpone a fuller discussion of this unlikely claim till then.

(v) Hume's argument fails to acknowledge the possibility of a priori synthetic knowledge, a possibility that Kant exploited so famously after having been 'woken from his dogmatic slumbers' by Hume.

Kant saw the necessity imposed as a condition of thinking and of perception. Kant proposed in the *Critique of Pure Reason* that a so-called *transcendental argument* can be used to establish that what seem to be very general factual principles, like that which says that every event has a cause, and even more specific ones like the Newtonian laws of mechanics and gravitation, are necessary because they are *preconditions of knowledge*, the inbuilt framework within which we structure experience.

Answer. The problem with Kant's theory is the undeniable fact that we can sensibly and consistently conceive alternatives to the principles Kant held to be 'necessary' conditions of cognizing—the 'law' of cause and effect, Newtonian gravitational theory, and Euclidean geometry as the only possible geometry for space—all of which, moreover, are now deemed false! In other words, the Kantian 'transcendental deduction' is unsound. Furthermore, even if there were ever a sound deduction, it would have to employ some non-tautological premisses, and we should then need to enquire how they were established (at this point Hume enters again). Either that or there is an infinite regress of justification, and nothing is achieved.

The modern descendant of Kant's transcendental argument is the claim, supposedly based on Darwinian theory, that the expectational structures we inherit are likely to be the product of evolutionary pressures. Assuming that they are, it then seems to follow that as adaptive structures they are also likely to generate broadly successful cognitive strategies. There is in principle nothing wrong with such a Darwinian explanation of why we might find it impossible not to think or expect in certain ways, but turning it into a justification would be assuming science to justify science, a palpably circular procedure, and one to which we shall return in Chapter 6.

(vi) Nature does not, as Hume claimed, give us only information about particulars. Nature's answer to a properly conducted experiment is itself a universal statement (in fact, an AE one, that is to say one starting with a phrase of the form 'For all x there exists a y such that . . . [A stands for 'all', E for 'exists']; Hintikka 1992: 24). Thus we can learn generalizations from Nature.

Answer. Nature's answer is nothing of the sort. Hintikka's objection is based on a notion of experiment as an already richly structured affair in which the experimental outcome is regarded as discriminating between a very small finite number of theories (Hintikka cites Newton's 'deductions from the phenomena' as an example). But, as we shall see in due course, the finiteness assumption is unjustified.

(vii) One of the commonest of responses to Hume is to concede the insolubility of the problem as it is stated, and say that what it reveals is the need for an '*inductive principle*', that is to say an additional premiss permitting the passage, deductively, from appropriate observation-reports to conclusions asserting either the truth or the high probability of some prediction of even general theory. Russell famously was the first to diagnose the problem in this way (1971), followed by Keynes (1973). According to Russell, the principle should state that the more cases an event of type A has been found to be associated with one of type B, the more probable it should become, tending to certainty, that all A events will be associated with B events. Keynes's candidate principle specifies only a 'Limited Independent Variety' in the ways things can behave (in effect, it would limit the number of possible laws to a small finite number; the need to do so is brought out dramatically in his ch. 4). A recent advocate seems to be Maxwell (1998), who calls it a 'principle of the comprehensibility of the universe'. However it is precisely characterized, such an inductive principle, according to these thinkers, enjoys the status of a postulate whose justification is its indispensability for factual knowledge.

Answer. This is clearly not a critical response to Hume's argument, whose validity is the only question we are concerned with here; the inductive-principle advocates explicitly or implicitly acknowledge the validity of the argument.

(viii) Hume's own argument that there is no justified procedure for showing that the future will resemble the past is question-begging. 'Past' and 'future' are theoretical concepts meaningful only within some theory of the way the universe behaves. Thus Hume's argument already presupposes the truth of some physical theory, namely that which postulates the existence of an oriented universe.

Answer. Exercise!

Conclusion

None of these replies meets the challenge posed by Hume's argument. What did Hume himself think? His own response is no less famous than the argument itself and, like so much in Hume, it is two centuries before its time. It was to *explain* where he could not justify, in this case the apparently universal psychological propensity to induce, and to explain it in terms of *inborn characteristics*. Hume argued that humanity, like all the animal kingdom, has an inborn expectation that factors observed to be constantly conjoined in the past will continue to be conjoined in the future. This belief may be wrong for certain pairs of factors, and weaker and stronger for others, but the propensity to extrapolate such conjunctions is always there. He called it, with remarkable prescience, *Instinct*:

the experimental reasoning itself, which we possess in common with beasts, and on which the whole conduct of life depends, is nothing but a species of instinct or mechanical power, that acts in us unknown to ourselves; and in its chief operations, is not directed by any such relations or comparisons of ideas, as are the proper objects of our intellectual faculties. Though the instinct is different, yet still it is an instinct, which teaches a man to avoid the fire; as much as that, which teaches a bird, with such exactness, the art of incubation, and the whole economy and order of its nursery. (1748: 108. The invariable elegance of Hume's prose style is at its most apparent in these final cadences.)

Both Hume's strategy, 'explain where you can't justify', and his explanation, an appeal to something non-rational and innate, anticipates the current vogue for a 'naturalized epistemology' based on Darwin's theory of inherited adaptive traits. Unlike 'naturalized epistemology', however, it keeps clear the distinction between explanation (by appeal to a theory whose truth is for the purpose at hand simply assumed) and justification which, according to Hume, is invariably wanting. We shall resume this discussion later; for now we leave the last word to Broad:

There is a skeleton in the cupboard of Inductive Logic, which Bacon never suspected and Hume first exposed to view. Kant conducted the most elaborate funeral in history, and called Heaven and Earth and the Noumena under the Earth to witness that the skeleton was finally disposed of. But when the dust of the funeral procession had subsided and the last strains of the Transcendental Organ had died away, the coffin was found to be empty and the skeleton still in its old place. Mill discreetly closed the door of the cupboard, and with infinite tact turned the conversation into more cheerful channels. Mr Johnson and Lord Keynes may fairly be said to have reduced the skeleton to the dimensions of a mere skull. But that obstinate *caput mortuum* still awaits the undertaker who will give it Christian burial. May we venture to hope that when Bacon's next centenary is celebrated the great work which he set going will be completed; and that Inductive Reasoning, which has long been the glory of Science, will have ceased to be the scandal of Philosophy? (1952: 143)

2

Reliabilism

Reliable Methods

Consider the following two ways in which a goal-directed procedure might be justified. There is the 'internalist' way, which means looking at its structure and seeing whether that underwrites an ability to achieve the goal in question. Thus deductive justification is internalist, since whether a putatively deductive inference is valid or not depends on nothing but its internal logical structure. If the inference is valid this can, in principle at any rate, be proved by means of a so-called soundness theorem. Hume's argument appears to rule out any similar internalist justification of induction. But it could also plausibly be argued that a procedure, like induction, is justified if *in fact* it achieves the goal sufficiently more often than not, even though it may have no intrinsic character that could provide a demonstration that it is reliable: it just happens to be the case. This sort of justification, if it is a justification, is called 'externalist', indicating that its reliability depends on factors extrinsic to it. But since the bottom line is actually achieving the goal, it might be wondered what better justification could exist. Whether one goes along with this view or not, some sort of further insight into Hume's problem might be forthcoming by finding out for what sorts of worlds reliable methods exist, and how robust they are.

A good deal of technical work has been done on this problem, work which forms the subject-matter of a new mathematical discipline called *formal learning theory*. As its name partly suggests, this is an abstract formal model of learning from experience. Its conceptual apparatus is, first, algorithms, that is, computable procedures, whose inputs are finite segments of infinite data sequences and whose outputs are either hypotheses about the structure of the data source or else conjectured truth-values of specified hypotheses, and, secondly, a variable set of data sequences whose particular constitution represents the constraints imposed by the relevant background information. 'Learning the truth' for a given data sequence consistent with the specified background information is modelled by the convergence of the outputs on that data sequence to the 'correct' hypothesis or class of hypotheses for that sequence. The condition that the procedure be computable is supposed to reflect the fact that a methodology of evidential assessment is usually regarded as an effective, rule-governed affair; were it not, it could hardly be humanly implemented. A famous thesis independently advanced by the mathematicians Alonzo Church and Alan Turing in the 1930s, and called, appropriately, the *Church–Turing thesis*, states that any effective procedure can be implemented on a suitable digital computer (somewhat idealized); hence the equation of 'methodology' with 'algorithm'.

A simple example of a hypothesis for which an algorithm exists which will reliably identify its truth across all possible data sequences, if it is true, is a simple existential hypothesis H: 'There exists some element of the data which has property Q', where Q is some decidable property of data elements: the algorithm consists of the instruction to examine each data element to see if it has Q, and if it does to register 'yes' and keep registering 'yes' on all subsequent elements (on the other hand, no algorithm will identify the falsity of H if H is false on an infinite data stream). This is a rather trivial example; the most impressive technical results of formal learning theory concern the way imposing various constraints—under the generic title of 'background information'—on the possible data sequences determines a corresponding logico-mathematical structure for the hypotheses which can be learned, or whose truth-values can be learned, in the sense described above.

These results are presented in Kelly (1996), which also provides a general discussion of the aims and his own assessment of the achievements of this programme. The results which relate to Hume's Problem are, as might have been expected, almost wholly negative. For example, positive results for strictly universal hypotheses tend to be forthcoming only when the background information, usually symbolized as K, is very strong indeed; and where general extrapolations are 'learned', K must be of a strength where it already contains information of universal generality. If any weaker prior restriction is placed by K on the class of possible data streams then, as might be expected, no provably reliable method exists for determining the truth-value of any universal hypothesis relative to arbitrary data sequences. I say 'as might have been expected', since it is pretty well the starting-point for discussions of Hume's Problem that there can be no 'internal' demonstration of the reliability of any method of assessing truth-values of general hypotheses relative to the class of all logically possible data streams, that is, across all possible worlds (cf. Kelly 1996: 46). Suppose, for example, that H is a hypothesis asserting that in specified circumstances an outcome A will always be observed. Suppose M is some proposed method which is claimed will detect the truth-value of H, if H is true, on *any* sample data, in whichever 'possible world' that data might inhabit; that is, the sample is input to M, and the claim is that after some sufficient amount of it M will output a T or an F, indicating the truth or falsity of H respectively, and this verdict will be correct over all possible samples. Clearly, the claim is untenable: whatever the software and hardware driving M, a demon able to select any from among all possible data streams can always confound M. For the demon, being a demon, knows M's algorithm, and can therefore select a data stream which it also knows will cause M after some finite stage n to output T, but which will contain a non-A at the (n + 1)th stage. Belief in a demon is of course not necessary to appreciate the problem: as Kelly, who uses demons to great effect, points out, demonic selection of the future course of events is merely a picturesque way of presenting Hume's argument for inductive scepticism (ibid.).

Being successful across all possible worlds is a very strong sense of the word 'reliable'. After all, we only inhabit one such world. This poses the question whether the extrapolation of observed data to the future is a reliable method in *this* world. It is clearly *possible* that it is. Its reliability would mean that our world does not systematically generate suitably induction-defying data sequences; it is a 'normal world', in the terminology of Goldman (1986). But now of course we are back to the old problem. How could we know, or have grounds for believing, any such thing? Once more we run up against Hume's Problem. We know there can be no method of evaluating predictive hypotheses that is reliable across all possible worlds, so how could any claim that induction is reliable in this one possibly be backed up?

Rule-Circularity

According to the so-called *reliabilist* doctrine, we can indeed know, or at least rationally believe, induction to be reliable precisely because there is *factual evidence* for it: induction has been observed to be reliable sufficiently often in the past. But what about Hume's charge that such reasoning is circular, for it in effect uses induction to justify induction? Having pointed to the circularity, Hume presumably felt that his work was done, no doubt assuming as self-evident that *no procedure can be self-justifying*; and the fact that his argument has been given the prominence it has is that up to now virtually everybody else has concurred in this apparently reasonable view of the matter. One of the more startling novelties of the reliabilist position is that it explicitly challenges this assumption. Ramsey, probably the first reliabilist ('We are all convinced by inductive arguments, and our conviction is reasonable because the world is so constituted that inductive arguments lead on the whole to true opinions.'), averred that 'An indispensable means for investigating [induction] is induction itself, without which we should be helpless. In this circle lies nothing vicious' (1931: 197), defending the position with a parallel with memory:

It is true that if any one has not got the habit of induction, we cannot prove to him that he is wrong. If a man doubts his memory or his perception we cannot prove to him that they are not trustworthy; to ask for such a thing to be proved is to cry for the moon, and the same is true for induction. It is one of the ultimate sources of knowledge just as memory is . . . It is only through memory that we can determine the degree of accuracy of memory; for if we make experiments to determine this effect, they will be useless unless we remember them. (ibid.)

But this is not a good argument. Some people can test other people's memories, and even if their own memories are involved there is nothing remotely circular in this, for it is not the general faculty of memory that is tested, but one person's. Even a suitably programmed machine could in principle carry out such experiments and evaluate them. It is true that computers have something called 'memory', but it is not any human memory, nor is there any evidence that it operates in the same way; quite the contrary, in fact.

The response of the later reliabilists is again to deny that the circularity is vicious, but to argue the case more systematically. Their ground is that the circularity involved is 'rule-circularity' rather than 'premiss-circularity', and that while 'premiss-circularity' is undeniably vicious, 'rule-circularity' need not be. Van Cleve (1984), a prominent exponent of this view, starts by considering the following putative justification for induction; call it A:

Most of the inductive inferences I have drawn in the past from true premises have had true conclusions.

Therefore the majority of all inductive inferences with true premises have true conclusions.

Suppose the ground-level inductive rules also have the form 'Most observed x's have had the property y; therefore the majority of x's have y'. Thus the justification A of the ground-level rule looks palpably rule-circular. Van Cleve proceeds to argue that though it is rule-circular, it is quite possible none the less that A is an argument, van Cleve calls it a 'probable argument', which does *as a matter of fact* transfer a justified belief (if it is justified) in the premiss to a justified belief in the conclusion, even though we may be unaware of the fact. He then uses this observation to argue that, though the rule by which the conclusion is apparently drawn from the premiss in A appears to beg the question, it actually need not. For if A is a probable argument then a justified belief in the conclusion given a justified belief in the premiss would not depend on a justified belief in the soundness of the rule itself. Hence there are inductive arguments which, though rule-circular, are not viciously circular: they *can* give you a justified belief in their conclusions without requiring justified belief in their own soundness.

That is all very well, but to draw the conclusion of A with any confidence we presumably would need to be confident both that the premiss is true—well, that's OK—*and* that the argument is sound, or, in van Cleve's sense of soundness, a 'probable argument' from justified belief in the premiss to justified belief in the conclusion. Van Cleve points out that on the externalist criterion of justification we do not need to know that A is a probable argument to be justifed in using it, because

our condition [that it is a probable argument] is an *external* condition, that is, one of which the inference-drawing subject need not be cognizant. In a world in which inductive arguments were probable, persons who used them would be able to acquire justified beliefs thereby, regardless of whether they *knew* inductive arguments to be probable. (1984: 558–9; italics in original)

This does not, though, as it stands, answer the question: *Am I* justified in drawing the conclusion, that is, *is* this a probable argument? According to van Cleve the question can be answered, *affirmatively*, and again by appeal again to the external standard of justification. For the conclusion of A tells us that induction is reliable, and according to the externalist, reliabilist, criterion any process that reliably leads from true beliefs to true beliefs is a justified one. Hence argument A is a probable one. QED.

But there is still an obvious objection. I may have proved by using that argument that the conclusion is justified, but *since the question at issue is the soundness of the argument itself* surely I have not really proved anything. To do that I would need to know not only that the premisses are justified, *but also have good reason to believe that the argument is sound* (i.e. probable, in van Cleve's sense). If I do not have that information I have proved nothing. Van Cleve's answer is to insist that I *do* have that information, because it is precisely the conclusion of the argument above that A is a probable argument, and hence a sound one. Moreover, there seems also to be a decisive *tu quoque* ('you too') counter to this type of objection, which is to invoke a damaging parallel with deductive logic, where, if an argument from A to B is deductively sound, the truth of B can justifiably be inferred from the truth of A without requiring as a further premiss the statement that the inference is sound. To suppose otherwise is both incorrect and courts an obvious infinite regress, as Lewis Carroll pointed out a century ago in the dramatic persona of the tortoise in his dialogue 'What Achilles Said to the Tortoise' (1895), between Achilles, who took the line above, and the more sagacious tortoise who exposed the inevitable regress. But if this is the case in deductive theory why insist on stronger conditions being satisfied by the theory of induction? As van Cleve remarks, 'if this must be true in some cases, why not inductive cases too?' (1984: 560).

There is an answer to this question, however. In the deductive case there are *proofs* of the soundness of any deductive rule or set of rules. Indeed, their use would not be authorized without them, evidenced by the fact that a standard feature of good textbooks of deductive logic is that the introduction of a particular deductive system is usually accompanied by a *soundness theorem* for that system. But that answer seems only to raise the rather obvious further question of what premisses and rules these proofs themselves employ. Perhaps the *tu quoque* will succeed after all. This is certainly what Goldman,

who now takes up the running, intends. In Carroll's dialogue the particular example discussed was a *modus ponens* inference (*modus
ponens* is the rule that from A and 'If A then B' you may infer B). The
doubters required that before they could infer B's truth from that of
A and 'If A then B' they had also to accept that the inference was
deductively sound, that is, they had to accept additionally the statement 'If A and "If A then B" are true, so is B'. But to be prepared to
infer the truth of B from this and the truth of A you would be making a *modus ponens* inference. Therefore the regress is stopped only
by using the rule whose soundness was in question. Goldman proceeds to generalize what he sees as the conclusion: 'Would one say
that a person could not be justified in believing in the validity of
modus ponens if he used modus ponens to arrive at this belief? . . . If
a process deserves to be permitted, then its permission should extend
to all subject matter, including its own performance and its own per-
missibility' (1986: 394).

But Goldman's conclusion, that *modus ponens* is justified deductively only at the cost of using *modus ponens* itself, is easily shown to
be incorrect. Suppose that some antecedent proof, using assumptions Σ, had established the soundness of *modus ponens*. Then it is
true that from premisses consisting of the statement that *modus
ponens* is sound, and the statement S that A and 'If A then B' are true,
we can infer by *modus ponens* that B is true. However, a general
deductive principle called 'Cut' (Machover 1996: 121) tells us that
there is a proof of the truth of B from Σ and S alone. Moreover, *this
proof need not use modus ponens*. In other words, there is a deductive
justification for detaching the conclusion of a *modus ponens* inference
which, *pace* Goldman, need not employ *modus ponens* at all. In fact,
there are a number of familiar complete deductive systems, some of
which have no rule in common (the tableau/tree system has none in
common with either natural deduction or sequent or Hilbert-style
systems; see Howson 1997*c*: ch. 10). Thus we can finally and successfully turn the *tu quoque* on its wielders: there are *independent* arguments for the soundness of deductive rules; that is to say, there are
rules which are not, as they are in the inductive case, circular.

To sum up. The demand for a patent of trustworthiness—a soundness argument—for a putative rule, deductive or inductive, is not an
idle or pointless one. It is not pointless because without it you have
no reason for confidence in any reasoning which employs it, and this
also goes for any 'justification' which employs that rule itself: if you

can only argue for its soundness by appeal to the rule itself then you have shown nothing, or nothing worth having. And the demand is not idle because such an argument, at any rate in the case of deductive rules, can be given which is not circular: neither 'premiss-circular' or 'rule-circular'. It might still be objected that any justification of any piece of deductive reasoning itself will in its turn employ deductive reasoning: a demonstration of the joint soundness of a set of deductive rules will be some chain of reasoning in its turn and hence rest upon the implicit claim that the links in this chain are themselves sound. It will also employ some non-trivial mathematics, in the form of some set theory and the principle of strong induction. So where, it might be asked, is the difference, in terms of the patent of security allegedly conferred, between a proof of deductive validity and an inductive argument like A? Is there any difference in principle?

Yes, there is. I am not in any way defending an absolutist position with regard to logic, that logical principles cannot be doubted, etc.: for some time there has been a debate about the necessity attaching to the law of excluded middle, and more recently there has been some questioning from another quarter, quantum physics, of the distributivity 'laws' and even *modus ponens* itself. But we have seen that in deductive logic there are independent arguments for any given logical principle, while there seems to be only one for van Cleve's rule, that rule itself. And we have still seen no convincing rebuttal of the simple yet compelling charge that self-authentication is no authentication. It may be, as Ramsey claimed, 'crying for the moon' to ask for a way out of the circle of justification for inductive reasoning, but that is beside the point. This, as another reliabilist reminds us, remains and will always remain 'whether [an inductive argument for induction] gives us a positive base for *trusting* induction' (Papineau 1993: 158; italics in original). Quite so. Papineau himself believes that it does, on the ground that since there is nothing obviously 'problematic' about induction, we can conclude that an inductive justification of induction is perfectly acceptable (p.160). Alas, were it only so. Papineau's remark brings us to the crux of the matter, for the inductive rule which extrapolates from a sample containing a sufficiently large percentage of successes, far from being unproblematic as he claims, is actually problematic in the worst possible way: it is *inconsistent*.

'Grue'

The construction which shows this is extremely simple. Due to
Goodman, it has become justly celebrated, and because it is a touch-
stone that a surprising number of apparently plausible methodolo-
gies of inference fail, it will play a leading role in much of the
subsequent discussion. Think of an emerald mine. Define the predicate 'is grue' of objects x that might be dug up as follows: x is grue
just in case (i) x is an emerald and (ii) x has been observed up to now
and is green, or x has not been observed up to now and is blue. It follows that any observed emerald is green if and only if it is grue, and
so all observed green emeralds are also grue emeralds and conversely.
An inductive rule that tells us that after observing a large number of
As we can infer—either outright, or with justified belief, or with high
probability, or whatever—that the next object observed will be an A,
or that all future objects in the reference class will be As, clearly tells
us (i) that after observing enough green emeralds we can infer that
the next emerald to be observed will be green, and (ii) that we can
infer that the next emerald observed will be grue. In other words the
rule tells us that the next observed emerald will be both green and
blue. Extrapolating past behaviour is therefore not just an unreliable
procedure: it is *maximally* unreliable.[1]

Worse still, *we can use the rule itself to 'prove' its own unreliability*,
just as, according to van Cleve, Goldman, Papineau, *et al.*, we can
use it to 'prove' its own reliability. Call an inductive inference made
by the rule 'right' if it concludes to a true assertion, and 'wrong' if it
concludes to a false one. Call an inductive inference 'ring' if it has
been checked and found to be right, or not been checked and is
wrong. Suppose the majority of checked inductive inferences have
been found to be right. It follows that they are also ring. Using as the
justified premiss 'The majority of checked inductive inferences are

---

[1] Goodman invented these 'grue' hypotheses (1946) as part of the process of testing
a putative rule—in this case 'Extrapolate the observed data'—against actual inductive
practices. We saw in Ch. 1 that Goodman believed that the same sort of validation
procedure is used to test and establish sound inferential procedures in deductive logic.
In the Goodman view of things, the grue problem shows that in practice we have
means of distinguishing 'projectible' from 'non-projectible' predicates: the projectibility of a predicate depends on its degree of 'entrenchment', i.e. the extent to which it is
embedded in existing inductive practice. The circularity problem clearly appears again
here, but it is likely that Goodman would have taken the same line as Goldman, claiming that the circularity is of a type both unavoidable and endemic.

ring' in van Cleve's argument A, we conclude from A that the majority of all inductive inferences are ring. But only a finite number have been checked, leaving a potential infinity unchecked. It follows that the majority of all inductive inferences are wrong, and hence that the rule is unreliable!

These easily manufactured counterexamples show dramatically the futility of circular justification, 'rule-circular' or not. The favourite, but hopeless, defence against them is to claim that an inductive procedure should only apply to 'natural kinds', and 'green' and 'right' denote natural kinds and 'grue' and 'ring' don't, and natural kinds are by nature more 'projectible' to the future. This is presumably the answer which van Cleve has in mind when he tells us that there is at least a 'partial answer to the "new riddle of induction"—which are the good inductive inferences, the ones that are justified if any are?' (1984: 556). But it doesn't work. On this understanding natural kinds are exactly as difficult to identify as projectible kinds. And the problem of identifying projectible kinds is just the problem of induction. An appeal to past evidence to show that what we intuitively understand as a natural kind is projectible begs the question, as Goodman's grue problem so dramatically shows. Indeed, what that evidence does show is that being a natural kind as that term might be intuitively understood is neither a necessary nor a sufficient condition for projectibility. Science is full of successful theories whose subject-matter is increasingly anything but natural kinds like 'green'. Time in the classical sense of a parameter completely invariant across frames would presumably have been regarded a century ago as a natural kind, but it was a natural kind that was displaced after 1905 by two distinct and very *un*natural kinds of time, an invariant 'proper time', not intuitively a time at all but a distance furnishing the metric structure of Minkowski space-time, and a non-invariant frame-dependent time in which temporal orderings between spacelike-separated events can be reversed from one inertial frame to another.[2] On a more banal level, the scientific concept of work is nothing like work as usually understood, nor that of energy like that of energy as normally understood; and so on: the examples are too numerous to enumerate.

---

[2] O'Hear points out that post-1905 we do in fact generalize our observations of moving bodies in terms of these unnatural kinds (1997: 42), just as we might in principle choose to describe green emeralds as grue.

The notion of a natural kind is anyway a very difficult one to pin down. If 'grue' is not a natural kind because as a parameter (time in this case) increases the possessor of that predicate changes discontinuously, then even such a basic term as 'water' must plead guilty as well, since as the parameter 'temperature' increases water will at 0 and 100 degrees Celsius pass discontinuously from one phase to another, just as do grue emeralds at their characteristic time. Why single out time for special treatment? The only recourse of the natural kinds defender is to define them in terms of their use in stable, perduring theory. But then to say that natural kinds are projectible and other kinds are not is empty, a mere tautology.

So much for natural kinds. A little reflection shows that the Goodman paradox arises because the number of observations after which A-ness is extrapolated to the next observed individual is taken to be uniform across the class of properties A. Consistency can be restored, but only by making that number be dependent on the property A itself. Thus the point at which it is 'safe'—according to the rule—to conclude that the next emerald will be green must come before the point at which it is 'safe' to conclude that it will be grue, or vice versa. This observation may seem to offer a way out of the Goodman paradox which does not appeal to the doctrine of natural kinds. But it brings with it the problem of identifying the characteristic 'projectibility-point', the point at which it is safe to extrapolate, for each property A. That can certainly not be a function of A's syntactical form, because, as Goodman further showed, the difference in syntactic form between 'green' and 'grue' is conventional. If we define the predicate 'bleen' to hold of x just in case x has been observed and is blue or is unobserved and green, the pairs {green, blue} and {grue, bleen} are interdefinable: x is green just in case x has been observed and is grue or is unobserved and is bleen. But this means that we have no independent means of telling at which stage in the accumulation of data it is 'safe' (the scare quotes are meant to signify that there is no assumption that it ever is safe) to project A-ness, for each A. We shall return to this point in the discussion of probabilistic induction in Chapter 4.

The 'Pessimistic Meta-Induction'

Recall Popper's famous picture of the progress of science as conjecture followed by refutation. An inspection of the history of science certainly seems to support his view. Even the most entrenched theories have been eventually undermined. Here is a rather ironical example: for Poincaré the Newtonian theory was so overwhelmingly probable as to be practically certain, given the enormous variety and number of the observations which supported it (Poincaré 1952: 186); yet in the very year that this opinion was published (1905) Einstein was to present the theory of special relativity, paving the way to the general theory and the complete overthrow of classical mechanics and gravitational theory. But the principal assumption on which the attempt to explicate a sound inductive method has always rested is that science exemplifies a particularly rigorous standard of inductive acceptance. Recall Broad's words: induction is the glory of science. If that is so, then it seems to have all the glory of a Pyrrhic victory. From a quite different quarter we appear to have induction showing that induction is an unreliable belief-forming process: a 'pessimistic meta-induction' indeed.

By now we should not be particularly surprised at this. But the majority view remains that to accept that induction is unreliable is to abandon any hope of a rational analysis of empirical knowledge and belief formation. Popper, usually regarded as the principal opponent of this view, believed that the acceptance procedures of science are rational but not inductive: his claim that induction plays no part in them rests, however, on a very narrow view of induction as the sort of fairly uncritical extrapolation from experience that van Cleve's argument A exemplifies and Bacon himself condemned. For those people for whom induction is what science is in practice and who also accept the 'pessimistic meta-induction', the only way out of the looming paradox is to cut the link between induction and truth. This has duly been done. Non-truth-based goals for science are of course the province of the anti-realist and pragmatist, but another option that preserves the spirit if not the letter of truth-oriented induction is to regard not truth pure and simple, but either of probable truth or near-truth as the goal of induction. Probable truth is quite consistent with all the members of what is over all of time probably a small sample turning out false, and we shall look at the probabilist programme in depth in Chapter 4. The near or approximate truth of theories which are strictly false is a notion employed by Popper (who despite his professed anti-inductivism accepted the view that all scientific theories will eventually be falsified) in proposing a Whiggish view of the history of science as an asymptotic progress to the 'whole truth' of a temporal sequence of strictly false but nevertheless more truth-like, or 'verisimilar' (his terminology) theories.

The idea that the evidence justifies concluding to the approximate but not actual truth of theories tends also to be combined with a view of inference from evidence as a quite different procedure from simple extrapolative inferences of the 'Most observed As are Bs. Therefore most As in the entire population are Bs'. This other view is often associated with the name of Popper, but it was the idea of lawyer Bacon himself that reliable information comes only from asking searching questions designed to make manifest the falsity of testimony where it is false. Suppose it is possible to devise a test which, if a hypothesis is false, is almost certain on the occasion of test to detect its falsity. And now suppose the test is performed and no negative outcome is revealed. If there are reliable procedures anywhere, surely this is where they are. And there certainly seem to be such tests. In the next chapter we shall see whether this approach to inductive inference lives up to its—apparently very considerable—promise.

Conclusion

Reliabilists have undoubtedly pointed out something of interest in the possibility of an external standard of justification. On the other hand, the literature has provided no shortage of highly counterintuitive consequences of the view. Nor does reliabilism assist you in telling, *from the information that you have available to you*, that you are on the right track, even if as a matter of fact you are. The problem of induction is precisely what, if anything, you *can* legitimately infer from the knowledge available to you. Hume's answer was nothing. The reliabilist appeal to the external standard does not succeed in showing Hume to be wrong. In particular, the distinction between 'premiss-circular' and 'rule-circular' arguments which is intended to cordon off a type of circular justification of an inductive rule from the obvious—and correct—charge of proving nothing is as specious as the rule itself turns out to be. Nor does the *tu quoque* charge of reliabilists against deductive justifications of deduction stick: there may be a potential regress of deductive justifications of a deductive rule, but it does not have to loop back upon itself.

3

Realism and the No-Miracles Argument

Introduction

Sophisticated advocates of the claim that there are reliable procedures for acquiring factual knowledge do not usually have the 'Most
observed As are Bs; therefore most As are Bs' rule—often called
'induction by enumeration'—in mind when they make it, nor do they
usually invoke 'rule-circular' justifications, at any rate consciously.
They tend to echo Bacon's condemnation of induction by enumeration as puerile, and endorse the other Baconian claim that the only
reliable inductive inferences are those from the confirmation of new
predictions to, if not the truth then the 'approximate' or 'essential'
truth (we shall come to what these scare-quoted qualifiers mean in a
moment) of the hypotheses which made them. Their argument,
implicit in Bacon's remarks about the need to *interrogate* nature, has
come, for reasons which will soon be clear, to be called the *No-
Miracles argument*. This is adduced in support of the following
CLAIM: If a hypothesis H predicts *independently* a sufficiently large
and precise body of data then on that ground, we can reasonably
infer H's 'approximate' truth.

A good deal of current scientific theory seems to satisfy the
antecedent of CLAIM. Given that, and CLAIM itself, we infer that the
experimental record is good enough evidence for the approximate
truth of current science. This conclusion is the doctrine of *scientific
realism*. If the No-Miracles argument is valid, then, we can infer that
scientific realism is 'essentially' true, and that thereby the problem of
induction is, in effect, solved.

The No-Miracles Argument

Note that if the qualifiers 'approximately', 'essentially' etc. were not
there CLAIM would be flatly inconsistent. For 'current science' is

indexical, and 'current science' in later epochs is in general inconsistent with 'current science' in earlier; this is the premiss, recall, of the so-called pessimistic meta-induction. The scare quotes remind us that no one has yet been able to give a very good, or at any rate uncontroversial, account of what 'approximate truth' means in the context of scientific theories (for a recent survey of the attempts see Niiniluoto 1998). This does not greatly matter from the point of the view of the No-Miracles argument itself, however, because the role—a crucial one, as we shall see—played in that argument by 'approximate truth' does not depend on any precise characterization. What that role is will become quickly apparent from the argument itself, which proceeds in the following four steps:

  (i)   If a theory T independently predicts some observational data E
        and T is not approximately correct, then its agreement with the
        facts recorded in E must be accidental, a chance occurrence.
 (ii)   The facts recorded in E are such that a chance agreement with
        them is exceedingly improbable. Here is just one example.
        Quantum electrodynamics predicts the observed value of the
        magnetic moment of the electron to better than one part in a
        billion, in natural units.[1] The odds against a chance agreement
        are therefore truly stupendous just for this piece of data, let
        alone for the total observational and experimental evidence
        that has been accumulated.
(iii)   We can regard such small chances as being so extraordinarily
        unlikely that we can confidently reject the hypothesis that they
        are *just* chance occurrences, at any rate if there is an alternative
        explanation which accounts better for them.
 (iv)   Hence we can confidently infer that T is approximately true,
        the smallness of the chance in (iii) being an index of the degree
        of confidence justified.

And so we have CLAIM. It all sounds very plausible. It has certainly sounded sufficiently plausible to others for the No-Miracles argument to become the argument of choice for scientific realists. Here is a sample:

The positive argument for realism is that it is the only philosophy that doesn't make the success of science a miracle. (Putnam 1975: 73)

---

  [1] The last calculated value up to 1987 was 1.00115965246 ± 0.00000000020, and the observed value was 1.00115965221 ± 0.00000000003.

It would be a miracle, a coincidence on a near-cosmic scale, if a theory made as many correct empirical predictions as, say, the general theory of relativity or the photon theory of light without what the theory says about the fundamental structure of the universe being correct or 'essentially' or 'basically' correct. But we shouldn't accept miracles, not at any rate if there is a non-miraculous alternative. . . . . So it is plausible to conclude that presently accepted theories are indeed 'essentially' correct. (Worrall 1989: 140; note the scare quotes)

it cannot be just due to an improbable accident if a hypothesis is again and again successful when tested in different circumstances, and especially if it is successful in making previously unexpected predictions . . . If a theory h has been well-corroborated, then it is highly probable *that it is truth-like.* (Popper 1983: 346; italics in original)

We have spoken of the experiment as testing a certain null hypothesis, namely, in this case, that the subject possesses no sensory discrimination whatever of the kind claimed; we have, too, assigned as appropriate to this hypothesis a certain frequency distribution of occurrences . . . the frequency distribution appropriate to a classification by pure chance. (Fisher 1935: 17)

Fisher is not usually included in the roll-call of No-Miracles workers. He is included here because he was the first to see that a familiar chance model, on which the No-Miracles argument is based, could be turned into a methodological tool of apparently very great power (though subject to an important qualification that we shall examine in due course). The chance model is that of a simple guessing game. Suppose someone correctly predicts a sequence of apparently random numbers. We tend to infer that the predictor must have *some* knowledge of how those numbers were selected, because had they none their success at prediction would have been too great a coincidence to be due simply to chance.

Mutatis mutandis, the No-Miracles argument appears to say just this. Steps (i) and (ii) say that if T is not some fairly substantial approximation to the truth about the structure of the data source then its success is that merely of a lucky guess, and a very lucky one indeed because the probability of it being true just as a guess, that is, by chance, is minimal. Consider again the case of guessing correctly each of nine digits after the decimal point in the magnetic moment of the electron. This has, or appears to have—the importance of the qualification will become apparent shortly—a probability of 10^{-9} on the chance hypothesis, which is very small indeed, so small that surely we can invoke (iii) to dismiss the chance hypothesis and claim with a commensurately high degree of confidence that the confirmed theories of current science are indeed 'approximately' true. And we can say this even without having any precise theory of approximate or 'essential' truth. In cases like the amazing prediction by QED of the magnetic moment of the electron, and that is only the most extreme, Nature is obviously trying to tell us that we are on the right track. To think otherwise is not 'exercising the faculty of reasonable doubt'. It is not even scepticism. It is *paranoia*.

The model of science as an 'active' game of guessing nature therefore seems to offer a very real hope of answering Hume, whose totally negative view of the problem of induction seems now as if it might be the result merely of presenting it in a falsely passive way. The analogy here is of setting someone the task of identifying an infinite sequence of numbers from the knowledge of just a short initial segment. If that is the only information supplied, then it offers no guidance at all in selecting the correct one from the infinity of possible continuations. Presented like this, Hume's negative view of the problem does indeed seem unanswerable. But suppose that the data are the outcome of a *dynamic interaction* between predictor and Nature, in which Nature is forced to confirm guesses which would be most unlikely to be correct by chance; as in the example of someone correctly predicting the first n digits of the sequence for n greater than, say, 10. In that case the 'passive' presentation omits highly relevant information, and when that information is added Hume's Problem seems suddenly far less intractable—apparently, not intractable at all. Moreover, the guessing-game model, Bacon's model in effect, seems a more realistic representation of the way the data that we do feel we can 'induce' from are obtained.

'Approximate Truth'

Or so it might seem. But now let us be a little more critical. First, what does it actually mean to say that current science is approximately true? The answer given by the No-Miracles argument: 'Because if it is not approximately true then its enormous predictive success would be due to chance, and the chance is so small as to be not rationally credible', suggests that each accepted scientific theory has a sufficiently extensive *core* of truth, extended and refined by its successors like a fruit shedding successive outer husks as it grows and matures. The problem is to turn a suggestive metaphor into an adequately precise explication which will explain the increasing accuracy with which physical magnitudes are successfully predicted.

There have been many attempts to define a precise notion of the approximate truth, or truthlikeness, or verisimiltude, of theories; just how many and diverse can be gathered from Niiniluoto's survey (1998). But relatively few promise to be able to explain how truthlikeness according to their account satisfies the additional explanatory constraint of accounting for the increasingly accurate predictive success of science. One that does, and is not included in Niiniluoto's list, is developed by Worrall (1996). It is that the core can be identified with the basic mathematical equations of the theories, given that these do seem to be the components retained in the succession of theories, often as limiting cases in the succeeding theories as a parameter approaches a fixed value: for example, classical kinematics and dynamics are recovered from relativistic for sufficiently small values of v/c. This seems promising because we can see a link between the stability but increasing refinement of the predictions made by the successive members of the theory-chain, and the retention of their equations as special cases restricted to what the succeeding equations tell us is the relevant domain of application:

Fresnel's equations are taken over completely intact into the superseding theory [Maxwell's]—reappearing there reinterpreted but, as mathematical equations, entirely unchanged . . . the [Correspondence] principle applies *purely* at the mathematical level, and hence is quite compatible with the new theory's basic theoretical assumptions . . . being entirely at odds with those of the old. (Worrall 1996: 160)

For all its promise there are nevertheless two quite distinct reasons for doubting this account. First, the Fresnel/Maxwell case is a very special one. It is stretching the notion of identity a good deal, and probably beyond what it can bear, to claim identity even at the mathematical level between the corresponding equations, say, of quantum and classical mechanics. There is almost a better case for talking of an identity of *interpretation* of *different* mathematical formalisms. Quantum mechanics talks about observables in an apparently similar way to classical physics, but in classical physics the observables are real-valued functions while in quantum mechanics they are types of linear operator on a vector space over the field of complex numbers. As is frequently observed, the mathematical apparatus of each couldn't be more different. It is true that the classical equation of motion of an observable, $df/dt = \partial f/\partial t + \{H,f\}$, is derived within quantum mechanics by 'identifying' the classical functions f and H with appropriate operators **f** and **H**, and the Poisson bracket $\{H,f\}$ with another linear operator, the commutator **[H,f]** of **f** and **H** (Landau and Lifschitz 1958: 27, 28). But there can clearly be no identification in the literal sense since **f**, **H**, and **[H,f]** are mathematically quite distinct objects from f, H, and $\{H,f\}$. Moreover, states in classical mechanics are not closed under addition (a formal property). In quantum mechanics they are.

'Structural realists' who take the view that there is continuity in the mathematics between successive theories might claim to be defending a purely *formal* identity in the equations, but even this is very questionable. The claim cannot rest on the fact that one can extract equations from one theory that, ignoring the differences between the mathematical objects respectively denoted by them, look formally identical to those extracted from another. If the mathematical-identity hypothesis is to explain how the predictive success of one theory is maintained and refined by its successor there must be some element of interpretation present, otherwise we should have to start crediting physics with the successful predictions of population genetics, and vice versa, because both use the same diffusion equations. But even a minimal interpretation of the equations of quantum mechanics would mention the fact that they are not identical to the classical ones for the reasons given above.

Counterexamples

All in all this particular 'approximate truth' account seems unlikely, for the reasons suggested, to live up to its promise. This is one source of difficulty for the No-Miracles account. Another, more immediately threatening, is that it is not difficult to show that CLAIM is *false*. Indeed, doing so is surprisingly easy, for there are recipes for producing simple counterexamples. Here is one due to Harold Jeffreys (1961: 46). Suppose T(x) and T′(x) are two mutually inconsistent law-like hypotheses about some class of physical objects, possibly just space-time points, x and let R(x) mean that x is located in the observer's past. Then the hypothesis T′: 'For every x, if R(x) then T(x) and if not R(x) then T′(x)' agrees with T: 'For every x, T(x)' on all points up to the present. Suppose also that up to now every x in the observer's past to have been examined satisfies T(x). It follows that both T and T′ agree with the observational data, and disagree on all future possible observations. T′(x) can be chosen in infinitely many different ways. This is particularly obvious where T(x) says that x satisfies some equation, which without loss of generality we can write $f(x) = 0$ (x can be multi-dimensional). If the data specify values $x_1, x_2, \ldots, x_n$ satisfying this equation, they also satisfy the equation $T'(x): f(x) + d_{x_1}(x)d_{x_2}(x) \ldots d_{x_n}(x)g(x) = 0$, where $d_u(x) = 0$ when $u = x$ and $d_u(x) = 1$ otherwise, and $g(x)$ is any function not identically equal to $f(x)$ (Jeffreys uses Galileo's law of free fall as an illustration). There are more such functions even than there are real numbers.

The other recipe is one we are already familiar with: Goodman's grue construction, which can be generalized to produce infinitely many alternatives. The different choices of the function g in Jeffreys's recipe create a 'horizontal' infinity of alternatives, but we can create a 'vertical' infinity of alternatives by specifying different epochs t, other than the 'now' characterizing grue, for some discontinuous change to occur. In the emerald example we should then have, for discretely increasing values of t, an infinite sequence of hypotheses 'All emeralds are grue t', which agree with 'All emeralds are green' for emeralds observed up to t but diverge after. Clearly, observational evidence gathered up to t for 'All emeralds are green' at time t will be equally consistent not only with 'All emeralds are grue$_t$', but also with 'All emeralds are grue$_{t'}$' for all $t' > t$. The extension to arbitrary hypotheses other than those about the colour of emeralds is straightforward. All these hypotheses describe distinct types of logically possible world in which T is presumably not even approximately true, for they disagree with T at all points past some epoch. Assuming that there are many more epochs to come than have elapsed, each grue$_t$ hypothesis has much more disagreement with T than agreement. And they all predict the data.

Hume himself had much earlier pointed the way to such possibilities:

Let the course of things be allowed hitherto ever so regular, that alone, without some new argument or inference, proves not that the future will continue so. In vain do you pretend to have learned the nature of bodies from your past experience. Their secret nature, and consequently all their effects and influence, may change . . . This happens sometimes, and with regard to some objects: Why may it not happen always, and with regard to all objects? What logic, what process of argument secures you against this supposition? (1739: IV)

None, of course. Nor even does the 'course of things' have to change: we might simply have misidentified it all along: the hypotheses embodying the infinitely many distinct possibilities equally predict the existing data and equally extrapolate it ('All emeralds are grue' is no less an extrapolation from a sample of grue emeralds than 'All emeralds are green' is an extrapolation *from exactly the same sample*— of green emeralds!). But they can't all be true, and they can't all be 'approximately true' either: the grue$_t$ alternatives all diverge from T on a potentially infinite data segment and agree only on a finite one. Unless some very non-standard meaning is being given to 'approximately true', this cannot be correct. But CLAIM says it is. Therefore CLAIM is false.

It might be objected that these concocted alternatives did not predict the data *independently*, as did T. They are parasitic on T: without its guidance they would never be thought of. Since, therefore, it is really T doing the predicting, not them, it is T, not them, that should receive the credit. This might sound plausible, but on closer analysis the objection collapses. It is true that the prediction of the data did as a matter of fact occur via T, but that means only that, for whatever reason, T was considered seriously as an explanatory theory while the others were not (and were it not for philosophers would probably never be considered at all): as Miller reminds us, 'we all know that "All emeralds are grue" is false' (1994: 37). Any grue alternative to T, indexed to the current epoch, could have been proposed before now, in which case it would have predicted exactly the same phenomena as T. The fact that nobody seriously did so is because, as Miller's observation attests, they in effect assign it a prior plausibility weighting of 0. But that is not the issue here: in every respect it would have been just as predictive of current evidence as T.

This answer seems only to raise another objection, however, and one moreover with a long and distinguished pedigree. Suppose some hypothesis H is deliberately constructed from the current evidence to 'predict' it. In this case H clearly did not *independently* predict the evidence. According to the argument above, though, it did: it too *might* have been proposed before the fact; it just wasn't. So if that is the argument for claiming that a hypothesis independently predicted data, the argument must be wrong. Furthermore, the structure of the

No-Miracles argument itself explains exactly why such a hypothesis is no counterexample to CLAIM: because, far from agreement with the evidence being highly unlikely if it is false, agreement is certain, guaranteed by the fact that H was constructed to deliver it. As Giere points out: 'If the known facts were used in constructing the model and were thus built into the resulting hypotheses . . . then the fit between these facts and the hypothesis [*sic*] provides no evidence that the hypothesis is true [since] *these facts had no chance of refuting the hypothesis*' (1984: 161; italics added). In other words, step (i) of the No-Miracles argument is blocked.

Giere is only one of many, in a line going back to Peirce and Whewell if not before, who have advanced this argument which, despite the concurrence of venerable opinion, is fallacious and rather obviously so. For E either conflicts with H or it doesn't: there is no *chance* to the matter. Giere is confusing an experimental set-up, call it X, with one of its possible outcomes, E. This is similar to identifying a random variable, like X a *function* on a possibility space, with one of its values: thus, there may be a chance that the outcome of this flipped coin will be as predicted—heads, say—but it makes no sense to talk of a tail (the actual outcome) being heads. We shall discuss the point further in Chapter 8, but it should be clear that it is simply not true that the chance of X producing an outcome agreeing with H must be 100 per cent: the chance is the chance, whatever it might be (and we shall consider that shortly), of the facts turning out other than they did. To sum up: the counterexample to CLAIM really is a counterexample, and CLAIM is really false.

The falsity of CLAIM implies that the No-Miracles argument is fallacious. Arguably at least a suspicion to that effect should anyway have been kindled by the claim that all the mutually inconsistent theories which in the past have made successful predictions are 'approximately true'. At any rate, there are now independent grounds for that conclusion and it is time to look at each of the inferential steps (i)–(iii) to determine which is at fault. The result, perhaps surprisingly, is that *they all are*.

Start with (i) and (ii), and consider once again the probability of predicting the digits in the magnetic moment of the electron by chance. Describing a real number down to k significant figures after the decimal point determines not, of course, a single number but an interval of length 10^{-k}. The space of all possible values the quantity might logically take is represented by the half-open interval consisting of the non-negative real line (or maybe even the entire line). There is a general procedure, adopted since the time of Bayes himself, for computing chances where the possibilities can be represented as points in a measurable region of Euclidean space of some finite number of dimensions. The whole-number ratios appropriate to discrete space transform 'naturally' into ratios of Lebesgue measures (Lebesgue measure is basically the familiar measure of length, area, and volume). In this case the space has one dimension and the regions are one-dimensional intervals. But there is a problem: the length of the interval representing the space of *possible* values is infinity, and dividing by infinity is not a defined operation. This might sound pedantic. After all, the usual rule of thumb when infinities appear in a denominator and not in the numerator is to say that the quotient is zero. So why not say that the chance is zero?

There is more than one answer. One could start off by noting that according to that rule the chance of the true value falling in *any* finite interval, however large, is still zero, which sounds odd. Not only does it sound odd: it also implies the violation of a principle called *countable additivity*. Each finite interval gets zero probability, but the half-line or the whole line, whichever is appropriate, can be represented as the 'sum' of as many such intervals as there are positive whole numbers (this is what is meant by the term 'countable'). But since this is all the possibilities, it has probability one, while the sum of a countable number of zeros is zero. We shall discuss the status of the principle of countable additivity later (it will turn out to be a principle that we shall actually want to endorse), but its violation suggests that something may be wrong. Indeed it is. Here is another problem. If B is any finite interval and A any subinterval of B, then by the definition of a conditional probability the chance of A conditional on B is undefined (for according to the rules of probability that conditional chance is the chance A divided by that of B; see below p. 62), though intuitively it would seem that it should be equal to the length of A divided by that of B.

There are, however, more decisive reasons against concluding that the chance is 0, or even that it takes *any* determinate value. First, there is the problem of transformations. By a suitable bicontinuous one–one transformation the non-negative part of the real line can be mapped onto a finite interval, depending on the mapping function (for example, the function $\tan^{-1}(x)$, $x \geq 0$ maps it onto the interval $[0,\pi/2)$; another, $x/(1 + x)$, maps it onto the interval $[0,1)$; it is not difficult to see that there are infinitely many analytic functions which will map it onto some finite interval). Such a transformation can be regarded merely as a relabelling of the outcomes, but under the relabelling the denominator of the chance-ratio is no longer infinite but a finite number, and 'the chance' is now well-defined but no longer 0! Indeed, by varying the choices of transformation judiciously 'the chance' can be made to take almost any value one likes. This non-invariance under transformations of the numerical coordinates gives rise to the so-called paradoxes of geometric probability, of which Bertrand's chord problem is the most famous example (Kac and Ulam 1968: 37–9.); another well-known example is the 'water/wine paradox', which we shall encounter in the next chapter.

And there is worse to come. So far we have been considering a possibility space consisting just of the possible values of a single physical magnitude. But that is an entirely artificial restriction, since implicit in the discussion are in addition all those possible states of affairs determined by the theories which make predictions about such magnitudes. Once we do include these explicitly the relatively tidy picture we have viewed up till now becomes much less tidy; in fact, it becomes ungovernably untidy. Let us see why. We want to know the chance of theory T agreeing with the data if T is not approximately true. Suppose T is not approximately true, but agrees in its predictions about the data with another hypothesis T' (such a T' can always be found, by Goodman's method). Therefore the chance of T agreeing with the data were T' true is 1. Similarly, if T agrees in its predictions on the data with T'', then the chance of T agreeing with the data given the truth of T'' is 1. And we know that we can always find *infinitely* many theories strongly disagreeing with T outside the data but such that, given their truth, the chance of T agreeing with the data is 1 (the grue alternatives will always furnish an infinite set). Theories correspond to classes of possible worlds (i.e. to each theory corresponds the class of possible worlds which would make it true), and the chance of T agreeing with E and T not being approximately true is the combined chance of all the infinitely many worlds in which E is true and T not approximately true.

The simple guessing-game we started with is simple no more. From guessing finite numbers of integers we seem to be faced with classes of possible universes, and the class of all these, to the extent that it is determinate at all (it is too vast to be counted even by the infinite counting numbers, the transfinite ordinals), not only does not have a metric structure like that of a Euclidean space, but it does not have a natural metric structure at all. Nor is it clear that it can even be given one (though where the universes are of the type describable within the sorts of formal language familiar to logicians it has a familiar topological structure, whence the compactness theorem for first-order logic gets its name: see Bell and Slomson 1969: 157, 158). Any Laplacean computation of chances in such an unstructured possibility-space seems out of the question.

The mention of Laplace brings us to possibly the most fundamental difficulty facing anyone trying to give an unambiguous and meaningful value to 'the chance' of T agreeing with the data when T is not approximately true. This difficulty is not mathematical at all but philosophical. So far it has simply been assumed that, where it makes mathematical sense, the chance is measured by the Laplacean ratio of number of favourable to number of possible cases. But Laplace himself cautioned that the use of the ratio is valid only if each of the possibilities is *equally* a priori possible (1915: 11). If they are not, 'we will determine first their respective possibilities, whose exact appreciation is one of the most delicate points of the theory of chance' (ibid.; Laplace uses 'possibility' interchangeably with 'probability' at certain points of his essay). This is not just an arbitrary condition imposed by Laplace. According to the mathematics of probability, the chance of any event is the sum of its chances given each possible world in which it might occur, multiplied by the chance of that possible world being the true world. Where, and only where, all those a priori chances are equal, is the Laplacean ratio the chance. But how could one possibly know a priori the chance of any possible world being the true world, and whether they were equal or not? One would have to be God.

It might be asked why we should need to guess chances a priori. Why not a posteriori? And a posteriori, on the basis of the scientific evidence itself, we know that most purely logical possibilities, for example those represented by the grue hypotheses, are just that, mere logical possibilities, not possibilities that are to be seriously entertained. In particular, the grue hypotheses are clearly mere philosophers' games. The possibilities that it is realistic and sensible to entertain are those that current science, after evaluating the total evidence, actually does entertain (under the title of 'Tempered Personalism' such a view was proposed as the foundation of a Bayesian methodology by Shimony (1993: 202–26), developing an idea of Harold Jeffreys).[2] And these are very few indeed. It is, one is frequently reminded, a far from trivial matter to think of *any* alternative that satisfies the sorts of powerful constraints (e.g. covariance, gauge invariance, other symmetry conditions, Correspondence Principle, and so forth) that the evidence appears to indicate are those that a satisfactory theory should satisfy, constraints which, when conjoined with the evidence itself, are very restrictive indeed.

We know how to answer this. If the constraints are sufficient to cut down the size of the class of alternatives in any effective way then the content of those constraints must extend far beyond the evidence, since the evidence is consistent with an uncountable infinity of alternatives to the theories of current science. They are implicitly, if not explicitly, *theories*, or classes of theories (a constraint is extensionally equivalent to such a class), about the world, and very strong theories at that. To say that the evidence justifies their adoption is to beg the very question that the No-Miracles argument was intended to answer. Such an a posteriori defence of it makes that argument presuppose the answer, nicely corroborating Hume's claim that any inductive argument will have either explicit or implicit inductive premisses.

To sum up: it is very difficult not to believe that a theory T which predicts among other things a quantity correctly to within one-billionth of its observed value should not be in some fairly intimate rapport with the truth. But it is equally if not more difficult to justify this belief by appeal to the chance of this occurring should the theory predicting it not be approximately true, for there seems to be no way to compute this chance without begging the very question that the exercise of computing it is supposed to answer. The existence of an uncountably infinite number of alternative possibilities which, while being in strong disagreement with T, would also explain that agreement, makes the 'miraculousness' of the agreement between T and the data at least questionable. And when these alternatives are taken into account the computation of the chance of agreement with the data when the theory is not approximately true is a far from straightforward or uncontroversial matter. There are the severe if not intractable mathematical problems of determining Laplacean

---

[2] 'The theory [of how scientific theories are evaluated against data] must provide criteria for testing the chief types of scientific law that have actually been suggested or asserted' (1961: 10). 'The theory', for Jeffreys, would be the Bayesian theory equipped with a Simplicity Postulate (see below, p. 204).

chances in such enormous and metrically unstructured possibility spaces, and there is the even more intractable philosophical problem of justifying in any non-question-begging way any assignment at all of probabilities to all these alternative possibilities.

Fisher's Solution

Fisher was aware of the problems attending any simple-minded identification of what he called the *null hypothesis* (in the No-Miracles argument the null hypothesis is that currently accepted science is not even approximately true) with a determinate chance distribution. Indeed, he used the transformation problem with devastating effect against it. But the work for which he is most celebrated in the field of scientific methodology was by no means merely destructive: possibly his most influential contribution was to find what many people, including both he and for long the statistical establishment, thought was a solution to the problem of alternatives while maintaining the essential form of No-Miracles reasoning. He presented this solution in the illustrative context of a famous thought-experiment which otherwise contains all the essential ingredients of the No-Miracles argument.

The thought-experiment is as follows. A lady claims to have the ability to detect by taste whether a cup of (milky) tea had the milk added before or after the tea was put in the cup. To test this claim the following experiment is performed. She is given eight cups, of which four had the milk added first and four the tea first. She has no knowledge of the order in which the different cups are presented, and is asked to identify the four cups in which the milk was added first. The null hypothesis in this experiment is that she has no appreciable faculty of sensory discrimination. A *significant* test result is one which has a sufficiently small chance of occurring, if the null hypothesis is true, to warrant rejection of it (this outcome will be the lady correctly identifying all four milk-first cups correctly). A significant result is thus the analogue of the 'miraculous outcome' in the No-Miracles argument for realism that refutes, or is alleged to refute, the hypothesis that current science is not even approximately true.

The additional constraint that Fisher believed needed to be satisfied to justify inferring a determinate chance distribution from the null hypothesis was a systematic *randomization* of the order in which the different types of cup are presented. It remains true that after any performance of the randomized experiment there will still be a potentially unlimited number of alternative explanations of any success the lady might have which are consistent with the falsity of the null hypothesis: she might have been told the sequence of random numbers determining the order in which the milk-first cups were presented; she might have guessed it; she might be using some personal algorithm that happened in this case to give the correct order; and there might be more occult reasons. All these things, and more, might be true. But now they pose no problem, for in the context of a properly randomized experiment we are looking, not at the single case, *but at the long run.* Why the long run? Because Fisher's view of chance was that it was a phenomenon that manifests itself only in the long run. This was a common view at the time, and still is. It is what is called a *frequency theory* of chance. According to it, chances are properties of generic events, like 'landing heads up' for tossed coins, and evaluated numerically as the relative frequency of occurrences of such events in an indefinitely large number of repetitions of the random experiment—in the long run, in other words. Fisher, with most working scientists, believed that the evidence supplied by very long sequences of observations pointed to characteristic long-run frequencies as invariant physical properties of the sorts of random devices he had enumerated. So telling was this evidence felt to be that Richard von Mises, author of the most worked-out and sophisticated frequency theory of chance, accorded it law-like status, calling it the Empirical Law of Large Numbers. We shall look at the frequency theory in more detail later, in Chapter 9; our concern here is limited to seeing what follows from accepting it.

What follows, Fisher believed, is that the randomization, by means of 'the actual manipulation of the physical apparatus used in games of chance, cards, dice, roulettes etc., or, more expeditiously, from a published collection of random sampling numbers' (Fisher 1935: 11) will ensure that each of the $^8C_4 = 8!/4!4!$ possible combinations of four milk-first and four tea-first cups has the same chance of occurring, in the frequency-sense that it *will occur with approximately the same frequency in the long run.* These random mechanisms, as far as Fisher was concerned, were chosen just because they were 'known' to yield their outcomes with approximately equal frequency in the long run (never mind how they were 'known' to do this; this is a problem we shall address in Chapter 9; for now let us simply assume it for the sake of argument). To sum up: only in the context of a properly randomized experiment is the identification of the null hypothesis with a determinate chance distribution possible, Fisher believed, and then not only possible but mandatory. The randomization 'is the only point in the experimental procedure in which the laws of chance, which are to be in exclusive control of our frequency distribution, have been explicitly introduced' (1935: 19). A corollary, of course, that there is no such chance distribution implied by the null hypothesis of No-Miracles argument for realism, for the data were not obtained from experiments deliberately randomized to produce their outcomes with equal frequencies; indeed, how could they be?

Suppose all this granted, and that the lady really has no discriminatory ability of the sort claimed. In a well-controlled experiment, therefore, she should (I say 'should' for reason which will be apparent shortly) have no knowledge at all of the order of milk-first, tea-first, cups. In that case the chance of her picking the correct one is simply equal to the frequency with which that particular combination is selected by the randomizer, which will be, in the long run, 1/70. The corresponding long-run frequency distribution for K correct identifications given the null hypothesis is then as below:

$$K = 0 \quad \text{chance} = 1/70$$
$$1 \quad \text{chance} = 16/70$$
$$2 \quad \text{chance} = 36/70$$
$$3 \quad \text{chance} = 16/70$$
$$4 \quad \text{chance} = 1/70$$

The task now is to identify a set R (for 'reject') of 'significant' values of K, that is, values which (*a*) are all in better agreement than any outcome outside R with the hypothesis that the lady has some power of discrimination and (*b*) are sufficiently 'miraculous', that is, have collectively a sufficiently small chance, say α, given the null hypothesis, to warrant rejecting it in accordance with step (iii). R = {4 cups correctly identified} has a suitably small α, and it is in better agreement with the hypothesis of some discriminatory power than any other outcome.[3] The force of the inference to the falsity of the null hypothesis should K = 4 be observed, Fisher observes, is 'logically that of a simple disjunction: *Either* an exceptionally rare chance has

---

[3] Though it is hardly highly probable merely given *some* power of discrimination. More probable would be the set {4,3} but, as Fisher pointed out, the probability of getting 3 correct by chance is too high to warrant dismissal of the null. A more sensitive test would be obtained by increasing the number of cups.

occurred, *or* the theory of random distribution is not true' (Fisher 1956: 39; italics in the original).

We shall look again at that last step in due course. The question that we have to ask at this point is whether Fisher is right that randomization secures the link between the null hypothesis and a determinate chance distribution. Despite Fisher's genius it is not difficult to see that the answer is no, no more (surprisingly) than in the unrandomized circumstances in which the No-Miracles argument is applied to conclude that current science is 'approximately true', and for just the same sort of reason: *there are too many alternative explanations of success other than that the lady can discriminate by taste.* For example, if a random number table is being used to randomize the combinations the lady might know which part of the table of random numbers is being used to determine the positions of the milk-first cups (Good 1983: 87, 88); she might have a stooge signalling the correct answers; she might be informed by a divine source; she might be a seer; and so on. By the rules of chance the chance of a 100 per cent success-rate in repeated experiments with the eight cups if the null hypothesis is true is the total chance of all these alternatives. And we are back again to trying to calculate something that does not seem calculable. What we can say definitely, however, is that, *pace* Fisher, it does not follow from the truth of the null hypothesis that the long-run frequency of successful identifications is the same as the frequency of the corresponding combinations generated by the randomizer. Just as the truth of the null hypothesis failed to determine any chance distribution without randomization, it continues to do so with randomization.

It is, of course, the problem of alternative explanations all over again. Randomization does not solve it. Nothing does. Some if not most of the possible causes of a high success rate unconnected with the lady's sense of taste would of course be considered outlandish, but considerations of a priori plausibility were just what the No-Miracles argument was intended to avoid, as unreliable and subjective. Steps (i) and (ii) of the No-Miracles argument, either in the grand arena of testing physical theory or in the homely and circumscribed ambit of a lady tasting tea, remain unsecured.

The Doctors' Dilemma

It is time to move on, for worse is to follow. The result of subjecting step (iii) to a similarly critical scrutiny will be, perhaps surprisingly (but in view of the already impressive list of casualties perhaps not), that it does not survive it. Let us take the story up from where we left it. Suppose that Fisher had been correct in believing that the chance distribution 1/70, 16/70, 36/70, 16/70, 1/70 for K = 0, 1, 2, 3, 4, *was* implied by the truth of the null hypothesis. It would then follow that if the null hypothesis were true it would be rejected incorrectly only very rarely: 1/70 of the time. That *sounds* good. But if we could show that there are choices of R where, as in this one, the chance of an incorrect rejection is very small, and yet where there is nevertheless a very *large* chance—say, close to 100 per cent—of the null hypothesis being true given an outcome in R, the small frequency of incorrect rejections clearly could not justify concluding that the null hypothesis is false; we should, in effect, have a counterexample to the claim that step (iii) is sound.

It might sound impossible that counterexamples like that could exist, but in fact they can be produced to order. The following, for which I am indebted to Korb (1991), is yet another celebrated fictional experiment which has become almost as well known as Fisher's tea-tasting lady. It is known as 'The Harvard Medical School test': it was actually performed on staff and students at Harvard Medical School to see how accurately they could reason from statistical data which intuitively suggest a conclusion quite opposite to that which should be drawn. The result, presented and discussed in Casscells, Schoenberger and Grayboys (1978), is of great interest to anyone concerned (justifiably, as it turned out) about the ability of the present and future medical profession to understand elementary statistics. It is very interesting from our somewhat different perspective too.

The problem was set to the subjects as follows. Suppose we consider a population of people, members of which are tested for a specified disease. The test has the following characteristics. The so-called *false negative* rate, that is, the chance of a person having the disease testing negative, is zero, and the *false-positive* rate, that is, the chance of a person not having the disease testing positive, is 5 per cent (recall the 5 per cent significance level in the tea-tasting test; not having the disease is the null hypothesis). Note that the false-negative rate of 0 is equivalent to a *true-positive* rate of 100 per cent. This combination of false-negative and false-positive rates means that a positive result has a very small chance of occurrence when the null hypothesis is true, but is predicted with certainty when it is not. The conditions of step (iii) are clearly met. Finally, suppose the chance of anyone having the disease is 1/1,000.

I should emphasize that the example is entirely hypothetical. We want only to see what follows from the assumptions; how or even whether they could ever be established with any definiteness is not our concern here. What does follow is something most people find quite surprising. There are standard formulas to elicit the consequences we want, which we shall become familiar with later, but while they do their work very effectively they are less illuminating about what is actually going on than a more heuristic method that has been used in illustrating these concepts for the last three hundred years: drawing randomly from an urn. Urn drawing is another classical chance mechanism that Fisher might well have listed with 'cards, dice, roulettes etc.'; like them, it was also one which he believed generated corresponding long-run frequencies.

In this particular urn we imagine black and white balls each of which carries just one of the numerals 0 or 1. The urn models the population; a black ball is a person having the disease, and a white ball is a person not having the disease. A ball numbered 1 is a person testing positive; a ball numbered 0 is a person testing negative. Suppose there are 1,000 balls in the urn, and a ball is drawn randomly. For the chance of the ball being black to be equal to 1/1000 there must be just one black ball in the urn. The false-negative rate implies that this same ball is numbered 1. We have to approximate the false-positive rate but supposing that, of the 999 white balls, 50 must also be numbered 1 is very close. Hence 51 balls are numbered 1, but of these one only is black. Hence the chance of the drawn ball being black, conditional on it bearing a 1, is 1/51. In other words, *the chance of a person having the disease conditional on their testing positive is 1/51, less than 2 per cent.* We can see easily from the urn model how this chance depends on the *base-rate*, that is, the chance of anyone having the disease at all. If it had been 100 in 1,000 instead of 1, the chance of a person having the disease given a positive test result is 100/150, or 2/3; if it had been 500 in 1,000, the conditional chance would have been 500/550, or about 91 per cent. The message is clear:

the lower the base-rate for a fixed false-positive rate, the smaller the chance that H is true given the data E. The example tells us in a dramatic way that *the respective sizes of the false-positive and false-negative rates do not determine the chance of a rejection of the null hypothesis being incorrect.* In particular, the condition that the null hypothesis be incorrectly rejected only a very small proportion of the time is, surprisingly, entirely consistent with an arbitrarily high proportion of those rejections being incorrect.

The majority of the respondents at Harvard Medical School, ignoring the base-rate, regarded the false-positive rate as the chance of subjects not having the disease if they test positive, and accordingly gave the answer as 0.95. To reason thus has accordingly become known as *the base-rate fallacy.* Not merely trainee and professional members of the medical profession commit the base-rate fallacy. Even very eminent scientists do, as we have seen. And all the philosophers who use the No-Miracles argument do so as well. It is committed anew in every generation. The central methodological claims of a recent book on methodology (Mayo 1996) are based on committing it. In this book a version of the argument very similar to Fisher's is proposed. As in the tea-tasting, there is a notion of outcomes agreeing better or worse with some hypothesis H (though Mayo calls the relation that of 'fitting'). Similarly, spelling out explicitly what is implicit in Fisher's discussion, if E 'fits' H, while there is a very small chance that the test procedure 'would yield so good a fit if H is false', then 'E should be taken as *good grounds for H* to the extent that H has passed a severe test with E' (Mayo 1996: 177; my italics). In the Harvard Medical School test we have Mayo's formal criteria for H 'passing a severe test with E' satisfied. It is of course true that a positive result in the Harvard test *increases* the chance of the subject's having the disease from the base chance of .001 to (roughly) .02, an increase, in percentage terms, of 2000 per cent. To that extent the test result enhances the support of the hypothesis that the subject has the disease. But it leaves the overall, or posterior, chance still at only 2 per cent or so. If the chance were 50 per cent it would mean, intuitively, that it is as likely on the evidence that the subject has the disease as not. It can only be in a Pickwickian sense of 'good', therefore, that a 2 per cent chance constitutes 'good grounds for H'.[4]

[4] Mayo discusses the example in Mayo 1997, but I cannot see that she in any way mitigates its force.

A Sounder No-Miracles Argument

Acknowledging the unsoundness of the No-Miracles argument nevertheless raises the question why it frequently *seems* to be sound to argue in that way (thus Worrall talks of the 'intuitions' underlying the No-Miracles argument; 1996: 151). It surely seems sound, for example, to infer from Fisher's lady getting all her answers right, on repeated performances of the test, under the most scrupulous supervision to prevent cheating and foreknowledge in general, that she almost certainly does have the discrimination she claims. It would surely be too fantastic a coincidence for all those conditions to be satisfied and for her not to have the ability. Yet we also know that there are too many other possibilities that would have the same observable manifestations for any such claim to be demonstrable. Nevertheless, part of the reason we accept 'No-Miracles' reasoning in practice is because these myriad other possibilities are reckoned to be just too remote from what we are disposed to entertain as being 'really' possible. Pigs might fly, but they don't and won't (except in aeroplanes): not here, not in any even mildly similar world to 'here'. There are possible worlds where pigs will freely take wing and sing hosannas into the bargain, but our world has a zero chance of being one of them—or so we believe.

These last observations bring us to a crux. The proponents of the No-Miracles argument regard it as sound reasoning *as it stands*, without need of any further assumptions, and in particular not estimates, which by their nature must be highly subjective, of how probable types of large-scale world are (C. S Peirce (1960: 117), who calls the argument 'abduction', actually regards it as a principle of *logic*). They are wrong. Such assumptions are precisely what it needs to be a sound argument (I am using 'sound' now in a sense that will become increasingly familiar as our narrative unwinds: namely, in the sense of an argument which contains no fallacious steps even though its questions may, and in this case definitely should, be questioned). To see what these assumptions are we shall end this chapter by reconstructing the No-Miracles argument as a sound argument in the sense above, in so doing exhibiting the assumptions it requires clearly as estimates, necessarily subjective and a priori, of how likely certain types of world are.

We already have all the ingredients for the reconstruction bar one. This is the fact, which will be proved later in this book, that the laws of chance are formally identical to those of epistemic probability. The reconstruction of the No-Miracles argument within epistemic probability will to a certain extent anticipate the developments in the next and later chapters, but no matter: the more often we see this sort of thing, the more familiar we shall become with it. So let us start. Let T be current theory, H the hypothesis that T is 'approximately true' and E the description of data that T independently predicted. The 'chance' of getting E if T is true is rendered by the conditional probability $P(E|T)$. Since E was predicted by T, the rules of probability which we shall encounter in the next chapter tell us that $P(E|T)$ is equal to 1. But we shall want to know $P(E|H)$ rather than $P(E|T)$. Recall that it was a constraint on any acceptable account of approximate truth, at any rate in the context of the No-Miracles argument, that the agreement with E should be expected if T is approximately true. Since we are talking about 'intuitions' rather than facts, let us suppose that this constraint has been satisfied, so that accordingly we can give some suitably substantial value to $P(E|H)$.

An important part of the earlier discussion concluded that even in the context of suitably prepared statistical experiments it is not possible to give any unambiguously objective sense to 'the chance of E if the null hypothesis of no effect is true'. But when people talk in that sort of way they arguably have quite another sense of chance in mind, an informal folk-sense that Hume captured in his well-known remark that chance is nothing but 'the absence of a cause' (1739: I. III. xi). Even this should not be taken too literally, since we commonly attribute things to chance that we do not thereby mean to consign to the realm of the uncaused: for example, a sequence of outcomes of successive flips of a coin; few would seriously deny that to a great extent these outcomes are caused by such factors as the force impressed by the flipper, the point on the surface of the coin where it is impressed, turbulence in the air, ambient air-density, and so on. Hume's remark is better understood to mean not the absence of causes in general, but the absence of a *single systematic cause*. Saying that the outcomes of the coin-toss are due to chance, understood in this way, is simply to say that the *pattern* of outcomes has no systematic cause, a hypothesis confirmed by repeating the flips and finding that a different sequence of heads and tails is generated.

Armed with this insight we can now resume our reconstruction. We saw earlier in the discussion that because of the illimitable number and variety of alternative possible explanations of the agreement with the data no sensible numerical value could be attached to the value of the 'chance' of its occurrence should the null hypothesis be true, even in principle. On the Humean understanding of what it means to happen by chance the task is no longer in principle impossible: 'happening by chance' simply means that no other systematic cause of that agreement exists if H is not true. While this is certainly not *known* to be the case, and indeed never could be known to be the case, it is often felt to be a plausible assumption in the light of what we know, or think we know, about the relevant circumstances. In terms of the epistemic probability calculus that by itself is sufficient. It means a negligible but otherwise unspecified probability, called *prior probability*, assigned to the union of all the H_i other than H which might explain E compared to $P(H)$, from which it can be shown to follow by the laws of probability that $P(E|-H)$ is itself very small. We are not in a position to perform the (approximate) calculation yet, but we can at least say in general terms why it turns out that way. It does so because, as we shall see in Chapter 8, $P(E|-H)$ is proportional to the product of $P(H_i)$ and $P(E|H_i)$ summed over i. The second factor might be considerable, since these are candidate explanations, but its effect is nullified by the extreme smallness of $P(H_i)$. So, subject to an orders-of-magnitude assumption, we have step (ii).

Now for the final step. The quotient $P(E|-H)/P(E|H)$ is called the *Bayes factor* (more elaborately, the Bayes factor in favour of –H against H), and since $P(E|H)$ is assumed to be considerable we see that this factor is very small. We know from the Harvard Medical School test that a small Bayes factor by itself tells us nothing (which is why step (iii) failed), and that it is only informative when taken in combination with the base-rate, which now corresponds to $P(H)$. Given that this is not itself too small, *those same laws of probability also tell us that, given these assumptions, $P(H|E)$ is large* (the reader may peek ahead to p. 182 to see why).

Does this mean that the No-Miracles argument is valid after all? Absolutely not. We have a sound probabilistic argument, but its conclusion, a large value for $P(H|E)$, depends on the assumption that $P(E|-H)$ was very small compared with the prior probability $P(H)$.[5] We anyway need a not-too-small value for $P(H)$; we have seen from the Harvard Medical School test how varying the value of $P(H)$ will

---

[5] This is the epistemic analogue of the base-rate.

lead to concomitant variation in $P(H|E)$ that we saw earlier. Here is another example. Suppose that person X's DNA matches that found on a murder victim's clothing. The chance of a match if X is the murderer is very high, of course, and very low indeed—of the order of 10^{-7}—if the match is 'due to chance'. But suppose there is highly reliable evidence from a number of independent witnesses that X was far distant at the time of the murder. Given the usual assumptions we make about the universe, it is extremely unlikely on this information that X was the murderer, sufficiently unlikely that the smallness of the Bayes factor $P(E|-H)/P(E|H)$ cannot dominate it.

To sum up: far from showing that we can ignore even possibly highly subjective estimates of prior probabilities, the consideration of these quantities is *indispensable* if we are to avoid fallacious reasoning. Different streams converge at this point. I remarked earlier that the various soundness theorems for deductive proof-systems are actually applied mathematics, but that that did not affect Hume's argument. In fact, Hume was quite happy to accept all of what he regarded as mathematics without a sceptical murmur, because for him mathematical reasoning merely displayed internal logical 'relationships between ideas': Hume was an early logicist. Whether logicism is correct or not is beside the point here. What is germane is that in the case of deductive logic a *mathematical* theory is used to give a precise meaning to the deductive concepts of deductive consistency, logical consequence, etc. and thereby to establish their properties and interrelationships. A more interesting search for parallels with deductive logic than the fruitless 'rule-circularity' might therefore enquire whether there could be a similar way of identifying and investigating sound *inductive* arguments.

For a long time it was widely thought that another mathematical theory might well be able to do just that. This mathematical theory is the theory of probability, and for well over two hundred years many people believed that in that theory they could define and justify a notion of sound induction that had the desired property of being able, *and without circularity*, to establish the existence of sound inductive reasoning in the form of arguments from observed data to conclusions of the form 'it is more likely than not that the future will resemble [in certain specified ways] those data'. From what we have seen so far it doesn't sound hopeful. Indeed, the conclusion of the systematic investigation we shall conduct in the next chapter will reinforce Hume's argument that the only sound arguments of this type that can be constructed incorporate strong inductive premises: so in effect they *prove* nothing inductive at all. We have seen that this is certainly the case with the No-Miracles argument. As it is usually presented it is fallacious, thoroughly fallacious, and we saw exactly how it can be transformed into a non-fallacious argument only at the cost of making explicit its implicit inductive assumptions, assumptions which we shall see are typical, about prior probabilities.

EXERCISE: The Anthropic Principle

'Reasoning' according to the fallacious logic of the No-Miracles argument is, sadly, widespread. One of the most egregious examples is the so-called Anthropic Principle. 'The' Anthropic Principle suggests a perfected statement, but the suggestion is belied, as so often, by a messier reality. In fact, there is a considerable variety of anthropic principles on offer at the present moment. They nevertheless fall into two groups, the Weak and the Strong. The Weak Anthropic Principle appears to say no more than that the existence of human beings imposes certain constraints on the way the universe must have evolved. As such it is something of a truism. The Strong Anthropic Principle is more variegated, but what its instances have in common is the following teleological argument: the restriction of certain fundamental physical quantities within the very narrow bounds which permit an orderly universe, and in particular one permitting the development of life, is too unlikely to have occurred by chance, and therefore points to the existence of some purposive structuring whose ultimate goal is human existence. Perhaps 'The Hubristic Principle' would be a more accurate name for this argument. Here are a couple of samples from the (extensive) literature, the first explicitly theistic:

The basic constants of nature need to be exactly what they are to produce life. This . . . 'may have the flavour of a miracle'. Well, it is just what one would expect if an immensely wise God wished to produce a life-bearing universe, if the whole thing was purposive. Whereas it is not at all what one would expect, if it was a matter of chance. *Every new scientific demonstration of the precision of the mathematical structure needed to produce conscious life is evidence of design. Just to go on saying 'But it could all be chance' is to refuse to be swayed by evidence.* (Ward 1996: 51, 52; my italics)

and

A force strength or a particle mass often seems to need to be more or less exactly what it is *not just for one reason, but for two or three or five* [*sic*] . . . So, you might think, mustn't it be *inexplicable good fortune* that the requirements which have to be satisfied do not conflict? (Leslie 1989: 64; italics in original)

Do you think so?

4

Probabilism

Probable Reasoning

When Hume wrote the *Treatise* the contemporary mathematical theory of probability seemed to be restricted in its applications to simple games of chance. It is true that James Bernoulli, the author of one of the most systematic treatises up to that time (*Ars Conjectandi*), had attempted to transfer the mathematics of chance to the problem of induction, in the course of which he proved his famous theorem about converging probabilities based on large numbers of events (there is a brief discussion in Chapter 9). But though Bernoulli's theorem was highly suggestive it was also widely regarded as being in the last analysis unsuccessful in providing a sound link from past observations to the probabilities of future events. By a historical irony, it was Hume's almost exact contemporary Thomas Bayes, a Nonconformist clergyman, who showed, in a mathematical *tour de force*, how to 'invert' Bernoulli's result so that instead of being able to deduce the probability of obtaining some sample data, for example, seven heads in ten tosses of a coin, given some specified parent distribution, one could deduce the probability that the true parent distribution is as conjectured, given the sample data.[1]

At the time of writing the *Treatise* and *Enquiry* Hume was unaware of Bayes's work, and never referred to it subsequently. It has been left to posterity to try to determine whether the application of the mathematical theory of probability can in any way undermine Hume's argument that no 'probable reasoning' can justify inferences from past to future. Impregnable though the argument seemed, it

---

[1] This is set out in Bayes 1763, a posthumously published memoir communicated after Bayes's death to the Royal Society of London by his friend and editor Richard Price, who thought that Bayes had refuted Hume. Bayes's famous calculation is too technical to go into here, but for a clear account of it, together with a judicious appreciation of what it achieves, see Earman 1992: ch. 1.

appeared to rest on a notion of probable reasoning—reasoning 'concerning matter of fact and existence'—that is not related by Hume to the formal rules of probability. It was noted, without endorsement, in Chapter 1 that some people have seen this as revealing a hole in Hume's argument through which might escape a probabilistic justification of induction. In the earlier discussion I gave Hume's own answer to this question: that probability theory is a piece of mathematics which by itself conveys no information on any matter of empirical fact. I myself believe Hume's position to be correct, but we must face the fact that there are people, from Bayes (somewhat hesitantly) in the eighteenth to Carnap and others in the twentieth century, who nevertheless believe that there are valid probabilistic arguments for induction. Nor is the position totally implausible, as we shall see. To adjudicate the issue we must, however, first get acquainted with the basic principles of formal probability theory.

The Probability Axioms

These basic principles were actually first set out in anything like a modern form by Bayes himself. Let A, B, C, . . . below be a class of factual propositions (about exactly what we shall settle as the book proceeds). The probability axioms, in the now-standard form due to Kolmogorov (1933), are the following three conditions on a function P defined on these propositions:

  (I) $P(A) \geqq 0$.
  (II) If A and B are mutually inconsistent then $P(A \text{ or } B) = P(A) + P(B)$.
  (III) Where T is a necessary truth then $P(T) = 1$.

Accompanying these axioms is a definition of a function $P(A|B)$ of two arguments: If $P(B) > 0$ then $P(A|B)$ is defined to be $P(A\&B)/P(B)$. $P(A|B)$ is undefined if $P(B) = 0$. $P(A|B)$ is read '*the probability of A conditional on B*'.

Modern mathematical texts tend to identify A, B, C, etc. with *sets*, subsets of some set S, and in the axioms replace the connective 'or' with set-theoretical union (the union of two sets is the set containing all the members of either) and the necessary truth T with S. Why sets? Because sets are a convenient way of representing propositions when these might not be expressible linguistically, at any rate in any non-formal language. S is to be thought of all the logically possible states of affairs in some universe of discourse, possibly subject to constraints determined by some sort of background information. The sets identified with A, B, C, etc. can then be regarded as the subsets of S making corresponding propositions true. Where the set-apparatus becomes almost indispensable is in considering propositions for which there are no corresponding natural-language sentences. Later on in the book we shall consider theories, bodies of hypotheses which make up a single cognitive unit, but which cannot be represented as single statements within our standard systems. Examples are mainly theories in mathematics, one of the simplest being the basic principles of ordinary whole-number arithmetic known as Peano's Axioms. At any rate, we shall equivocate on the nature of propositions, regarding them as either ordinary statements or when necessary sets of possibilities.[2] This may sound a little cryptic at this stage; it should get clearer as we go on.

Nearly all texts on mathematical probability also adopt a sort of Axiom 0, usually stated as a preamble to I–III, saying that if A and B are already in the domain of P, then so are 'not A', 'not B', 'A&B', and 'A or B'. In technical jargon, Axiom 0 says that the domain of the probability function is a *field*. It is useful for some specific applications, as we shall see in Chapter 7, to require closure under these operations, as well as types of 'infinite' disjunction and conjunction. But we shall let the applications dictate how much of the modern measure-theoretic mathematics of probability is used. For most of what we do there will be none at all.

What Does It All Mean?

The axioms themselves will no doubt appear unmotivated and abstract. We can nevertheless give some preliminary informal explanation of what they say, admittedly at this stage only in a very general way. But that is better than nothing. Axiom III does not explicitly state that 1 is the upper limit, but that is the intention. The usual criterion determining choice of axioms is that they should provide as concise as possible a set of assumptions from which you can

---

[2] In earlier treatments it is not unusual to see, instead of P(A), etc. where A is a set, the notation $P(X \in A)$, i.e. the probability that X is in A, making the propositional nature of what lies inside the scope of the P-operator explicit (see e.g. Khintchin 1949).

derive everything you think is true about the area of study axiomatized, and merely stating that P(T) = 1 turns out to be enough, in
combination with the other axioms, to guarantee that the scale is the
closed unit interval. In other words, the axioms are implicitly telling
us that P(A) is a *normalized non-negative function*. This suggests that
P might be a ratio of quantities with the numerator not exceeding the
denominator. As we shall see, in one of the two main interpretations
of the axioms we shall consider P will be such a ratio.

The additivity principle II is best thought of in terms of the associated subsets of possibilities from S corresponding to the propositions
A and B. To take a simple example, suppose S is the space of possibilities admitted by throwing a die and observing the number of dots
on the upmost face when it comes to rest. Then the subset corresponding to 'an even number occurs' is the set {2,4,6}. Of course, S
may be relatively unlimited—when we are considering propositions
which are general hypotheses about the structure of the physical universe, for example. However extensive, though, we can always think
of it as like a set of points in a plane, with the sets of possibilities corresponding to A, B, etc. as regions in this subset of the plane. We can
also imagine (here I follow van Fraassen's nice metaphor: 1989:
161–2) that on these regions are spread amounts of *mud*, possibly not
evenly, but with the proportion of mud on any subregion equal to the
probability distributed over it by P. Suppose we signify the region
corresponding to A by *A*. So the probability of A is the proportion
of the total mass of mud on *A*.[3] Where A and B are mutually exclusive propositions *A* and *B* have no point in common, and the amount
of mud/probability over the sum *A* + *B* of the 'areas' *A* and *B* is
therefore equal to the sum of the amount of mud/probability over
each. Now notice that where A and B are mutually exclusive, *A or B*
is just *A* + *B*. Putting these observations together, we infer that for
mutually exclusive A and B we should have that P(A or B) = P(A) +
P(B), *i.e. axiom II*.

This little story is of course far from being a rigorous justification
of Axiom II. Such a justification would require that the mud analogy
be the appropriate one for the particular interpretation given to P.
However, if we think of the epistemic interpretation, it is certainly
not unnatural to regard the amount of belief heaped on A as measurable in principle by a proportional amount of mud heaped on *A*

---

[3] This of course implies that P(A) ≥ 0 (and ≤ 1).

(this implies no disrespect to the quality of that belief!). Now let us look at the definition of the function P(. |B) where P(B) > 0. Again, it is helpful to think in mud-theoretic terms (*nostalgie de la boue* has its uses). The idea is that P(. |B) will signify the *restriction* of P to the subdomain of possibilities admitted by B, i.e. for any proposition A, P(A|B) is to mean 'The probability of A assuming that the domain of possibility is curtailed to B', i.e. *assuming that B is true*. So now the new set of possibilities admitted by A is not A but only those points common to both A and B, which set-theorists call the intersection $A \cap B$ and which, it is easy to see, is the set of points represented by the conjunction A&B. But we can't simply set P(A|B) equal to P(A&B), because the total mass of mud/probability left by excising the points not in B is P(B), which if probability is to be equal to the proportion of mud-mass relative to the universe, should now be 1. But the solution is obvious: we have to scale everything up by a factor of 1/P(B). Thus we must have P(A|B) = P(A&B)/P(B), assuming P(B) > 0.

I repeat that this little exercise is *not* a rigorous justification of any of I–III, or anything near one; it is more of a heuristic first approximation to one. A rigorous justification will depend on what exactly P is supposed to mean. Unfortunately there is not a single answer to this question, for it turns out that there is more than one distinct way of interpreting the formalism, two of which are regarded as principal. In one, which we shall call the epistemic, or from now on more often the *Bayesian* interpretation (we shall see why shortly), A, B, etc. are factual propositions about particular states of affairs whose truth-values are (normally) unknown and P(A), P(B), etc. are, roughly (we shall be more specific later), the degrees of belief which some consistent individual might hold in A. The first reasonably rigorous justification of I–III from the point of view of this interpretation was given by Bayes himself, in his work cited. Because of its historical interest, and because it is both easy to follow and, with certain qualifications (concerning rather subtle utility considerations, whose discussion I shall postpone to Chapter 7), still regarded as essentially sound, I give a slightly modified version of Bayes's derivation of the axioms in Appendix I to this chapter.

The other interpretation of I–III has nothing to do with our beliefs or even with us at all. It is an interpretation of P(A) as an *objective property* of an event-*type* described by A occurring in the context of some repeatable observation or experiment. The great French mathematician and probabilist Poisson gave this property a much older name, *chance*. In his words, chance 'pertains only to things in themselves and independently of what knowledge we have of them' (1823: 2). What I have called the epistemic or Bayesian interpretation Poisson called '*probabilité*'.[4] I should emphasize that these two interpretations have since become more or less broad categories, with many variants; for example, Popper has proposed a type of objective chance interpretation which he calls the *propensity theory* of probability. To avoid terminological confusion I should also point out the notion of chance discussed in the context of the No-Miracles argument in Chapter 3 is more akin to the older tradition in which it was usually intended to denote something objective, but what that something was was never clearly defined except in the very special classes of circumstances in which symmetries in the apparatus were held to justify assigning the same chance to each in the space S of possible outcomes. If there was a finite number n of such outcomes then each individually was held to have the same chance 1/n of occurring.

There is also a further distinct concept—perhaps 'theory' would be the better word—of probability which I shall mention now but not dwell on, and whose status is anyway still controversial. That is *quantum mechanical probability*. It is not just another interpretation of axioms I–III, but a quite different theory of the semantics *and syntax* of probability, with the latter based not on the classical logic or 'ordinary' propositions but on a non-classical logic generated by the lattice of closed subsets of an appropriate vector space, a *Hilbert space* of quantum states. This logic differs fundamentally from the classical one in being non-Boolean (for a discussion of what this means see Hughes 1989: ch. 7). As a consequence, the 'quantum probability' postulates differ fairly radically from I–III above. The condition in the additivity axiom III is no longer that the two propositions over which the probability adds are inconsistent with each other, but that they are represented by orthogonal subspaces, while conditional probability is governed by a completely different type of rule, the so-called Lüders rule (Hughes 1989: 224–6). Whether it is

---

[4] Poisson's distinction between 'chance' and 'probability' as the names of quite different quantities was new in the history of mathematical probability, and very quickly became established; they are just Carnap's well-known 'probability$_2$' and 'probability$_1$' respectively (1950). Before Poisson the terms were regarded as synonymous; thus on the first page of his Memoir Bayes says that by 'chance' he means the same as 'probability' (1763).

necessary to transfer to such a non-classical logic and probability theory for the discussion of quantum phenomena is a very controversial issue, though the majority view is probably that it is not; though we should note that even those who deny that it is are nevertheless forced to concede that there is something rather strange about quantum-mechanical probability.[5] It would be interesting to take the quantum-mechanical discussion further, but it would also take us away from our current objective, which is to see how inductive inference has been modelled within the epistemic, Bayesian interpretation. For this reason also a more detailed account of the chance interpretation will be postponed until the stage at which its relationship with epistemic probability becomes an issue (in Chapter 9).

In the subsequent discussion it will be useful to have at hand a few fairly easy consequences of the axioms. I shall list them below without proof (the interested reader can find proofs in Howson and Urbach 1993: ch. 2).

   (i) $0 \leq P(A) \leq 1$.

  (ii)   If F is a necessary falsehood then $P(F) = 0$.

 (iii) $P(-A) = 1 - P(A)$ (read $-A$ as 'notA', i.e. the negation, or denial, of A).

 (iv) $P(A\&B) \leq P(A), P(B) \leq P(A \text{ or } B)$.

  (v)   If A entails B then $P(A) \leq P(B)$.

 (vi)   If A entails B and $P(A) > 0$ then $P(B|A) = 1$ and $P(-B|A) = 0$.

 (vii)   Logically equivalent propositions receive the same probability.

(viii)   If $A_1, A_2, \ldots, A_n$ are all mutually inconsistent then $P(A_1 \text{ or } A_2 \text{ or } \ldots \text{ or } A_n) = P(A_1) + P(A_2) + \ldots + P(A_n)$. This is known as the *finite additivity principle* (cf. Appendix 1, (III′)).

 (ix)   Where $P(B) > 0$, the function Q defined by $Q(\, . \,) = P(\, . \, |B)$ satisfies I–III (this justifies the terminology 'conditional *probability*').

---

[5] For example, while the so-called statistical algorithm of quantum mechanics delivers numerical probabilities for any finite number of commuting observables being measured in any joint interval of their eigenvalues, it is impossible to define a joint probability distribution over noncommuting observables.

Epistemic Probability: Modelling Inductive Inference

That probability is a measure of uncertainty is familiar and has a long history—as long as that of probability itself. In his *Ars Conjectandi* ('Art of Conjecturing') James Bernoulli had explicitly advanced the idea: 'Probability is degree of certainty, and differs from absolute certainty as a part differs from the whole' (1713: 8). He also suggestively linked this measure of uncertainty with the uncertainty of *hypotheses* ('conjectures') in the light of evidence: 'To conjecture about something is to measure its probability' (ibid.). Nevertheless, the Great Step Forward which definitively linked the mathematical theory of probability with the justification of inductive inferences was taken not by Bernoulli but by Bayes over half a century later. Bayes made the crucial identification, which thereafter became canonical, of a 'probable argument' from data E *with a conditional probability $P(\ . \ |E)$* (it is assumed that $P(E) > 0$). Thus a probable argument tells you the probability, on the supposition that E is true, of any hypothesis plugged into the space marked by the dot. Of course, strictly speaking, $P(H|E)$ is a *term* and not an argument in the way an argument is usually understood. But it seems to be transformable into an explicit argument-form by the following obvious rule: *if you learn E then you can infer that the credibility of H is equal to $P(H|E)$*. This principle is known as *conditionalization*. It sounds reasonable enough, even obvious, given the interpretation of $P(H|E)$ as the probability of H on the assumption that E is true. But one qualification must immediately be made: E must be the logically strongest statement you learn. If you learn a proposition A then arguably you learn some of (some strong idealizers say all) the consequences of A; but it may be that $P(H|A)$ and $P(H|A')$ differ, where A' is a consequence of A. To condition on both A and A' would be to generate inconsistent evaluations; the qualification ensures that you condition only on one, the logically strongest, of the propositions that you learn.

So things are not quite so absolutely straightforward after all. We shall see later (in Chapter 7) that this is not all that is not straightforward about conditionalization, but the issue is not all that relevant here because the rule only acts on $P(H|E)$ to detach from the acceptance of E, provisional or otherwise, a conclusion about the probability of H, a probability which will be formally equal to

P(H|E) itself. The meat of the discussion of whether probabilistic induction is possible or not therefore depends directly on the properties of P(H|E), and the Big Question, which has occupied people since the time of Bayes, is how to evaluate P(H|E) for interesting cases of H and E. From the definition of conditional probability we can deduce that P(H|E) = P(H&E)/P(E) if P(E) > 0. But the axioms seem to give little or no guidance on the evaluation of P(H&E) or P(E). One interesting context from the point of view of the problem of induction is that in which H is a predictive hypothesis which entails E, modulo some background conditions, whose satisfaction is assumed to be reflected in the behaviour of P (so that P assigns them probability 1). Then modulo these same conditions H&E is logically equivalent to H, and so by (vii) above P(H&E) = P(H). Then P(H|E) = P(H)/P(E). Even so, at this point we have as yet no way of further determining the unconditional or *prior probabilities* P(H) and P(E), and most of the work done trying to model induction probabilistically has been an attempt to use additional heuristic principles to try to determine values for them; sometimes for special cases of H and E (as was the case with Bayes's famous essay), sometimes in a more ambitiously global way (as in Carnap's monumental *Logical Foundations of Probability* 1950).

In order not to get involved in a lot of technical work which might turn out to, and in fact mostly does, lead nowhere, it will be better at the outset simply to regard the axioms as imposing constraints on any probability function P, and then seeing whether, though they do not determine P anything like uniquely, they nevertheless force P to be inductive. If it turns out that this is the case, then we can reasonably regard Hume as defeated without going further into the issue of exactly how many probability functions are consistent with those constraints—an interesting question, perhaps, but not our concern here. If, on the other hand, it turns out not to be true, then we have to look at further principles which might be invoked.

The Case For

Remarkably, the following results appear to show that the axioms do force P to be an inductive measure in the sense defined. Relatively simple to prove, some of these formal consequences of the probability axioms are so striking that the mathematician and statistician

I. J. Good even calls them *induction theorems* (1983: 164,165). First, though, some suggestive terminology will help to point the way (whether the suggestion conveyed is wholly, or at all, accurate is something that will be carefully questioned, but later). Call a probability function P *dogmatic with respect to a contingent proposition H* if $P(H) = 0$ or $P(H) = 1$.[6] We call people dogmatic on a question if, whatever you tell them, you know they won't change their mind. Well, similarly for dogmatic probability functions, as the following shows:

(a) Suppose that $P(H) = 0$. Let E be any information to which P awards *some* chance, however small, of being true; i.e. $P(E) > 0$. According to the definition of conditional probability $P(H|E) = P(H\&E)/P(E)$, and by (iv) above, $P(H\&E) \leq P(H) = 0$. Hence $P(H|E) = 0$. In other words, there is *no* information, given only that it is minimally credible, which P would regard as causing it to change its 'mind' about H were E true.

(b) Now suppose that $P(H) = 1$, and $P(E) > 0$ again as in (a). By (iii), $P(-H) = 0$, and by (a) $P(-H|E) = 0$, whence by (viii) and (ii), $P(H|E) = 1$. So learning E wouldn't cause P to change its 'mind' about H in this case either.

Dogmatic probability functions are also *blind to the contingency of contingent statements*, in the following sense: if $P(H) = 0$ then H is assimilated by H to a necessary falsehood (by (ii) above), while if $P(H) = 1$ then H is assimilated by P to a logical truth (by axiom III). In the light of these facts it seems an obvious desideratum for a 'reasonable' probability function that it should not be dogmatic with respect to any contingent hypothesis; if it is dogmatic then it will not provide a faithful model of how a paradigmatically rational individual should measure uncertainty, since it will *irrevocably* tell us to be certain either that a hypothesis is false which might be true, or that a hypothesis is true which might be false.

These mild and apparently reasonable modelling assumptions appear to be all that is needed to refute Hume, since it seems that we can now very easily prove that valid inductive arguments exist! Suppose that H is some simple predictive hypothesis that says that if

---

[6] The term 'dogmatic' was inspired by a passage in Jeffrey 1992: 45. Probability functions vary between the totally non-dogmatic, also called *strictly positive* functions, which assign 0 only to logical falsehoods, and the totally dogmatic, which assign every proposition the value 0 or 1 (such functions are formally identical to Boolean truth-valuations).

observationally verifiable conditions C are met, E will be observed. To keep the discussion simple suppose that P is relativized to C, that is, C is regarded as background information to which P has already assigned the value 1. Another simple derivation from I–III establishes

Theorem 1 If $0 < P(E)$, $P(H) < 1$, and if H entails E, then $P(H|E) > P(H)$.

The proof is extremely easy. For by the definition of conditional probability $P(H|E) = P(H\&E)/P(E)$ and since H entails E, H&E is logically equivalent to H. Hence by (vii) above $P(H|E) = P(H)/P(E)$, whence the theorem immediately follows. Jeffrey, who calls it 'Huygens's Rule', gives a simple geometrical proof of it (in terms of corresponding regions in the state space S) which makes it intuitively obvious (1992: 58).

Theorem 1 tells us that if P is not dogmatic with respect to H and E then any prediction that H gets right increases its initial, or prior, probability. In other words, *if P is not dogmatic for H and E and if H predicts E then the occurrence of E inductively supports H*. Not only that: it follows almost immediately that each succeeding prediction H gets right increases its probability still further. For let $Q(.)$ be $P(. |E)$ for fixed E. By (ix) above Q satisfies I–III. By Theorem 1, therefore, if H entails E' then $Q(H|E') > Q(H)$, whence it easily follows that $P(H|E\&E') > P(H|E) > P(H)$. Of course, there is a considerable idealization involved in supposing that any hypothesis predicts observed values exactly. Generally there will be some spread, due to ineliminable experimental errors, around predicted values even for so-called deterministic hypotheses. This is true, but the issue here is one of principle, not of practice. Hume had argued that there can be no probable argument from the data to anything beyond it. Subject to an idealizing assumption in which such errors are ignored, Theorem 1 seems to be just such an argument.

Perhaps we can save Hume's position by interpreting it as saying that no evidence can raise the probability of a prediction to the point where the prediction is more probable than not. A further consequence of I–III seems to knock that on the head too. To see why, we shall look at a model that is widely used in these sorts of investigation. This is an idealized form of a *universal hypothesis* which, whenever specified experimental conditions, call them C, are instantiated, and it is assumed that in principle there is no limit to the number of times they can be, predicts outcomes of some determinately observable character. Let H be such a hypothesis. The outcome space, that is, the set of all possible outcomes of an indefinite series of repetitions of C, can be represented simply as the set of all infinite sequences of Es (the outcome predicted by H) and –Es (any other type of outcome), and H itself can be represented by the single sequence consisting only of Es. Let E_i mean that E occurred at the ith repetition. The consequence in question of I–III, which I shall give without proof, is

Theorem 2   Suppose that P(H) > 0. Then for some i, $P(E_{i+1}|E_1\& \ldots \&E_i) > \frac{1}{2}$, and indeed tends to 1 as i tends to infinity.

In other words, an inductive principle of the sort Russell thought had to be postulated (Chapter 1, p. 19) *actually follows from the apparently natural requirement that P be not dogmatic with respect to at least one universal hypothesis.*

In fact, P(H) > 0 is a sufficient but not necessary condition for $P(E_{i+1}|E_1\& \ldots \&E_i)$ tending to 1. It is known that this limiting behaviour, even where the progress to the limit is monotone or even strict, is consistent with the hypothesis that says it will always occur having prior probability 0. All the measures in Carnap's λ-continuum are of this type, for example, and de Finetti in a celebrated theorem showed that a very weak condition consistent with P(H) = 0, so-called *exchangeability*, will generate that behaviour (1964: 121). Suppose the outcomes of a repeatable observation are classified in some way. They are said to be exchangeable if the probability of any sequence of them depends only on the *number* of outcomes of each type in the sequence. Now suppose that the classification is merely in terms of whether E occurs or not. De Finetti's theorem shows that if we consider infinite sequences of such binary exchangeable events then the probability of getting r Es and s not-Es in the first n observations depends on how the prior probability distributions over the different possible numbers n_j of Es in the first j observations, j = 1, 2, 3, . . . behave as j grows very large. If, for example, for each j all the possible numbers of Es, i.e. 0, 1, 2, . . . , j are judged equally probable then we obtain the following special case of *Laplace's Rule of Succession*:

$$P(E_{m+1}|E_1\&E_2\& \ldots \&E_m) = m + 1/m + 2, m = 1, 2, 3, \ldots,$$

which clearly tends to 1 as m tends to infinity. In general, as long as none of those prior distributions over n_j vanishes anywhere, that conditional probability will still tend to 1.

Grue Again

By now any defender of Hume might well be feeling pretty bad. Worse is to come: *we actually seem able to solve the grue paradox*! Within the simple formal model of an indefinitely repeated experiment we can represent the hypothesis space for H and its grue variants as the set of all infinite sequences of Es (green emeralds) and –Es (blue ones),[7] describing the potential output of a data source (sequentially observing an unlimited supply of emeralds). H, 'All emeralds are green', corresponds to the single sequence consisting entirely of Es. Each of the 'grue$_t$' alternatives H_t, where t is now an integer, corresponds to that sequence with Es up to the tth place and –Es at t and thereafter. H and its grue variants constitute a *denumerably* infinite set (i.e. one which can be indexed by the positive integers). All the members of a denumerably infinite set of mutually incompatible alternatives can be assigned positive prior probabilities (for example, from the sequence ½, ¼, ⅛, ¹⁄₁₆, etc.), and we shall assume that all these hypotheses are assigned them. The consequence of I–III we now need is this:

Suppose that H_n, n > 0, is an infinite family of hypotheses such that for each n, H_n agrees with the predictions of a hypothesis H for all individuals observed up to epoch n and disagrees after n. Let E_i be the evidence gathered up to i and suppose it is as predicted by H. Then for all n < i, H_n is inconsistent with $E_{(i)}$, and for all n ≥ i H_n predicts $E_{(i)}$. Given that P(H) > 0 and for all n, $P(H_n)$ > 0, it follows that there is a k such that for all n > k, $P(H_n|E_{(k)})$ < $P(H|E_{(k)})$, and that this inequality will persist for all k' > k (for a proof see Appendix 4 to this chapter).

We can gloss this complicated-looking result in a simple way as follows. Suppose P is not dogmatic with respect to H ('All emeralds are

---

[7] In this 'universe' emeralds are only either green or blue.

green') or all the $grue_n$-alternatives to it (assumption (i)). Then as data of the form 'All emeralds observed up to i are green' ($E_{(i)}$) accumulates, H will eventually be left as the most probable hypothesis despite the fact that infinitely many $grue_k$ alternatives remain unfalsified. *We seem to have shown that we can generate, in a familiar, concrete example, a probable argument that extrapolates past experience into the future in just the way our intuitions tell us is correct.*

Those who remember the cautionary remarks about inductive rules in Chapter 2 will recall that the grue problem showed that on pain of inconsistency no such rule can say that after some number n of positive instances of any property A we are justified in predicting an A at the next occurrence of the appropriate conditions, *where n is independent of A*. On the contrary; we saw that consistency demands that the point at which the evidence is sufficient, according to the rule, to justify extrapolating to a future occurrence of A must be highly *non-uniform* across the class of properties A. It is not difficult to see that any rule based on a probability function, like the conditionalization rule, has this property, since it is a straightforward consequence of the additivity principle II that it is impossible for both A and –A to have probabilities greater than ½. To see what else is implied, recall that, subject to $P(H) > 0$, $P(E_{i+1}|E_1\& \ldots \&E_i)$ must exceed ½ for some i. Hence if $P(H_k)$ is also positive, as we assumed above, we must also have $P(E_{j+1,k}|E_{j,1}\& \ldots \&E_{j,k}) > ½$ for some j, where we define $E_{n,k}$ to be E_n if $n \le k$ and $-E_n$ if $n > k$ (if the domain is emeralds sampled over discrete time and E is the predicate 'is green' then E_n says that the nth emerald is green, and $E_{n,k}$ says that the nth emerald is $grue_k$; H_k says that all emeralds sampled will be $grue_k$). This does *not* imply that for some r, both $P(E_{r+1}|E_1\& \ldots \&E_r) > ½$ and $P(-E_{r+1}|E_1\& \ldots E_r) > ½$,[8] since the first n for which $E_{n,k}$ becomes more probable than not given a uniform run of previous $E_{j,k}$s must exceed k. So 'grue' is no problem in principle for probable arguments; it just shows that a type of convergence cannot be uniform.[9]

[8] Popper thought it did, and that it showed that $P(H)$ and $P(H_k)$ for every k must be zero (1959: 370–1)!

[9] Mathematically speaking this is exactly what is shown: that the functions $f_k(n) = P(E_{n+1,k}|E_{1,k}\& \ldots \&E_{n,k})$ converge pointwise to 1 over the set $\{k:k > 0\}$ but not uniformly.

The Case Against

Suspicion that perhaps these results, despite their knock-down, drag-out character, do not provide the non-circular 'probable reasoning' for induction that Hume denied possible, is aroused by the realization that non-dogmatism is for mathematico-logical reasons not possible as a uniform policy. We return to the fact that there are infinitely many mutually exclusive possible laws over infinite domains. It was pointed out that those we can actually refer to in ordinary language are the least infinity in number, denumerable infinity, and hence that it is possible in principle to assign all of them positive initial probabilities. But that is not by any means the end of the story. It is because natural language is not ideally suited for mathematical representation that it was superseded in the seventeenth century by a dedicated mathematical language, which most certainly does have resources for referring not just to the members of denumerably infinite collections, but to those of larger ones as well. Indeed, we shall consider later a set of hypotheses of the form {X: X∈I}, where I is a non-degenerate interval of real numbers and hence *uncountably* infinite.[10] Nor need we stop there: when we consider all the possible smooth functional relationships that specified real or complex variables have to each other we ascend to a yet higher infinity, which again we can denote in a standard mathematical notation.

So we are neither conceptually nor notationally restricted to the countable. It is not very difficult to see that the additivity principle implies that there at most n elements of any possibility-space with probability at least $1/n$, from which it follows that *at most* denumerably many members can have positive prior probability. Since the difference between an uncountable and a countable set can itself be shown to be uncountable, this implies that *uncountably many possibilities in an uncountable possibility space must have probability 0.* This puts the notion of dogmatism, as we defined it earlier for probability functions, in a quite different perspective. For it shows that with a large enough hypothesis space any probability function will

---

[10] Nobody knows how large, in the sense of where exactly in the hierarchy of alephs it lies, this infinite cardinality is, except that it is somewhere above the least, $\aleph_0$. That it is $\aleph_1$ is Cantor's famous continuum hypothesis, known since 1963 to be logically independent of the standardly accepted axioms of set theory.

necessarily be dogmatic for the vast majority of the hypotheses in that space. In other words, the desideratum on p. 70 above that 'reasonable' probability functions are not dogmatic with respect to any contingent proposition must fail in big enough possibility-spaces. But we definitely need to consider as big spaces as we can conceive if we are really to face up to the problem of induction, and indeed even in practical contexts such large spaces are routinely considered, for example in mathematical statistics: all the continuous distributions studied there actually assign probability 0 to *every* point of the possibility-space.

Armed with this information, we can now get a clearer idea of what is going on in the 'solution' of the grue paradox. Recall that in the solution of the grue paradox we assigned positive probabilities to all the grue variants of H; we could do so because that set was only denumerably infinite. But the set Ω of all possible infinite sequences of Es and –Es is actually *uncountably* infinite. To see this, just replace E by 1 and –E by 0. It is a mathematical fact that every real number x such that $0 \leq x \leq 1$ has a binary representation: x can be expressed as a sum $a_1/2 + a_2/4 + a_3/8 + \ldots + a_i/2^i + \ldots$, where $a_i = 0$ or 1, and x is represented in binary by the sequence $a_1, a_2, \ldots$. The representation is not as it stands unique because of recurring digits (e.g. $1.000000 \ldots$ is the same number as $.1111111 \ldots$) but this tells us that there is at least the same number of things in Ω as there are real numbers in the unit interval (in fact, it can easily be shown that there are *exactly* as many in the sense of infinite cardinality). The real numbers in any nondegenerate interval are known to be uncountably infinite. *Hence any probability measure must be dogmatic with respect to almost all the hypotheses in Ω.* Had we let H be one of these the 'solution' to the grue problem obviously wouldn't have worked. In other words, the grue paradox was 'solved' probabilistically only by a prior decision to give positive prior probability to the 'correct' hypothesis! The decision cannot be justified on the ground that otherwise the probability measure would be dogmatic with respect to that hypothesis, for as we have seen it will necessarily be dogmatic with respect to uncountably many other hypotheses any one of which might, a priori, be the true one. Thus H ended up being the best confirmed *only because a prior decision was taken to allow it to be 'confirmed' at all.* Similarly, Theorem 1 shows that such an assignment in the form of a positive probability assignment to H is a necessary and sufficient condition for H to be confirmed by its positive instances. It is beginning to sound as if we have here the probabilistic version of the inductive postulate Hume declared would be present in any inductive argument. Indeed it is, and we shall come to that presently. In the restriction of a positive prior probability to at most denumerably many incompatible hypotheses we also have something akin to Keynes's *principle of limited independent variety* (1973: 289), not as a separate postulate as he imagined it would have to be, but as a condition implicit in the very laws of probability themselves.

It might be objected that most of the hypotheses in Ω can't be named because they are infinite random sequences (this is true). At most a denumerably infinite number of possible sequences can be named explicitly, and these correspond to those which are generated by some algorithm (there are only denumerably many algorithms, in the sense of computer programs which generate infinite sequences of binary digits). Surely, the objection continues, only these should, indeed can, be the bearers of probabilities, since only these represent genuine discussable hypotheses. And if this is granted then the problem is solved, at any rate in principle. For then as we have seen all these hypotheses can be assigned positive prior probabilities. Not only that; a solution in practice also beckons. For these hypotheses have a natural probability ordering in terms of *simplicity*: the simpler any is, the more a priori probable it is. Harold Jeffreys, an eminent mathematical physicist and geophysicist, adopted such a principle, which he called the *simplicity postulate*, in his pioneering work advocating probabilistic methods in inference in the sciences, though he talked of the simplicity of mathematical equations, and proposed to measure it in terms of the number of their independent adjustable parameters (1961: 47).

We shall look at Jeffreys's idea later (in Chapter 8), but it is to no avail in solving this problem. For it is just not true that we can only consider denumerably many hypotheses. We have seen that in the language of ordinary analysis hypothesis spaces of uncountably many elements are dealt with as a matter of course. The fact is that these are all possibilities and they cannot be ignored at the behest of an arbitrary restriction on language. They cannot all be assigned non-zero probabilities, and consequently any assignment of a positive probability is not something that can be justified by appeal to considerations of non-dogmatism. We have to be dogmatic, or so it appears, whether we like it or not.

Non-Additivity?

It might seem that the root of the problem lies in classical probability theory itself: the combination of the additivity principle with a finite upper bound on probabilities implies that certainty, represented as a finite upper bound (1, in fact), is the sum of (the measures of) a finite or at most countably infinite number of exclusive alternatives. One option that might be considered is to abandon the assumption of the finiteness of the measure of certainty, allowing it to become infinite. Harold Jeffreys, in all other senses a standard epistemic probabilist, himself suggested this as a possibility (1961: 21). Indeed, there is a very familiar measure of uncertainty which has this property, the odds measure: the odds on certainty are necessarily infinite (odds ω are related to probability p by the equation $\omega = p/1-p$). But odds are too close to probabilities to give the desired result, since it is also a mathematical fact (look at the equation in the preceding parentheses) that only a countable number of hypotheses can have positive prior odds. That aside, introducing infinity as the value of anything is not anyway a particularly good idea, since 'infinity' does not really stand for anything at all. To say that a function takes the value infinity at a given argument is just an elaborate way of saying that it is undefined at that argument. In fact, the suggestion is something of a red herring, because all that is desired (at any rate by some) is to disengage the 'probability' assigned to A from the 'probability' assigned to any proposition inconsistent with A. So why not just stipulate that these may be independent of each other?

Uncertainty functions having this property have actually been proposed. For obvious reasons they are called *non-additive functions*. The most prominent developments in this area have been Glen Shafer's theory of belief functions (Shafer 1976) and Zadeh's fuzzy logic and probability theory (see the survey in Dubois and Prade 1988). I shall not describe these in any detail, because I think that though non-additivity seems to offer a way out of the seeming impasse it is not an acceptable one, *precisely because it uncouples P(A) from P(-A)*. For if anything should be taken as fundamental to the measurement of belief, surely it is that as your belief in a proposition's being true increases, so your belief in its falsity correspondingly decreases. To deny this would be like denying that the positive integers are obtained by successive additions of 1 to 0.

Granted it, and here I am simply going to take author's prerogative and assume it is granted, non-additive functions do not solve the problem.

Infinitesimal Probabilities

An alternative diagnosis of the problem is that the 'dogmatic' priors inevitably accompanying uncountable possibility spaces are merely an artefact of the structure of standard probability-*values*, that is, of the real numbers. Here the suggestion is that the real numbers do not permit a fine enough resolution of possibility-space: the system of reals simply gives up at a certain level, so to speak, and assigns measure 0 to things that should have a positive measure. In other words, the problem arises not because there are too many *possibilities*, but because there are too few *numbers* to measure them with. On this view, the various number systems—the integers, the rationals, the real and complex numbers—are to be seen as a continued attempt at increasing resolution that has prematurely stopped short. The integers are the coarsest numerical measure, with big gaps. The rationals, that is, fractions, are finer, since they are dense: between any two rationals there is another. Yet they also have gaps, as the discoverers of the irrationality of $\sqrt{2}$ found out over two thousand years ago; indeed, there are 'only' denumerably many rationals. So we get to the reals, which are a continuum. But even the reals have a sort of discreteness property, in that they obey the so-called Archimedean axiom: this says that however small a real number x is, so long as it is not 0, there is a *finite* number of times x can be added to itself such that the resulting sum will exceed any finite number specified. In other words, the objection continues, the reals, despite forming a continuum, are still too coarse: they can't measure down to truly infinitesimal magnitudes, for that would be to deny Archimedes' axiom.

This defence, though noble, fails. The Archimedean property of the real numbers isn't really the root of the problem posed by the failure of probabilistic induction over uncountable sets. There is now a consistent theory of non-Archimedean, infinitesimal and reciprocally infinite, quasi-real numbers occupying the 'spaces' between the genuine reals. If we set P(H) = x where x is infinitesimal, then by Corollary 1 we still have P(H|E) > P(H) if H entails E. But we have also $P(H|E) = P(H)/P(E)$, and, since $P(E)$ is real, it follows that $y = 1/P(E)$ is also real, and so yx, i.e. $P(H|E)$, remains infinitesimal. But precisely *because* this enlarged number system is non-Archimedean there is no finite number y such that xy is non-infinitesimal if x is infinitesimal (we would need an infinite y for that). Nor can we go to superinfinitesimals, because these are just infinitesimals. The problem really is that the space of possibilities represented by the uncountable set of all infinite sequences of 0s and 1s is just too immense. So resistant is it to any normal standard of measurement that even the fundamental axioms of set theory, our only theory in which infinite magnitudes are assigned explicit numerical values (infinite ones, of course) which can be manipulated according to definite arithmetical rules, are insufficient to determine its size!

Popper's Arguments

We have seen that we cannot be non-dogmatic in our probability assignments across the board, in the sense of universally assigning non-zero prior probabilities to the members of big enough possibility-spaces. But it has also become less clear that such assignments really are non-dogmatic, for, as we have seen in Theorems 1 and 2 above, they bring in their train what appear to be very strong inductive principles. In a puzzling way, being non-dogmatic in one sense seems to entail a type of dogmatism in another. The status of non-zero priors thus looks somewhat confused and unsatisfactory. A more settled view, and one very congenial to our Humean stance, will emerge in the course of examining the arguments of Popper claiming to show that any reasonable prior probability for a universal hypothesis *must* be dogmatic. To these we now turn.

Must General Hypotheses Have Zero Probability?

These arguments are presented in Popper (1959: app. *viii). They in their turn are criticized in Howson (1973), and Howson and Urbach (1993: ch. 15). The technical arguments are, I believe it is fair to say, now recognized to be fallacious (we saw one of them in footnote 7 above). But there is a more philosophical argument which seems more robust. This employs a principle which we, following Keynes (1973: ch. 4), shall call the *principle of indifference*. In fact, it can be traced back to the dawn of mathematical probability; it was called the *principle of insufficient reason* by James Bernoulli, and was employed in Bayes's seminal memoir where it appears as a special postulate (called Bayes's Postulate in subsequent discussions of Bayes's work). The Principle makes the following apparently tauto-logical statement: if {H$_i$} is some family of hypotheses about which you have no relevant information other than that they are mutually exclusive, their initial probabilities relative to that (null) information should be equal. For finite possibility spaces the Principle has as an almost immediate corollary (using the additivity axiom) Laplace's famous 'definition' of epistemic probability, since then often called the *classical* definition of probability (whose acquaintance we have already made in Chapter 3): the probability of an event 'is thus simply a fraction whose numerator is the number of favourable cases and whose denominator is the number of all the cases possible', where by 'cases equally possible' is meant 'such as we may be equally undecided about in regard to their existence [this is a standard trans-lation; the last word would be better rendered by 'occurrence']' (1951: 6–7).

Popper's contention follows very quickly from the principle of indifference. For we have already noted that over an infinite domain the class of mutually exclusive hypotheses is infinite. With 'All emer-alds are green' and the infinitely many grue$_t$ alternatives, for exam-ple, we have a denumerably infinite family representing the various ways in which an unbounded sequence of possible observations can 'flip over' from being homogeneous in one way to being homo-geneous in another. By the principle of indifference, the initial prob-abilities of all these a priori 'equally possible' hypotheses must all be equal, and there is clearly only one value that that common prob-ability can consistently have, namely 0. QED.[11]

Let us consider this argument critically. First, far from being the tautology it appears at first sight to be, the principle of indifference is in fact a highly non-trivial assumption. *It says that you should regard alternatives as equally likely because you have no information about them.* In fact, this assertion is highly non-trivial—it is certainly not a logical truth; indeed, so non-trivial is it that it generates 'para-doxes' with great ease. Consider the following (adapted from the 'book paradox' in Keynes 1973: ch. 4). I have a book with a cover

---

[11] This is very similar to the example that Popper uses, except that his infinite space is uncountable and this is countable (1959: app. *viii).

which is coloured with a primary colour. I do not know what the colour is. Well, it is either green or not green. Both possibilities receive probability ½ by the principle of indifference. Similarly, the colour is either red or not red; again the probabilities are ½ each. Do the same for violet/not violet. Now we have a contradiction because by the additivity principle the probability that the book is green or red or violet is ⅓, contradicting consequence (i) of I–III.

But is this a real paradox? Isn't it rather that an elementary mistake has been made? There are three primary colours, green, red, and violet. 'Not red' (similarly 'not green' and 'not violet') is a disjunction of two of them. Therefore the principle of indifference does not really assign 'not red' (ditto 'not green' and 'not violet') the probability of ½, but ⅔. This objection might sound very plausible, but on closer inspection it becomes less so. Why, for instance, must the principle of indifference be applied to the set {red, green, violet} rather than to each of the sets {red, not red}, {green, not green}, {violet, not violet}? All of these are sets of exhaustive and exclusive possibilities: why pick out one rather than any other(s) for special attention or privilege? Of course, you get the contradiction back if you do, but we are looking for a *principled* reason. It might be replied that one such reason is that the set of primitive possibilities implicitly specified in the original problem is the set of the primary colours, whereas {blue, not blue}, etc. are sets each consisting of one primary colour and one implicit disjunction of primary colours. But so what? The principle of indifference merely assumes as the condition of its application that there is no relevant knowledge discriminating between the possibilities. If we know nothing that relevantly discriminates between 'red' and 'green' and 'violet', then we presumably also know nothing that relevantly discriminates between 'red' and 'not red', 'green' and 'not green', etc. *except* that 'not red' (not green, etc.) is equivalent to a disjunction of the other two primary colours, and is therefore capable of being realized in more ways in the space {red, green, violet} than is 'red' (green, etc.). But to say that that is *relevant* knowledge is to presuppose that each of these 'ways' is in some sense equally weighted, which is just another way of saying that the bigger space is the one to which the principle is to be applied, and which, of course, simply begs the question. Hume, ever quick to see questions begged, identified this one with his usual unerring accuracy:

The question is, by what means a superior number of equal chances operates upon the mind, and produces belief and assent, since it appears that it is *neither by arguments derived from demonstration, nor from probability.* (1739: I. III. xi; my italics)

Indeed so. This is a beautiful example of what I pointed to in Chapter 1 as the strategy Hume would employ to refute the pretensions of mathematical probability to solve the induction problem: where it is pure mathematics, it can give no indication of how we ought to adjust our beliefs to evidence; where it does attempt to give such an indication, it ceases to be pure mathematics and will employ synthetic assumptions which effectively beg the question.

In addition, we have seen that the number of ways in which an event can be instantiated is not an *invariant* but dependent on the language, or the coordinate system, or the ultimate partition as probabilists say, in which the event is described. Generally speaking, if A can be realized in more ways than B in one reference system, another can be found in which that ordering is reversed. It should now be clear that the idea of a null information state cannot be used as the basis of an equal distribution of probabilities, since, as we have seen, it would apply to different families of related possibility-spaces over which uniform distributions cannot consistently be assigned. The lesson is driven home even more brutally when we consider certain types of infinite possibility-space. As such spaces constitute one of the principal applications of inductive probability (Bayes himself discussed one such space), the discussion has a good deal of practical interest. Suppose that we know only that some measurable magnitude X lies in a bounded interval I of real numbers. The principle of indifference applied to quantities like X would seem to assert that equal subintervals of I, being equally sized extensions of the possibility-space, should therefore have equal probabilities (technically, probability should be proportional to what is called Lebesgue measure). Thus, suppose X can take any real-number value between a and b, where we shall suppose for simplicity that a is positive. The principle of indifference now implies that if we divide up the interval into k (k a whole number) equal subintervals, all these subintervals will receive the same probability; and since probabilities must sum to 1, this implies that the probability of each is $1/k$. Since k is arbitrary, we can apply an intuitively obvious principle of continuity to obtain the flat *probability density*, where the density is obtained by dividing the probability by the length of the interval and letting the latter tend to 0. The probability that the outcome will be in one of the subintervals of length k is $1/k$, and the length of the subintervals is $(b–a)/k$.

Dividing the probability by the length we get $1/(b-a)$, which is independent of k and the subinterval, giving a constant density of $1/(b-a)$ through the interval (a,b). This extension to 'geometrical' outcome spaces sounds very plausible, and indeed, ever since the work of Bayes, it has been regarded as the canonical way the principle of indifference is to apply to them.

But now consider a famous problem, discussed by von Mises (1957: 77). All we know about a mixture of wine and water in a glass is that the proportion X of water to wine is somewhere between equal amounts of each, and twice as much water as wine. This unknown proportion X therefore lies in the interval $(1,2)$, and hence, by the principle of indifference, the probability that X is between $3/2$ and 2 is the same as the probability that X lies between 1 and $3/2$, namely $\frac{1}{2}$. But now consider the reciprocal ratio $W = 1/X$, of wine to water. Clearly, W must lie between $\frac{1}{2}$ and 1, and the probability that X lies between $3/2$ and 2 is equal (by consequence (vii) of I–III) to the probability that W lies between $\frac{1}{2}$ and $\frac{2}{3}$, and this probability we know to be $\frac{1}{2}$. But suppose we had first applied the principle of indifference to W. We would then have found that the probability that W lies between $\frac{1}{2}$ and $\frac{3}{4}$ was $\frac{1}{2}$. These probabilities are compatible only if the probability that W lies between $\frac{2}{3}$ and $\frac{3}{4}$ is zero. But this interval has length $\frac{1}{12}$, and dividing the range of W into twelfths, the principle of indifference asserts that the probability that W lies between $\frac{2}{3}$ and $\frac{3}{4}$ is not 0 but $\frac{1}{12}$. *So we have a contradiction*, and a contradiction unlike the earlier one, involving the colour of the book, in that in the present case both possibility spaces $1 \le X \le 2$, and $\frac{1}{2} \le W \le 1$, are equally 'elementary'. Such contradictions involving continuously distributed quantities began to be noticed in the nineteenth century: they were called 'paradoxes of geometrical probability', and considered merely puzzling at first[12]; only later was it acknowledged what a

---

[12] Consider also this one, mentioned by Edwards (1972: 61). Suppose E_1, E_2, and E_3 are three events about which nothing is known except that they occur in that order (in some frame of reference), they are independent of each other and that the time-intervals T_1 and T_2 between the first two and the last two are bounded above by specified values. Then a simple argument shows that if the probability distributions of T_1 and T_2 are uniform as required by the Principle of Indifference, the probability-density at the point $V = v$ of the sum $V = T_1 + T_2$ cannot be uniform but must be proportional to v. Edwards remarks that 'If a uniform distribution expresses complete ignorance, the distribution [proportional to v] evidently conveys information, so that we have achieved the remarkable feat of learning about the sum of two times, about each of which we know nothing, without making any experiment'. Edwards's point is sound, notwithstanding the initial non sequitur.

serious, if not fatal, objection they posed to the principle of indifference.

It is sometimes objected that in reality there are no continuous magnitudes: these, it is alleged, are a fiction employed merely to facilitate a smooth mathematical treatment. In the 'water–wine' case, for example, it is not true that the possible real proportions of water to wine are represented by all the real numbers in a non-degenerate interval, since proportions by definition are ratios n/m of whole numbers: in this example, whole numbers of molecules. The objection is both question-begging, as a *general* thesis about the values of physical magnitudes, and beside the point: the contradiction is there implicitly in discrete cases as well as continuous. It is there as soon as we try to define the idea of null information in terms of uniform distributions of probability.

The inconsistencies resulting from applying the principle of indifference in the context of continuous probability are real enough, but we should be careful about what they truly show. For example, it is often claimed that problems like the wine–water 'paradox' show that you cannot represent pure ignorance probabilistically. Shafer, who is one of those who claim this, uses the alleged fact to argue for a non-probabilistic theory of uncertain reasoning (1976; and see above, p. 78). But there is absolutely nothing inconsistent about using a uniform distribution over a bounded interval to represent your indecision. Obviously you must not try to do the same over an unbounded interval; such a distribution would correspond to an infinite probability. But then it is entirely reasonable to see the mathematical block as merely demonstrating that on pain of inconsistency ignorance cannot work like that over infinite spaces. Equally, the wine–water example shows that if I believe myself indifferent between all equal subintervals in the range of a variable X in its scale [a,b], then I cannot, again on pain of inconsistency, believe myself indifferent between all equal subintervals in the range of Y = 1/X in its scale [1/b,1/a], and similarly for any other non-linear transformation of X. But I am not likely to in any case. There is always some background knowledge for any parameter in nature or science (where after all do the end-points of the interval come from?), and it is hardly plausible that if my ignorance about, say, a temperature spreads equally over a positive range of degrees Celsius then it also should over the corresponding range of logt or t^4.

The principle of indifference, however, is genuinely hit by the paradoxes, for its role in the traditional Bayesian theory of Bayes and Laplace was as a fundamental methodological principle for determining neutral prior distributions. The idea was that anything other than a uniform (or in suitable circumstances log uniform) distribution over ultimate possibilities would not be epistemically neutral; it would import human prejudice into an objective evaluation of the data, thereby preventing Nature from speaking through the evidence alone. 'Objective Bayesians' today hold just the same view that anything other than a uniform a priori distribution adds to and thereby distorts the data of observation.[13] The inconsistencies strike home against this methodology because according to it there can be no justification for discriminating a priori between logt and t and in consequence adopting a uniform distribution over both, which is, of course, impossible. It is, in other words, the *methodology* of a priori neutrality, of which the principle of indifference is the probabilistic expression, that the paradoxes show to be untenable. And its conclusions, like Popper's that P(H) = 0 for universal H, based on applications of the same principle, must be judged not only unproven but suspect.

In one sense Popper's claim is definitely false. A theorem of Horn and Tarski (1948: theorem 2.5) implies that there is a strictly positive countably additive probability measure on the sentences of a language whose vocabulary is countably infinite, even where the logical axioms are supplemented by an 'axiom of infinity', that is, a set of sentences which can be jointly true only in infinite domains (Howson 1973: 153). This means that a probability measure exists on such a language which assigns positive values to every contingent general statement, including those which imply that they have infinitely many distinct instantiations. So there is certainly nothing in mathematics and logic to rule out probability functions not satisfying Popper's claim, and Popper even tells us that he regards the probability axioms as determining all the rules of what he calls logical probability (1968: 286). Having zero prior probability is admittedly a property of all the measures in Carnap's so-called λ-continuum (Carnap 1952), for $\lambda > 0$, that they assign universal hypotheses zero probability, but these measures are subject to so many additional, and as far as most commentators have been concerned unjustifiable, constraints that little significance can be attached to this feature of them.

---

[13] See e.g. Rosenkrantz 1977: 54.

Independence

In the process of developing his first attack Popper also produced a quite different argument for P(H) = 0 which, despite being fallacious, is very interesting in that it embodies reasoning of a type that seems, on the face of it at least, thoroughly Humean and which, correctly followed, leads to a resolution of the problem of how correct assignments of prior probability should be made. The resolution is that, outside trivial cases, there *are no* correct assignments. To see why, we need to start with a rather obvious reflection on the nature of inference. Canons of inference are generally regarded as within the province of logic, and we can plausibly assume that in so far as probability theory furnishes a theory of non-deductive *inference* it must thereby constitute some sort of logic in its own right. Indeed, Popper himself regards the formal calculus of probability as possessing, among others, a definite *logical* interpretation (1968). Can this logic also be a logic of inductive inference? Popper believes that it cannot, and for a reason which itself appears at first sight to be a very Humean one. It is that an inequality $P(E_{i+1}|E_1 \& \ldots \& E_i) > P(E_{i+1})$, or, with the sign reversed, would have 'the character of a *synthetic a priori* principle of induction, rather than of a . . . logical assertion' (1959: 370); indeed, 'we must consider [the E_j] as mutually *independent* of one another . . . if we are concerned with absolute logical probabilities then $p(a_i.a_j) = p(a_i)p(a_j)$; every other assumption would amount to postulating *ad hoc* a kind of after-effect' (1959: 367).

It is not difficult, however, to see that there is something self-defeating about Popper's argument for the probabilistic independence of all the E_i. If a probabilistic inequality expresses a synthetic principle, as according to Popper it does, then why should not an equality equally do so? If an inequality expresses 'a synthetic a priori principle', then why not an equality also? These simple questions seem quite fatal to Popper's case. The more natural inference would be that within a truly logical theory no *categorical* assertion, apart from trivial ones, should be provable, and that would include both probabilistic equalities and inequalities alike (strangely enough, this is a position that Popper claimed himself to be committed to; 1968: 286). That would of course mean that both Popper's independence condition and his claim that P(H) = 0 for universal hypotheses H were not theorems of such a logical calculus.

But it would also follow that P(H) > 0 is not a principle of logic either. We can note that to assign a finite prior probability to H is to judge (by Theorem 1) that the quantity of uncertain information in H *can* be reduced by acquiring appropriate finite data. It is not easy to see this, any more than P(H) = 0, as an a priori truth. Following on the reflections above, any ascription of a definite probability to a contingent statement is a claim that exceeds pure logic, and therefore if adopted as an assumption, like either P(H) = 0 or P(H) > 0, is at least as questionable as what is proved thereby. So, ironically, we can regard Hume's position as strengthened by the failure of Popper's attempted defence of it.

More than that. According to Hume's circularity thesis, every inductive argument has a concealed or explicit circularity. In the case of probabilistic arguments we argued there that this would manifest itself on analysis in some sort of prior loading in favour of the sorts of 'resemblance' between past and future we thought desirable. Well, of course, we have seen exactly that: *the prior loading is supplied by the prior probabilities.* What gets supported empirically and what does not will be determined by these: just how we shall see in Chapter 8.

Conclusion

Despite initially promising appearances the conclusion seems to be that probability theory does not supply a framework for making sound inductive inferences without the assistance of additional assumptions: in particular, about what is to be assigned positive prior probability. In the extensive universe of possibilities implicitly contemplated in discussing the problem of induction, a very large number of these will necessarily be assigned zero prior probability, with the corollary that what is even *allowed* to be inductively supported by observational data is our decision. To that extent the positive assignments seem to be Humean inductive assumptions, and this also seems to be true for whatever actual value is assigned to a hypothesis. We have seen that in certain circumstances P(H|E) depends on P(H), and we shall see later—it is a simple consequence of the probability axioms—that in general P(H|E) is an increasing function of P(H). That prior probability assignments appear to be tantamount to substantive assumptions, as they seem to be, vindicates Hume's circularity thesis, at any rate for probable arguments framed in the mathematical theory of probability. We shall have to wait until Chapter 7 for a final verdict, but it will bear out fully what has been said here.

Appendix 1

In section 1 of Bayes (1763), Bayes defines the probability (the epistemic, knowledge-based interpretation of probability) of an event A to be

> the ratio between the value at which an expectation depending on the happening of the event ought to be computed, and the value of the thing expected upon its happening (Definition 5).

We should bear in mind that Bayes construed the term 'event' very broadly, to include items which we would today call propositions. For example, one of the 'events' he considered was the 'event' that the true value of a chance probability is such and such. There is a similarity of structure, in technical language an *isomorphism*, between the algebra of events and that of propositions, and so formally speaking it does not substantially matter whether we regard the domain of a Bayesian probability function as a set of propositions or a set of events. It is usual these days, when discussing the Bayesian interpretation of probability, to regard the probabilities as probabilities of propositions. In what follows I shall let A stand either for 'event A occurs' or 'the proposition that A occurs is true'. Bayes always talks about events occurring, whereas here we are primarily concerned with the truth of propositions. I trust that no confusion will be caused by this harmless equivocation.

Bayes's definition is to be understood as follows. Suppose a promise to pay a sum of N units of currency is made on condition that an uncertain proposition A is true. The uncertainty of A means that you should pay a price in general less than N units for that promise, and Bayes is saying that we can use the ratio of the discounted value to N as a measure of the uncertainty of A (the ratio rather than the discounted value itself is chosen because only the former gives a common standard for the comparison of different probabilities). Such a contract is familiar, as it is essentially nothing but a *bet* on the truth of A, with odds given by the ratio $p/(1-p)$, where p is the Bayesian probability of A.

Bayes talks of the probability as the value at which N *ought* to be discounted, divided by N. This raises the question: 'ought' according to which criteria? Another feature of Bayes's definition which also calls for comment is that it assumes that the ratio of the value of N, discounted by the uncertainty of A, to N itself *is independent of N*. This assumption is often taken to conflict with the accepted view that money has diminishing marginal utility.

And there are other questionable aspects of the definition besides these: it seems to assume that the truth-value of A can always be veridically decided, and that there is a *unique* value of a which, through the ratio a/N, measures the uncertainty of A. I shall postpone till later (Chapter 7) a fuller discussion of these issues (Bayes himself would have been quite aware of them), and merely assume for now that they can be resolved in some more or less satisfactory way. The important thing here is to see what properties of Bayesian probabilities follow from his definition, and we shall do so in the order of Bayes's own exposition. Henceforward P(A) will signify the probability of A.

    (I)   P(A) ≥ 0.
Proof. Immediate.
    (II)   P(T) = 1 if T represents a necessary truth.
Proof. Also immediate.
    (III)   If A and B are mutually exclusive then
           P(A or B) = P(A) + P(B).
Proof (a slight modification of Bayes, Proposition 1). Suppose P(A) = a/N, P(B) = b/N. Suppose you were to buy the two options 'N if A' and 'N if B' for what you take to be their true values a and b. Thus if A or B is true you receive N, since given that they are mutually exclusive only one of the statements 'A [B] is true' can be true, as the table shows (T is 'true' and F 'false'):

A B	Payoff
T F	N
F T	N
F F	0

So if 'A or B' is true you receive N, and you have paid out the sum a + b. In other words, you have in effect bought the option 'Receive N if A or B is true', for the price a + b. If you are consistent in your pricing of options you should therefore regard a + b as the value of the combined option. Hence consistency requires P(A or B) = P(A) + P(B). QED. The proof extends straightforwardly to the case of any n exclusive events (see if you can say why).

These results were elaborated and refined by de Finetti and Ramsey in the twentieth century, but Bayes's central idea proved seminal and has become the foundation of nearly all work in what is now officially called Bayesian probability. No less seminal was his treatment of conditional probabilities. In the partial interpretation of the axioms given at the beginning of this chapter P(B|A), the probability of B conditional on A, was glossed as the probability of B given the assumption, which may be false, that A is true. Given the way Bayes proposed to operationally evaluate unconditional probabilities, the natural evaluation of a conditional probability P(B|A) is as the fair price for the option of receiving N if B is true (and of course nothing if not) *just in the circumstance that A is true*, that is, with the understanding that no contract exists if that condition is not satisfied. Granted that in proposition 3 of his paper Bayes proceeds to show that if $P(A) > 0$ then to be consistent you must set $P(B|A) = P(A\&B)/P(A)$; in other words, $P(B|A)$ must be numerically determined according to the standard definition. I give a slight modification of Bayes's own proof.

Proof (essentially Bayes, Propositions 2 and 3). Let $P(A\&B) = p/N$, $P(A) = a/N$ where $a > 0$, and $P(B|A) = b/N$, and suppose that you were to

(i) pay the fair price p for the option 'Receive N if both A and B occur', and

(ii) receive the fair price b for the conditional option 'Receive N if B occurs, conditionally on A occurring'.

The payoff table below sets out your net gains from (i) and (ii), for each of the three exclusive and exhaustive cases *A&B true*, *A true and B false*, and *A false*:

A B	gain from (i) +	gain from (ii)
T T	N–p	–N + b
T F	–p	b
F	–p	0

Hence if A occurs you gain b–p, while if A does not occur you lose p. In other words, you have implicitly contracted to pay p to receive b if A occurs. Where $b > 0$ consistency requires $p/b = a/N$ and where $b = 0$, p must therefore be 0. In both cases $ab = Np$, giving $a/N \cdot b/N = p/N$. Hence $P(B|A) = P(A\&B)/P(A)$. QED.

Axioms I–III together with the principle $P(B|A) = P(B\&A)/P(A)$ express what Bayes regarded as the *general* principles of the probability calculus. They are actually a *complete* set, in the sense that every proposition regarded as true of probability in general is known to follow from them (they are also complete in a much more precise sense which will be related in Chapter 7). Bayes at any rate seems to have recognized this, which is remarkable in the light of the fact that no other attempt to derive such general principles seemed to have been made at that time, as Bayes is reported to have remarked to his friend and editor Richard Price.

Appendix 2

Using a form of the rule of conditionalization (above, p. 68) together with the 'deliverances of experience', we can obtain a particularly strong dynamic model of *learning from experience*. This form of conditionalization states that on learning the experiential data E (and no more) one must proceed to a new, or updated, probability function Q(.) equal for all arguments in the dot place to P(. |E). From Q we can form new conditional probabilities Q(. |E') according to axiom IV, and on learning E' we proceed by conditionalization to a new function $Q'(\,.\,) = Q(\,.\,|E') = P(\,.\,|E\&E')$ (by (ix) above). Within this model, learning from experience is represented by a progression of sequentially updated probability functions, each member of which is obtained from the preceding one by conditionalization when one learns the appropriate conditioning propositions.

This model bespeaks a fairly radical empiricism, in which experience successively modifies some original, or prior probability function P, representing something like the ideal reasoner before the reception of any information whatever from 'experience' (a sort of Lockean *tabula rasa*). This picture of learning raises questions which seem impossible to answer sensibly, however. For example, if you have no experience, then it is doubtful that you could have any language within which to frame your conjectures, or the evidence that you will subsequently acquire, in which case it is also doubtful, to say the least, that any sense can be given to the expression P(H|E). Even if this problem is solved, it merely raises another, which is that the model makes no concessions to what most people now accept as the fallibility of even the most observational of observational evidence. For suppose you conditionalize on E, proceeding from P to Q in the manner described. Then by the definition of Q, Q(E) = 1, since Q(E) = P(E|E). It is not difficult to see that all later functions Q', Q'', etc. will assign E the same probability 1: once accepted as evidence to condition on, in other words, there can be no going back on the decision. Finally, there is the problem of deciding in some non-arbitrary way how the *tabula rasa*'s original, *ur*-probability function P is to be defined. Nearly everybody who has experimented with this model has tried to use the principle of indifference over some sufficiently large space of possibilities. Apart from the probably insuperable difficulties with that principle itself, discussed earlier, there is the equally insoluble problem of specifying all the possible hypotheses that science will ever consider. This model seems therefore a hopelessly unrealistic one, which indeed it is, and which is why most of the exponents of probabilism have either given it up after becoming acquainted with its more objectionable features, or refused to adopt it in the first place.

Appendix 3

The result is a simple application of the result popularly known as Bayes's theorem, though it was actually first proved by Laplace. Bayes's theorem has several versions, all of which are fairly simple consequences of the axioms: the one we use here is stated as follows (for a proof see Howson and Urbach 1993: 28):

$$P(A|B) = \frac{P(B|A)P(A)}{P(B|A)P(A) + \Sigma P(B|A_i)P(A_i)}$$

where $\{A, A_i | i = 1, 2, 3, \ldots\}$ is a set of exclusive and exhaustive alternatives. Now let H_i predict 1s up to and including the ith trial, and 0s thereafter. Let E_k say that only 1s have been observed up to and including the kth trial. Clearly, $P(E_k | H) = 1$ for all i, $P(E_k | H_i) = 0$ for $i \le k$, and $P(E_k | H_i) = 1$ for all $i > k$. Let $P(H) = r$. Suppose for simplicity that we give all other hypotheses about the evolution of the data sequence zero prior probability. This does not in fact affect the conclusion but it makes the application of the equation above more straightforward. It now tells us that

$$P(H | E_k) = \frac{r}{r + \Sigma_{k<i} P(H_i)}$$

By the additivity principle, $\Sigma_{i \le k} P(H_i) \to 1$ as $k \to \infty$, and hence $\Sigma_{k<i} P(H_i) \to 0$ as $k \to \infty$. Hence $P(H | E_k) \to 1$, so that eventually H will be overwhelmingly better supported than any of the still infinitely many surviving grue$_t$ alternatives to H.

5

Deductivism

This chapter is titled 'Deductivism' because, according to the views of the protagonists discussed herein, assessments of the merits of competing hypotheses in the light of evidence require no dedicated inferential machinery other than deductive logic, together with a clear statement of the aims which the assessments are intended to achieve. These authors firmly repudiate the idea that there is any specifically *inductive* logic, and in particular any probabilistic inductive logic, underwriting inductive inferences.

Popper

In the preceding chapter we became acquainted with Popper the scourge of probabilistic induction. Popper believed that there is no such thing as valid inductive inference, and certainly not probabilistic inductive inference. The problem—Hume's Problem as we called it— remains to justify any sort of 'forward-looking' claim to predictive success or even to truth (the truth of a general hypothesis implies continued predictive success), for hypotheses that have passed all the tests to which they have been exposed. Popper's novel suggestion is that Hume's Problem can be solved in a *positive* way *without invoking any inference procedures other than those of deductive logic*. To achieve this goal, Popper tried to drive a wedge between (*a*) having a good reason for preferring a hypothesis if one's aim is truth, and (*b*) having a good reason to suppose that some specified hypothesis is true or more likely to be true in the light of the available evidence; (*b*) is induction, which Popper repudiated. He tried instead to show that there can be a reason of type (*a*) for a rational preference for hypotheses in the light of evidence, *which does not appeal to any (b)-type reason.*

Popper's claim, indeed the whole of his celebrated philosophy of *falsificationism*, rests on an elementary consequence of the usual definition of deductively valid inferences. According to that definition, deductively valid inferences are just the truth-preserving inferences under all interpretations of premisses and conclusion (see Howson 1997*c*: ch. 1). The consequence Popper invokes is known traditionally as *modus tollens*: if a deductive consequence of a statement A is false, then so is A. The methodological significance of *modus tollens* is that if we discover a false consequence of a hypothesis then we know that the hypothesis is false (I shall ignore the fallibilistic objection, and one pressed by Popper himself, that we can never know with rigorous certainty the truth of any factual assertion, even an 'observation statement'; there are more fundamental objections). Hence, in a comparison between a hypothesis that has passed a test and one that has failed, we have a good reason of type (*a*) for preferring the former if our aim is truth. Hume's problem is 'essentially' solved, according to Popper, because such an argument demonstrates that we can have good, non-inductive, grounds for choosing between competing universal theories: 'For it may happen that our test statements may refute some—*but not all*—of the competing theories; and since we are searching for a true theory, we shall prefer those whose falsity has not been established' (1970: 8; my italics). It follows, according to Popper, that science does not need induction at all: deduction alone serves the purpose of discriminating between competing hypotheses even when our aim is truth.

As a solution of Hume's Problem this has been treated with a good deal of scepticism by most commentators; and with good reason. The catch to it is signalled by Popper himself in the phrase 'but not all' in the quotation above. 'Not all' indeed—for what about 'grue' and the underdetermination problem? The response: Test H against any grue$_t$ alternative H$_t$ and see which one survives, certainly will not work, since, as we have seen, there are infinitely many grue$_{t,t',t''}$, . . . alternatives to H, and there is no single test or even finite number of tests which will eliminate all but a finite number: any finite set of tests will still leave an infinity of alternatives unrefuted. Hence binary evaluations of the (*a*) sort cannot discriminate between H and its grue$_t$ variants, and hence cannot justify the knowledge-claims that Popper wishes to make on behalf of the currently accepted theories in science.

However, Popper has also developed a method of evaluating hypotheses which does not issue verdicts merely of the sort 'H has passed the test T and H′ has not', and which does seem, in principle

at any rate, to provide a means of evaluating any single hypothesis H
against the reports of experimental tests to which H has been subjected. This apparently more powerful method of evaluation involves
measuring what Popper calls the *degree of corroboration* of H by the
report of the test's outcome (or tests' outcomes). The underlying idea
is that corroboration reflects the *severity* of the test or tests passed:
the more severe and rigorous the tests, the greater is H's degree of
corroboration by successful outcomes. Moreover, according to
Popper, we have a natural measure of the severity of a test T, whose
outcome E is as predicted by H, in the smallness of 'the' probability
$P(E)$ of E (what 'the' probability is I shall come to shortly). So corroboration should increase with decreasing $P(E)$. Popper's choice for
the function $C(H,E)$ taken to be the formal measure of the corroboration of H by E is, he tells us, a suitably increasing function of the
arithmetical difference $P(E|H)-P(E)$ (1959: app. *ix), where P is suit-
ably relativized to some stock of background information. Indeed,
Popper tells us that we can regard $P(E|H)-P(E)$ itself as an admissible
measure of corroboration.

Those with a good memory for the probability axioms will notice
that, given Popper's view that the prior probability of any strictly universal hypothesis H is zero, then according to the definition of condi-
tional probability $P(E|H)$ is undefined even when H entails, that is,
predicts, E. But such hypotheses are *par excellence* the hypotheses science deals with. Because of this difficulty with the standard axiomatization of probability, due to Kolmogorov, Popper felt that a different
axiomatization of probability is called for in which $P(E|H)$ is always
well defined, and is equal to 1 when H entails E. Such an axiomatization is presented in Popper (1959, app. *iv). This is not the place for a
discussion of the competing merits of the standard axiomatization of
probability and Popper's. For the sake of argument we shall just
assume that $P(E|H)$ is well defined whether $P(H) = 0$ or not.

The probability function P in Popper's account determines what
he calls 'logical' probability. Popper's idea of 'logical' probability is
a function defined on sentences which reflects just the purely logical
relations subsisting between them. The trouble with this suggestion
is that there seems to be an infinity of such functions, as many indeed
as there are functions satisfying the probability axioms (for a longer
discussion of this point see Howson 1973). But question marks over
the nature of P are secondary to a much bigger one over corroboration itself. First, Popper insists that $C(H,E)$ is not to be regarded as

having any inductive significance. But in that case it is difficult to see what positive role it plays, and why such care should be taken to stress that it reflects the severity of tests passed. And what about this remarkable statement: 'If a theory h has been well-corroborated, then it is highly probable *that it is truth-like*' (1983: 346)? Popper even proposes an argument for this supposedly 'non-inductive' position, namely

the *valid* but *misinterpreted* intuitive idea that *it cannot be just due to an improbable accident* if a hypothesis is again and again successful when tested in different circumstances, and especially if it is successful in making previously unexpected predictions. (ibid.; italics in original)

The No-Miracles argument now has to support Popper's theory of corroboration. But we know that it cannot even sustain itself. The rider that the hypothesis in question has made 'previously unexpected predictions' will not save it, for we know from Chapter 3 that the same is true of all its grue variants. This brings us to the second problem. Inspection of C(H,E) shows that it is immediately vulnerable to the grue problem for the same reason: it cannot discriminate between them. C(H,E) has the same value for *all* hypotheses predicting E, for C(H,E) depends on H only through P(E|H), whose value is 1 for every hypothesis entailing E (note that C(H,E) cannot depend on the priors since by assumption all these are uniformly 0 in Poppers' theory). C(H,E) can't tell grue from green! Popper's quantitative theory of corroboration is therefore no advance on his earlier 'solution' of the problem of induction in terms of crucial tests among pairs of competing hypotheses.

While Popper never explicitly attempted to answer the objection that Goodman's 'Paradox' poses to his theory, other Popperians have. David Miller has recently tried to answer it, by first conceding that there is nothing in terms of a difference in empirical support to distinguish the 'grue' alternatives from 'All emeralds are green', but then denying that that is even an important consideration:

The difficulty entirely disappears once we discard the mistaken idea that empirical support is significant, and that it is empirical support that makes a hypothesis eligible for admission into the body of science . . . It is whether our hypotheses are true or false that matters, not whether they are empirically supported; and *we all know that 'All emeralds are grue'* is false. (Miller 1994: 37; my italics)

How do we know? No answer.

By contrast, Deutsch (who places Popper in a highly exclusive pantheon of twentieth-century thinkers) does give reasons which he thinks justify the 'summary rejection' of such theories (1997: 151). He lists two: (i) that they have not been subjected to criticism, including that of experimental test, and (ii) that they 'spoil' the *explanations* provided by existing accepted science; these latter explanatory properties 'justif[y] our relying on the prevailing theory' (ibid.). Now (i) does sound plausible, for a necessary condition for an experiment to decide between competing theories is surely that it be in their area of disagreement. Yet no such test has been performed to test between existing theory and any grue alternative to it; by construction all the existing data is in their area of *agreement*. It would seem, therefore, that Deutsch is quite correct in saying that none of the grue theories has never been subject to a proper test, and hence that the data do not favour them against existing theory. But that observation does not help his case, *for the situation is quite symmetrical*: just as no test has pronounced in favour of a grue variant and against existing theory, so no test has pronounced in favour of existing theory against a grue theory, and the data therefore provide no warrant for making the choice in either way. We must look elsewhere for a criterion.

Does consideration (ii) provide it? Deutsch considers a rather special grue variant to gravitational theory, in which a single exception is made to the rule that all bodies fall when unsupported (1997: 151), but his argument applies to the more general form we have been considering as well. The argument is that such 'theories' are not explanatory because they postulate unexplained exceptions to a rule. To the objection that they can be made syntactically universal by introducing appropriate predicates, like 'grue', Deutsch replies that these merely conceal the fact that unexplained anomalies are being postulated, a fact which ordinary English, which evolved to express faithfully what is genuinely problematic and what is not, makes clear (p.153). Thus there *is*, claims Deutsch, a relevant asymmetry: currently accepted theory is explanatory in a way that the grue variants to it are not. It is strange to find the authority of Popper of all people, a thinker vehemently opposed to 'ordinary-language' arguments, being enlisted in such an enterprise. But Deutsch is really doing no more than restate the Goodman criterion of projectability based on what is entrenched in common concepts, and the same objection applies that we brought against that: science introduces *unconventional* concepts, a fact that Deutsch, himself something of a scientific revolutionary, should be the first to appreciate. So while it is undeniable that we do not regard Goodmanized theories as explanatory, that is not to say that they are not, nor that they will never be thought so. And we do not regard them as explanatory because, as Miller correctly pointed out, we 'know' that they are false.

Another Popperian, Musgrave, claims that a rational preference for 'All emeralds are green' over 'All emeralds are grue' can be grounded on the alleged facts that the former is simpler than the latter, containing as it does implicitly the reference-point 'now', and if the simpler hypothesis is false then it will be easier to show that it is false (1993: 292). Neither of these claims stands up. As Goodman himself pointed out, 'All emeralds are green' is simpler than 'All emeralds are blue' relative to the {green, blue} language, but more complex relative to the {grue, bleen} language. True, Popper himself proposes a notion of simplicity—in fact, one proposed earlier by Jeffreys (1961: 47)—characterized by the number of free parameters occurring essentially in a hypothesis, a notion which is not language-relative. But on that criterion, both 'All emeralds are green' and 'All emeralds are grue' are equally simple since neither has any free parameter. Musgrave's second claim is false because ease of falsification is related only to the paucity-of-parameters notion; and the reader can easily verify that 'All emeralds are green' is exactly as easy, or difficult, to falsify as 'All emeralds are grue': both hypotheses make equally definite statements about the colour-characteristics of observed emeralds. But even were Musgrave's claims about differential ease of falsification true, he still faces what is, to put it mildly, an uphill task explaining why the more falsifiable theory should be preferable to the less. *Ease of falsification and actual falsity are logically independent.* If I am 99 per cent certain that H is false, and it is easy to establish that H is false whereas testing H′ may prove costly and difficult, why should I prefer H to H′ which I think stands a much better chance of being true than H? Such a preference would be absurd. Yet that is what Musgrave asks us to accept.

Falsifiability and ease of falsification are red herrings. They led Popper to give undue prominence to universal hypotheses, because these, in the simple world where observation statements are genuinely observation statements, are *modus-tollens*-falsifiable by a single counterinstance. Since the date of the first publication of Popper's principal methodological work, *Logik der Forschung* (best-known in the English-speaking world as *The Logic of Scientific*

Discovery), a class of statements *not* falsifiable in this way has assumed a growing importance in science, especially in particle physics and cosmology: these statements are pure existence statements, and some of the currently most important hypotheses are of this type ('Does the Higgs particle exist?'). To claim, as Popper does, that these are not scientific because they are unfalsifiable, is clearly to beg the question. *Modus tollens* is a false god. No purely deductive rule can solve the problem of induction. Jeffreys sums up the position with his usual succinctness:

the tendency to claim that scientific method can be reduced in some way to deductive logic . . . is the most fundamental fallacy of all: it can be done only by rejecting its chief feature, induction. (1961: 2)

The discussion has nevertheless been advanced. In more or less conceding that the empirical data cannot discriminate between a hypothesis and any of the myriad alternatives which stand in the same logical relation to it, Deutsch has pointed to a fact of fundamental importance, but one recognized explicitly only by the Bayesian model of the logic of scientific reasoning, in which posterior probability is shown to depend in general on prior probability. But that model, at any rate as it will be presented in Chapter 8, does not in any way propose to justify any distribution of prior probabilities, and therefore is not really an *inductivist* model. By contrast Popper, in conceding that evidence might justify a preference for a small finite subset of hypotheses over the literally uncountable remainder, did advance a view inductivist in everything but name. And in so doing he ran sharply up against the Humean argument. To his credit, and unlike other philosophers (Hempel 1945 is a notable example) who construct 'confirmation theories' without attempting to answer or even recognize the Humean objections, Popper did recognize the gravity of Hume's Problem. But the verdict must be that he has not solved it.

Fisher

The similarities between Fisher's and Popper's methodological views are quite remarkable, passing as they do right down to the details. Thus, both Popper and Fisher believed that probabilities of hypotheses are at best psychological indicators having no place in objective science (Popper 1959: 255 and 1960: 29; Fisher 1935: 6–7); both stated that the function of experiment is not confirmation but attempted refutation (Popper 1962: 197; Fisher 1935: 16); both stressed that a, if not the, crucial feature of their own measures of evidential import (for Fisher, so-called likelihood, for Popper, degree of corroboration, i.e. likelihood minus prior probability of E) is that they do not satisfy the probability axioms (Popper 1959: 394; Fisher 1925: 10); and both expressed the view that to show that a 'significant' result in statistics is not merely the coincidental 'chance in a million', repeatability of the result is required (Popper 1959: 203; Fisher 1935: 142).

Above all, both Fisher and Popper were revolutionary *falsificationists*. Both repudiated the fundamental Bayesian principle that experiments are well designed to the extent that they bring the posterior probabilities as close to the extreme value of 1 as possible. But Fisher was the deeper thinker (he was, after all, a great scientist). He realized that failing to be falsified even in the most searching and stringent of tests cannot not furnish a *positive* reason for adopting any theory, for there are too many alternatives also satisfying that condition. As we saw in Chapter 3, to disarm this problem Fisher had the ingenious idea of opposing a hypothesis asserting *some* degree of causal effect to its negation, the null hypothesis of no effect, and identifying the latter with chance agreement with the data. He thereby introduced the No-Miracles argument, on which in effect he based the decision to reject the null hypothesis and thereby accept a causal hypothesis, into official scientific methodology. But as we also saw, not only there is no legitimate way of identifying the null hypothesis with any determinate chance distribution, but to infer that the null hypothesis is false when a test outcome falls in the rejection class in a significance test can be, and in easily reproducible circumstances is, wildly wrong. The No-Miracles argument, if not as full of holes as a sieve, still has too many to hold water.

Neyman and Pearson

Just as Fisher seemed to have given falsificationism a relevance for ordinary scientific enquiry by finding what appeared to be a way of turning a falsification—of the null hypothesis—into a confirmation of the real hypothesis of interest, so Neyman and Pearson seemed in their turn to have found a way of rescuing the essence of Fisher's position by transposing it into a purely decision-theoretic problem. In an analysis of what it means to make an *erroneous* decision to accept or reject a hypothesis on the basis of test-outcomes, Neyman and Pearson seemed to come up with a rigorous justification of doing in many cases of practical interest pretty much as Fisher had been recommending.

The analysis proceeds in stages. First, it is assumed that on the basis of a suitable type of observational evidence we make a decision to accept or not a hypothesis H. More precisely, we have an experimental procedure X for which there is a space S of mutually exclusive and exhaustive possible outcomes. If the observed outcome is in a suitably defined subclass C of S, we accept H, and if it is not we reject it. Incidentally, the word 'accept' should not be taken too literally. The idea is to partition S into two classes, one of which, often practically the more important, is the rejection region. Tests based on such a partition are called *bivalent tests*, and in these 'accept' might mean little more than 'not reject'.

Let us resume the narrative. Neyman and Pearson next argue that their own novel analysis of reliability imposes sufficiently strong constraints on C to allow it to be uniquely determined. They point out that our decision, to accept or not, may be *erroneous* in one of two ways:

1 We may reject H, that is, the outcome does not fall in C, though H is in fact true.
2 We may accept H, that is, the outcome falls in C, though H is in fact false.

Neyman and Pearson argue that a decision procedure, namely the choice of C, is more reliable the more it jointly reduces the *chance of error*, that is, of a type 1 or a type 2 error above (the usual presentation focuses on the class of outcomes which *reject* H, that is, on the complement C* of C, and defines the errors in terms of C*; the reader who is more used to doing things that way round can make the necessary adjustments).

At this point a short digression on the nature of the hypothesis H is in order. There are two broad kinds of scientific hypothesis, generally called *deterministic* and *statistical*. A deterministic hypothesis predicts that in a suitable context a specified quantity will take a particular determinate value (hence the name 'deterministic'). A statistical hypothesis specifies a range of possible values of a quantity and a chance probability distribution over them. In practice, of course, as we observed in the previous chapter, there are inevitably smaller or larger small disturbances in recording observed values, which collectively fall under the heading of *experimental error* (not to be confused with the type 1 and type 2 errors defined above). These errors themselves are usually supposed to be subject to some chance distribution (often one such that the mean of the observed values is presumed to be the true value of the quantity), which can be estimated from previous observations of similar quantities with similar instruments. This means that when it comes to comparing observed and predicted values, even a deterministic hypothesis becomes in effect a statistical one. Again we shall freely idealize for the sake of simplicity, and forget about errors when it comes to evaluating deterministic hypotheses, assuming that they make exact observational predictions. The point at issue is an 'in principle' one: whether even in these admittedly idealized circumstances inductive inference is possible. If it is, then the practical complications can presumably be taken care of by suitably approximative methods.

There is one last preliminary. Much of what Neyman and Pearson say concerns *chances*, which they understood in a very similar if not identical way to Fisher: chances are registered in long-run frequencies of occurrence. Later (in Chapter 9) the issue of what chances 'really' are will be discussed in more detail. For now it is sufficient to know what Fisher, Neyman, and Pearson thought they are. We now resume the narrative. With all these considerations in mind, suppose that H predicts (correctly or incorrectly) the proportion of outcomes of the experiment which will fall in C, either because H is deterministic and says they all will, or all won't, or because H specifies a chance probability distribution over all the outcomes of the experiment, and so predicts the proportion of times the outcome will fall in C in the long run. Either way, we have a prediction by H of the proportion (relative frequency) of times the outcome will be in C: 0 or 1 if H is deterministic, and some intermediate value if not. In either case we shall call this predicted proportion the *chance according to H* of the outcome falling in C, and symbolize it $P_H(C)$. Finally, suppose (we shall return to this later) that H is false just in case some rival, equally specific, H′ is true. The chance of a type 2 error is $P_{H'}(C)$, and again we shall usually know how to evaluate this.

And now the final stage. Finding a C which maximizes $P_H(C)$ jointly with minimizing $P_{H'}(C)$ presents technical problems—there may be no such C. However, suppose that a maximum admissible value q for the chance of the type 1 error is first chosen. The problem is now reduced to that of finding a C such that $P_{H'}(C)$ is minimal among all the possible classes C' of outcomes for which $P_H(C'^*) < q$. This problem is soluble and was in fact solved by Neyman and Pearson themselves. They proved, in their 'Fundamental Lemma' (for a simple proof see Hoel 1971), that C is the set of outcomes E such that $P_{H'}(E)/P_H(E) < t$, where t is a constant whose value is determined by q. One minus $P_{H'}(C)$, i.e. $P_{H'}(C^*)$, is called the *power* of the test with rejection region C*. It may be that there is some other experimental procedure X' such that the $C_{X'}$ selected by the same criterion in the outcome space of X' has greater power, i.e. $P_{H'}(C_{X'}) < P_{H'}(C)$. Such an experimental procedure would plausibly be preferable because it has a smaller chance of a type 2 error. In other words, we have a clear and precise direction for obtaining a best, that is, most reliable, test of H: choose that experimental design with the best power characteristics.

Neyman and Pearson seem to have kept their promise of exhibiting a procedure which provably produces the most reliable decisions that can in principle be obtained (though they may not actually be very reliable, they will be the most reliable), and without any consideration of prior probabilities. However, on closer inspection the picture is much less clear-cut. The argument so far has depended on H being such that there is only one predictive alternative H'. But we know now very well that in general this will not be the case. Suppose then that H has more than one such alternative (remember grue!). How are we going to define the chance of a type 2 error? Without introducing Bayesian prior probabilities the expression 'the chance of C specified by –H' is meaningless, since –H, being the proposition merely that H is not true, will not in general itself specify a definite chance distribution. However, the following suggestion might seem to offer a reasonable way round this problem: select a C which minimizes $P_{H'}(C)$ for every alternative H' to H. In other words, select C such that for *every* alternative hypothesis H', and any other C' with no greater type I error probability, $P_{H'}(C) \leq P_{H'}(C')$: in Neyman–Pearson terminology, the test with rejection region C* is *uniformly most powerful* (standardly abbreviated to UMP).

It is instructive to look at this suggestion in the context of Fisher's tea-tasting experiment. The test that Fisher recommended possesses a rejection region for the null hypothesis (the lady lacks any authentic ability to discriminate on the basis of taste) consisting of the one outcome of her guessing correctly all the cups. The chance distribution given the null hypothesis is symmetrical about the mean value of two correct selections. Identifying no cups correctly and four cups correctly each has the same probability given the null, 1/70. Only the latter justified rejection because Fisher imposed the condition that the significant outcome must be one in some sort of agreement with the hypothesis of effect; and identifying more cups correctly rather than fewer is more in accord with the truth of the alternative hypothesis. In Neyman–Pearson terms, Fisher is implicitly appealing to power considerations. Modern treatments based on Neyman–Pearson theory do indeed present the tea-tasting experiment as a most powerful test of the null hypothesis against the alternative of having some discriminatory ability. In these treatments the experiment is usually described in the slightly more tractable form of a standard binomial experiment, where in a sequence of n trials a coin is tossed to determine whether at that trial the milk-first or the tea-first cup is presented. In this experiment the null hypothesis says that the chance p of the lady guessing correctly is a constant equal to $\frac{1}{2}$ at each trial and that the trials are probabilistically independent. The right 'tail' of the binomial chance distribution is uniquely determined by the Neyman–Pearson Lemma as the most powerful test of the null against the class of alternatives represented by all the values of p greater than $\frac{1}{2}$; the 'significant' (rejecting) outcomes are those in which the number of correct identifications exceeds some number related to n through the significance level required (see e.g. Bailey 1971: 283–326).

But $p > \frac{1}{2}$ does not, of course, represent *all* the alternatives to $p = \frac{1}{2}$, even restricting them just to alternative values of the parameter p (this is actually quite a restriction, since it includes only binomial models). The complete class of alternatives, given that constraint, is of course the set of all values of p other than $\frac{1}{2}$: those that correspond not just to some degree of positive discrimination, so to speak, but also those that correspond to some degree of *negative* discrimination as well. *But against even this class it is easy to see that there is no uniformly most powerful test.* The problem is a quite general one for the Neyman–Pearson theory. It is even more revealing to consider it in the context of deterministic hypotheses, for there we shall encounter again an old friend (or enemy, depending on one's perspective). Consider a sequence of experiments consisting of examining first one, then two, . . . , then i, . . . emeralds, recording the outcomes as green/not-green. There are events common to all the outcome spaces generated after any given value of i, e.g. 'emerald 1 is green & . . . & emerald i is green'. We want to fix appropriate acceptance and rejection regions in the infinite outcome space S_∞ extending all the finite subspaces. Since these must support corresponding *decisions* to accept and reject they must contain only outcomes in principle observable, which means that they must be restricted to the sets of outcome-sequences determined by finitely many observations. Without loss of generality we can restrict these to be subsets S_i of S_∞ generated by i-fold sequences of the sort above. Can any such region be uniformly most powerful? The answer is easily seen to be 'no'. For any given i the optimal acceptance region C_i for H: 'All emeralds are green' is the set of those sequences in S_∞ generated by the single conjunction above; C_i^* will therefore contain all the sequences generated by those i-fold conjunctions with at least one conjunct negated. Now consider the grue$_j$ alternatives H_j to H, which specify a change of colour at index j. For any i there will always be a k such that C_k^* has probability 1 relative to one of these which gives C_i^* probability 0; e.g. C_{i+1}^* has probability 1 relative to H_{i+1} and C_i^* probability 0. It follows that there is no i such that C_i^* is uniformly most powerful against all the H_j. It is no answer to say that the fault is with the experiment because it cannot discriminate between H and *some* alternative to H. The problem is that no experiment, according to the Neyman–Pearson criteria, can do this: the grue possibilities show that every experimental design will have zero power relative to some alternative to H. Thus grue strikes at the Neyman–Pearson theory too. Appeals to 'optimal' power functions $f_c(I) = P_{Hi}(C^*)$ will not help, as there is no C such that $f_c(i)$ dominates all other power functions $f_{c'}(i)$. So in the sorts of case which Popper and most scientists would find interesting, the analysis by Neyman and Pearson is simply inapplicable.

Actually, the situation is even worse. Applicability is one thing, the correctness of the inferences recommended even where the theory is applicable is another; and the underlying logic of inference recommended by Neyman and Pearson is fallacious. Neyman–Pearson theory, and variants and extensions of it like that of Mayo (1996) which we encountered earlier, are based on the principle that if the chance of getting a certain class of outcomes given the truth of some hypothesis is sufficiently less than the chance according to an alternative to it, then that by itself is sufficient for a sound rejection of the hypothesis. *But we know that this principle is wrong.* The Harvard Medical School test shows why it is wrong: depending on the magnitude of P(H) even a very small value of the ratio P(C|–H)/P(C|H) are consistent with a very small value of P(H|C). It is sometimes objected that in the more general context where H is some sort of *theory* it makes no sense to speak of the chance of H being correct, since there is no frequency with which H is true: it either is true or it is not. There are two things to be said to this. First, a fallacious inference does not cease to be fallacious because an additional term that needs to be there as input to render it not fallacious cannot always be calculated. Secondly, it is how confident we are entitled to be in H in the light of E that is really what we want to know. *This consideration places the problem where it always should have been, in the context of sound reasoning about uncertainty.* And that shows explicitly where the Neyman–Pearson criteria are insufficient: we know from Chapter 3 that P(H|C) will depend not just on the ratio P(C|–H)/P(C|H), but also on P(H).

It might be objected that Neyman and Pearson repudiated epistemic probability (as indeed they did, especially Neyman) as a foundation for inductive inference, and that Neyman provided an influential decision-theoretic rationale for the Neyman–Pearson criteria: that in a long-enough run of repetitions of the test you will reject hypotheses when they are true a very small proportion of the time and simultaneously minimize the frequency of acceptances of a hypothesis when it is false. But this will not save the position, for we know how to construct scenarios, like the Harvard Medical School test, where if you were to make your decision based on Neyman–Pearson criteria, *you would be incorrect nearly all the time.* This sounds odd, but only because, as numerous pieces of research have shown, people sometimes find it difficult to interpret probabilities, particularly conditional probabilities. Indeed, the Neyman–Pearson criteria are a classic instance. The informal statement of a type 2 error, as a small chance of the test passing a false hypothesis, could equally easily be read as a small chance of a false hypothesis passing the test. The two descriptions are virtually equivalent in ordinary English, which gives no firm guide as to whether to represent the chance of the test passing a false hypothesis as either (i) the chance of passing *given* that the hypothesis is false, or (ii) the chance of the hypothesis being false given that the test passed it. *But these are quite different chances*, and indeed they are independent of each other: as we saw, a small type 2 error chance puts almost no limit on how large the chance (ii) can be, and therefore how *large* what we might call the 'real' type 2 error can be. The Neyman–Pearson theory, aided and abetted by the equivocal nature of informal language, gives something that in ordinary English sounds like the right thing, but is not.

6

The Naturalistic Fallacy

No one has been able to knock Hume's argument down. But if the argument is valid, as I believe it is, there is a paradox that comes in its train. In this chapter we shall take time out to look at this paradox, and at one fashionable solution to it. Hume pronounced the paradox himself when he confessed of his sceptical arguments that they 'admit of no answer and produce no conviction'. A consequence of the argument that induction is invalid is that we do not seem justified in betting that the future will be as science predicts at shorter odds than that it will be as some mad soothsayer predicts. But we are convinced that anyone who didn't bet in this way would be quickly bankrupted or suffer some other calamity. If Hume's argument is valid, why are we so certain that the mere follower of whim will eventually, and probably quickly, do much worse than the prudent person guided by scientific research?

Put like that, however, as a request for *explanation* and not necessarily justification, the question may well have an answer. Nor, even though it is not the question we initially wanted answered, is answering it a waste of time. There is a good, non-question-begging reason why any consistent explanation of an apparently paradoxical result like this one has value quite independent of whether it is actually true. A paradox suggests an inconsistency in our reasoning: indeed, the word 'paradox' is used by logicians synonymously with 'inconsistency'. So if we can find a clearly consistent way of explaining how an apparently paradoxical situation might be true, that is, is true in some possible world, then we have shown at least that we have not unwittingly run into genuine inconsistency, which is true in no world. And there is an explanation of how it is possible to be convinced both that there are no sound inductive arguments from observation alone and also that a potentially enormous penalty would be exacted for not heeding the ones we accept. First pronounced by Hume and then elaborated in terms of Darwinian theory, it is that we are moderately efficient deductive reasoners but hard-wired, as it were, to be inductivists.

In other words we just can't help it. One of the more interesting developments in late twentieth-century science and philosophy is the realization of the possibilities Darwinian theory holds out, or seems to hold out (the issue is contested), for the explanation of all sorts of things. One of the more tempting possibilities which the Hume–Darwin hypothesis seems to offer is turning—the *naturalistic* turn—an explanation into a sort of *justification*. The temptation has proved irresistible, as we shall see.

Hume-Darwin

Hume believed that in common with the rest of the animal kingdom we inherit an instinctive expectation that the apparent stabilities revealed by the accumulation of data—how much depending on the particular situation—will be maintained in the future:

This belief is the necessary result of placing the mind in such circumstances. It is an operation of the soul, when we are so situated, as unavoidable as to feel the passion of love, when we receive benefits; or hatred, when we meet with injuries. All these operations are a species of natural instincts, which no reasoning or process of the thought and understanding is able either to produce or to prevent. (1748: 46–7)

The expectations that 'the future will resemble the past' in the appropriate ways are on the level of feelings in Hume's system, classified under the head of 'passions', or emotions. But we also inherit a reasoning faculty which may, and in this case does, inform us that there is no rational ground for the expectations. No matter: reason in itself, as Hume points out, is inert and powerless; the emotions provide the dynamic for action. Thus we inherit powerful expectations, and also the power to reason, but in the nature of things reason is doomed to play no active role: 'reason is and ought only to be the slave of the passions, and can never pretend to any other office than to serve and obey them' (1739: 415).

It is a nice explanation, and anticipates, in its disconnection of passive reason and active emotion, the classification of brain functions into the reasoning but unemotional frontal cortex, and the more ancient and highly active limbic system, the seat of the primal drives.

Hume's theory of a pre-established harmony between our beliefs on the one hand and Nature on the other also seems an uncanny anticipation of Darwin. In fact, it is not so uncanny. Hume's ideas are known to have been a powerful influence on Darwin's grandfather, Erasmus Darwin, who was himself a seminal influence in the genesis of his grandson's theory. And Darwin's theory is now often taken to complement Hume's by explaining in very general terms (i.e. with a lot of free parameters; some suspect far too many) *why* we should have these inbuilt expectations and why they seem to be successful. The explanation is that they are adaptively attuned to the way things really are; had they not been those organisms possessing them would have died out and the genes responsible with them. Our presence reflects expectational structures roughly harmonizing with the way things behave, on the macro level and at small to medium velocities:

a world in which intelligence emerges by anything like standard *evolutionary* processes has to be pervaded by regularities and periodicities in the organism–nature interaction that produces and perpetuates organic species. And this means that nature must be cooperative in a certain very particular way; it must be stable enough and regular enough for there to be appropriate responses to natural events that can be 'learned' by creatures. If such 'appropriate responses' are to develop, nature must provide suitable stimuli in a duly structured way. An organically viable environment—to say nothing of a knowable one—must incorporate experientiable structures. (Rescher 1990: 64; italics in original)

and in the same vein:

Nonetheless, because of how we are in fact constructed biologically and socially, we do not start inquiry utterly ignorant. We have evolved to favor certain behaviors and to organize our sensations in particular ways. Unless hindered in some serious way, infants rapidly learn to identify and reidentify objects, and they learn that objects continue to exist when unobserved; infants have available almost from birth some simple facts about size, distance and perspective. (Glymour 1992: 120–1)

And of course there was Ramsey himself:

If we actually . . . found out . . . on what a priori probabilities his present opinions could be based, we should obviously find them to be ones determined by natural selection (1931: 192)

All these people are or were quite aware that there is an infinity of distinct possible explanations of any observational data, and that despite its entrenched status Darwinian theory is a theory and no exception to that rule.[1] But weighing against this is the fact, which they feel it would be perverse to ignore, that we *are* reliable cognizers, possessing in our current science an incredibly rich body of highly reliable knowledge. Given that unaided reason, as Hume should take the credit for pointing out, could not have led us to this epistemic cornucopia, our achieving it is either an incredible accident, or there is some systematic and reliable guidance at work. The religious explanation quite properly no longer commands wide assent, and Darwinism supplies the explanatory deficit with the only account which it is scientifically respectable to accept. Equally perverse, on this view, is to impugn this explanation because it does not satisfy the most rigorous standards of proof. For those standards, it is claimed, are *unrealistically* high because, as Hume showed, virtually nothing satisfies them. Go the way they point and we should all die of inanition. It cannot be rational to do that. And since there is no evidence at all that adopting any other method of forming of beliefs will be as reliable, we are fully entitled to accept the standards of scientific proof, and with them good scientific explanations where they exist.

Doing so affords the opportunity for some creative bootstrapping. Since on Darwinian grounds we can expect our expectational structures to reflect in important respects the way the world actually is, we obtain corroborating evidence that the world is approximately the way we believe it is: it does indeed support 'past-to-future' inferences in a stable way, at any rate for 'entrenched' properties like 'green' rather than contrived and unnatural ones like 'grue'. And there is a further bonus. Accepting as our only warrantable standards those of science seems to solve an old philosophical problem *about* science, the problem of why anyone should be a scientific realist. Now the answer is simple: *science* itself tells us. Inference to the best explanation, also known as *abduction*, is *the* inferential method of science, and realism is the best, because the only scientifically acceptable, explanation of why the methods of science are successful:

the only scientifically plausible explanation for the reliability of a scientific methodology that is so theory-dependent . . . Scientific methodology . . . is reliable at producing further knowledge *precisely because, and to the extent that, currently accepted theories are approximately true.* . . . It is not possible . . . to explain even the instrumental reliability of actual recent scientific prac-

---

[1] See e.g. Hauptli's discussion (1994) of Rescher.

tice without invoking this explanation. (Boyd 1990: 223; italics in the original)

Starting only from the consideration that we must accept some beliefs or perish, and that there is no 'first philosophy' supplying indubitable first principles, not only do we seem to have arrived at some sort of solution of Goodman's paradox, but we have also implicitly turned the traditional philosophical programme on its head. For if there is only science, then it would seem that epistemology should be treated, not as the domain of 'first philosophical' a priori theorizing, but as the subject of empirical-scientific investigation, with a view to identifying successful cognitive strategies, and improving and extending them wherever possible. And so, building on the foundation supplied by what we know about our evolved cognitive apparatus, we are led to the empirical study of epistemology as a scientific subject in its own right: we are led to *naturalized epistemology*.

We are led, or possibly we have simply been carried away. For something must be wrong with an epistemic ascent which starts by accepting Hume's sceptical argument and ends by denying it. Something is wrong. In fact, several things are wrong. One thing that is wrong with it is systematic question-begging. Another is bad logic. Take the question-begging. The quasi-dominance argument, that concludes that we can't do better than less than impossibly high standards of evidence, begs the question that the evidence for current scientific explanations, let alone being incomplete according to 'the highest standards', is evidence *at all*. And there is also more than a suggestion of the No-Miracles argument in the wording of Boyd's 'abductive' argument for realism as the best explanation of the success of current science (Peirce invented the term 'abduction', and presented it explicitly as a No-Miracles argument (1960: 117)). From our earlier discussion we know that any claim that the only explanation of the success of current science is that it is approximately true is incorrect. There is a horde of possible explanations. Boyd, and following him Leplin (1997), try to preclude these from consideration by placing sufficiently stringent conditions on 'being an explanation' that it neatly turns out that the only explanations of what we observe are those of current science. While the conclusion is hardly surprising if it is accepted that science supplies the standard of explanatoriness, this strategy also rather obviously begs a question. Indeed, it is exactly as question-begging as the claim that you are justified in believing any part of current science to be 'approximately true'.

Nor will appeal to what is, scientifically or otherwise, plausible help. What is plausible and what is not is likely to be a highly context-dependent affair, if not an outright subjective one, unless it is tied to some objective standard. That of probability naturally comes to mind. There is nothing in principle wrong with combining the standard of inference to the best explanation with an explicitly probabilistic criterion of 'best': you simply 'abduce' to the most probable among a pre-assigned set of alternative explanatory hypotheses, if there is a uniquely a posteriori most probable one (cf. Pearl 1991: 181–2). The problem with this idea is, as we saw in Chapter 4, that a posteriori probability depends on a priori probability, and a priori probability assignments seem to be irretrievably dependent on either an arbitrary or a subjective decision which again begs the question. All this Hume said long ago, if not in as many words. It is remarkable that two hundred and fifty years after the *Treatise* and fifty years after Goodman's 'New Riddle of Induction' (1946) we can find in a leading philsophy of science journal remarks like 'the novel success of theories requires some kind of realism' (Ladyman 1999: 183).

But modern abductionists do know the Humean arguments; they even exploit them, as we have seen, in claiming that to seek an ultimate justification is futile because there isn't one. But they point out that there are nevertheless perfectly good *achievable* standards of justification which have in fact been achieved. The game, in other words, simply *has* to change from that of foundationalist justification to the less utopian appeal to the standards we, a successfully adapted cognizing species, have actually evolved as best practice. For it is indeed a fact that we are successful cognizers. That is the 'paradox' we started with, but a paradox, according to this point of view, only because the standards of justification were set unrealistically high. Lower them to the more realistic level exhibited in existing best practice, science, and the paradox becomes merely a fact calling for explanation, *scientific explanation*. And so we return again, to the Hume–Darwin theory as the explanation. Unfortunately, we also return to the observation that the Hume–Darwin theory is just one among an infinity of alternative possibilities consistent with the data, and that no amount of wordplay will alter that stark logical fact. We may have in the Hume–Darwin hypothesis an explanation but, *pace* Boyd, Leplin *et al.*, explanations are not in short supply. Good reasons for accepting them are.

Naturalism is a development akin to the phenomenon psychotherapists call 'denial'. Hume's powerful case that our reliance on induction is, in the last analysis, simply unfounded is often conceded by naturalists, but the concession is usually no sooner made than modulated into a positive programme for acquiring knowledge about the way we learn, or think we learn. Thus for Quine, who first introduced the term, 'naturalized epistemology' is no more than the natural response to accepting Hume's claim that we know nothing beyond what we sense: 'The stimulation of his sensory receptors is all the evidence anyone has had to go on, ultimately, in arriving at his picture of the world. Why not just see how this construction really proceeds?' (1969: 75–6).[2] Seeing 'how this construction really proceeds', for Quine, means identifying epistemology with empirical psychology. But empirical psychology deals in general hypotheses: it certainly involves generalizing from particular experiments on particular subjects. But if we are limited to what we perceive then what right have we to generalize in any way at all? If we are not justified in proceeding beyond the evidence of our senses (whatever that may amount to) then we are no more justified in accepting the hypotheses of empirical psychology than we are their Goodmanized analogues. Quine seems to be telling us not that we can have our cake and eat it, but something altogether more dramatic: that we cannot have our cake and we can nevertheless still eat it!

Glymour also nods, but only nods, in the direction of scepticism:

Naturalized epistemology is a program for snatching victory from defeat. *Metaphysical skepticism wins, true enough,* but in practice we are not and could not be in the circumstance of trying to learn from pure ignorance. Assuming the circumstances we cannot help but believe we are in, the powers of science to expand our knowledge are increased. (1992: 123; my italics)

This is a remarkable passage. How is conceding the day to metaphysical scepticism in any sense snatching victory from defeat? If metaphysical scepticism wins then, unless we are giving a very unfamiliar meaning to familiar words, we have no knowledge to expand. Of course, practically speaking, no one really does doubt that science has expanded and will continue to expand knowledge. But that wasn't quite the point. The point was to justify that conviction. The

---

[2] Knowingly or not, Quine is merely echoing Ramsey: 'all that philosophy can do is to analyse [induction], determine the degree of its utility, and find on what characteristics of nature this depends' (1931: 198)

Ramsey, the first modern reliabilist, was also the first epistemological naturalist.

problem is not solved, or even partially solved, by sanguine remarks. Perhaps the most apt response to the type of argument that commences from some alleged matter of fact, in this case that 'we cannot help but believe in' the reliability of our cognitive procedures, to conclusions about what we are justified in believing in is contained in these much-quoted and justly celebrated lines by an eighteenth-century philosopher:

I cannot forbear adding to these reasonings an observation which may perhaps be found to be of some importance. In every system of morality which I have hitherto met with I have always remarked that the author proceeds for some time in the ordinary way of reasoning, and establishes the being of a God, or makes observations concerning human affairs; when of a sudden I am surprised to find, that instead of the usual copulations of propositions, *is* and *is not*, I meet with no proposition that is not connected with an *ought*, or an *ought not*. This change is imperceptible; but is, however, of the last consequence. For as this *ought* or *ought not* expresses some new relation or affirmation, it is necessary that it should be observed and explained; and at the same time that a reason should be given for what seems altogether inconceivable, how this new relation can be a deduction from others that are entirely different from it.

The philosopher was David Hume (1739: III.i.i). Nowell–Smith aptly describes Hume's observation, an objection to eighteenth-century versions of naturalism, as 'crushing' (1961: 36–7), and G. E. Moore, more presciently than he knew, famously described the reasoning that Hume indicts as the '*Naturalistic Fallacy*'. And so it is.

For all that naturalism represents a dead-end as an attempt to salvage something from the programme of *justifying*, in however weak a sense, the general constructions we impose on experience, it has had profound effects in other ways. Most notably, it has encouraged a closer study of what scientists actually do, the way they make decisions, switch horses, and so on. Quine may have cited psychology as the appropriate empirical study of science, because Quine still felt that the main element in scientific activity was cerebral and ratiocinative, in a word, reasoning. Since then, inspired by Kuhn's justly celebrated work (1962) on the structure of scientific revolutions, reasoning has been demoted to a relatively negligible factor in the decisions of scientists compared with the social and other forces to which they are subject. The focus has shifted, and the more recent studies, such as those of Shapin and Shaffer (1985), Galison (1987), and Latour and Woolgar (1986), have turned to anthropology, economics, sociology, and linguistics, the precise mix depending on who is writing, as the appropriate empirico-theoretical milieu within which to model scientific activity.

Ironically, however, the laudable intention to find out empirically what goes on in science, particularly institutional science, has tended to issue in generalizations as speculative as those of the more speculative parts of science itself, and sometimes stranger, like the increasingly frequently voiced denial that any objective world of people-independent fact exists, and the contrary affirmation that what we take to be such a world is actually constructed by us, out of our linguistic and social practices (there is a greater or lesser amount of qualification, depending on the author). It should be clear by now that such inferences are no more warranted than the inference of scientific realists to the existence of an external world accessible in principle to scientific investigation. Both views, realism and anti-realism, go equally far beyond the data of observation. In particular, the impulse to generalize far beyond the limits of the data remains unquenched however anti-realistic the philosophical faith. Realism versus anti-realism seems in that light more a matter of opposing ideologies than anything else, at the extremes naïvely accepting the scientific establishment's view of what it is going on the one hand, and on the other seeing in that account nothing more than the propaganda of a privileged élite. More moderate versions are of course available. You pay your money and you take your choice.

Where Do We Go from Here?

Even conceding the force of Hume's arguments, it is admittedly difficult, if not impossible, to avoid the feeling that there must be something to science and scientific reasoning that is not entirely arbitrary (unfortunately remarks like that excite the ire of scientists at what they understandably see only as the hubris of philosophers). But 'naturalized epistemology' and 'abduction' are not the way to explain what that something is: the appeal to empirical science, admissible perhaps as an explanation—but only one among many— is not permissible as a justification. So let us look away from empirical science to the science of justification itself, to *logic* (though not, I hasten to add, 'abductive logic').

Deductive logic was the residue Hume felt untainted by Humean doubt (though not our ability to follow logical arguments). Some brave spirits have felt free to doubt it, and not all frivolously. For example Intuitionists, followers of the Dutch mathematician L. E. J. Brouwer who believe that mathematical entities, including proofs, are literally constructions of the mind, query the full classical deductive logic, and they are not easily shown to be wrong or even incoherent in doing so. If there is an answer to them, it is not a trivial one. On the other hand, it is objective, factual truth that is the topic here and even the Intuitionists have not denied that there is a logic for this, and that that logic is classical; so we can ignore, in this context, the Intuitionistic challenge. There remain others, however. There is for example Quine's famous objection (1953: 43) that no statement, whether a statement of fact or a statement even of logic, is in principle immune to revision. Early in the twentieth century the philosopher and physicist Duhem had argued that, because scientific hypotheses in general are able to make predictions about observables only in conjunction with a more or less large number of auxiliary hypotheses, including hypotheses about the normal functioning of experimental apparatus, the failure of any given prediction cannot, logically, unequivocally point to the falsity of the hypothesis under test; equally, one or more of the auxiliaries might be false (Duhem 1906). Quine (1953) took Duhem's arguments further, proposing the view, since called the '*epistemological holism*', that any part of the currently accepted body of science might in principle be revised in the process of establishing a harmonious agreement with experience. Quine's statement of this position was very influential, and as a result even the (classical) logic of factual truth is now regarded by many as in principle revisable. Indeed, some people argue that quantum mechanics *demands* the revision of classical logic (e.g. Putnam 1965); and so-called quantum logic has become a flourishing research programme (quantum logic, of whatever specific flavour, rejects the Boolean structure of classical propositional logic for a non-Boolean one whose 'propositions' are represented by the closed subspaces of a Hilbert space of quantum states).

Only a dogmatist would deny that a different logic *might* one day be adopted in preference to the current classical one. If so, it might well be some version of quantum logic, at any rate for the physics of the very small. This is not the place to investigate these issues, and any conclusion would certainly be premature. But even if we feel free to follow Hume and accept classical logic (this is anachronistic, of course: Hume knew nothing of quantum theory and anyway would not have understood the distinction between classical and non-classical logic; but never mind) as the logic of factual truth, there remains a problem with classical logic which has been familiar since Bacon famously animadverted on it four hundred years ago. The problem—the notorious problem—is that classical logic does not seem to get us very far; indeed, anywhere. Hume himself foreclosed its use in any positive way, saying that it merely described 'relations between ideas'. Bacon admittedly declared only syllogistic reasoning barren of useful progeny, but it has since become a commonplace that deductive inference in general is not (factual) content-increasing, merely the elicitation of what is implicit in any set of premisses, an opinion that is unlikely to change: indeed, it is more likely to act as a constraint on what will be allowed to call itself a logic (we shall have more to say on this point in Chapter 7). But Bacon, Hume, and just about everybody else, went on to draw the—apparently obvious— inference from the non-ampliative nature of logic that, far from promising anything in the way of underwriting the reasoning procedures of science, logic must therefore be hopelessly impotent on that score. This conclusion has been so generally accepted that it may come as a shock to find it denied. *Yet that is what I intend to do.* The remainder of this book will be taken up with arguing that, even conceding the soundness of Hume's argument, something of inestimable value nevertheless remains safe from his attack, and that is nothing less than the logic of science itself.

But what about Hume's argument? An assumption of the induction debate, sometimes tacit, sometimes not, and certainly one that Bacon and all his successors accepted, is that the endorsement of scientific procedure must also extend to the endorsement of truth-claims made on behalf of the appropriate scientific theories: that for the principles of scientific reasoning to be correct means that they should lead in some guaranteed way to truth, or to some surrogate, like 'approximate truth' or probable truth. Hume's reasoning is therefore usually taken as showing, if correct, that the procedures of science are without foundation. My claim is that it can equally be seen as a *reductio ad absurdum* of the assumption that sound inductive reasoning will point us the way to truth, or at any rate to justified beliefs about truth. Indeed, I shall try to show that the commonly accepted rules of scientific method are not truth- or probability-oriented in this way, which I shall do by showing that the rules of method are just rules of logic. It will follow that they are demonstrably sound, for they are only logic, and that they do not tell us which theories are true, for, being only logic, they cannot. I shall then proceed to show that, despite *just* being logic, these rules are nevertheless indispensable in the search for truth because, *as rules of logic*, they prevent us making fallacious inferences. That is the programme. In the next two chapters I shall try to deliver it.

7

'A New Species of Logic'

Recall from Chapter 4 the two broad interpretations of probability, one as objective chance, and the other epistemic, as a measure of the uncertainty of conjectures. It is now time to pursue the second further. The goal will be to show that Bayes's own derivation of the probability axioms leads naturally, indeed almost inescapably, to a view of those axioms as *laws of logic*: to be precise, as consistency constraints on quantified partial beliefs. That is the programme for this chapter.

We start with a problem, however. As we have seen (Chapter 4, Appendix 1), Bayes defined the probability (*qua* measure of uncertainty) of an event to be

the ratio between the value at which an expectation depending on the happening of the event ought to be computed, and the value of the thing expected upon its happening. (Definition 5).

But how do you determine 'the value at which an expectation depending on the happening of the event ought to be computed' in any given case? How 'ought' Bayes's probabilities to be evaluated?

It is not clear that there is a determinate answer to the question. The probability axioms, as we know, by themselves fail to determine values for particular probabilities except in special circumstances, as when the proposition A is a necessary truth or falsehood, or where deductive entailment relations hold between the As and Bs in the conditional probabilities $P(A|B)$ (recall that if B entails A then $P(A|B) = 1$, while if B is inconsistent with A then $P(A|B) = 0$; all supposing $P(B) > 0$, of course). Otherwise the axioms are silent. As we saw in the earlier discussion of prior probabilities, many people have appealed to the principle of indifference for computing probabilities where the axioms themselves provide no guide as to 'correct' values. But as we also saw, the principle is both arbitrary and inconsistent. Carnap, in his monumental *Logical Foundations* (1950; and then again in Carnap 1952, 1970, and 1982), attempted a systematic grounding of a priori probabilities in alleged logical principles, but the general consensus is that where these principles were strong enough to generate determinate probability values, they were dubiously logical; indeed, they were mostly variants of the principle of indifference. The general view now is that Carnap's work in this field amounted to no more than a heroic failure (for a more detailed discussion see Howson and Urbach 1993: ch. 4).

There have been a number of other attempts to supplement the probability axioms with additional principles, like invariance principles, 'informationless' prior measures, the use of maximum entropy, and others, but all are question-begging in one way or another (there is a longer discussion in Howson 1997*a*). At any rate, there is a growing feeling that the probability axioms may be *necessarily* incomplete in one sense, namely that a large class of probability values, like the unconditional, or prior, probabilities for example, cannot be determined a priori, except in the extreme cases cited. Perhaps surprisingly, such a view can be *supported* by stating that the probability axioms are actually *complete* in some different but important sense. Those familiar with deductive logic will understand how a set of axioms and/or rules can be incomplete (in one way) and complete (in another): the logical axioms and rules of inference of the relevant formalizations of deductive (first-order) logic, like the probability axioms (*mutatis mutandis*), do not determine truth-values except in extreme cases; but they are nevertheless complete in the sense that all universally valid sentences are formally deducible from them. Perhaps the probability axioms can be shown to possess the analogous property, that all generally valid probability statements are already derivable from them.

Indeed they can (in just what sense of 'valid' we must wait and see), but that still leaves the problem of how to evaluate particular sentences in particular contexts. One possibility is to bite the bullet, and say that where there is an objective chance distribution we should set the probability value equal to the chance, and where there is no such distribution, concede that the corresponding probability simply has no value. If there is no chance then, the argument runs, there is no objective way uncertainty can be discussed, let alone measured, and we should not try. Indeed, if there is no objective value that the probability 'should be', why worry about it? But if there is, that is what the probability should be.

This sounds plausible, but it faces some difficult problems, three in particular. First, chances, in the way we shall choose to understand them and the way Fisher understood them, are defined in terms of long-run frequencies. But why should we base our probability that a particular event will occur on what happens in the indefinitely long run (this is a problem we shall return to later, in Chapter 9)? Secondly, how do we actually know what the chance distribution over an outcome space is? We can certainly conjecture one but, when it is considered that the conjecture involves speculating about frequency in an arbitrarily long sequence of trials, its evaluation itself would seem to be of a serious order of uncertainty. It would seem that a satisfactory account of objective chance presupposes the development of a satisfactory theory of epistemic uncertainty rather than vice versa. The question is whether such a theory can ever be developed if the route via objective probabilities is initially blocked, as it seems to be. Finally, there are more or less uncertain events about which we should intuitively have epistemic probabilities but which don't seem to be in the domain of objective chance. For example, I may be more or less uncertain whether a theory, General Relativity say, is true, though it makes no sense to talk of the long-run frequency with which it is true.

But there is an alternative way of determining how Bayes's 'expectation depending on the happening of the event ought to be computed'. This is simply to compute it in the way *you*, given your current state of information, would estimate it, bypassing completely the issue of whether that belief is in any way secured by any objective feature of the world. In other words, you just nominate as Bayes's (or rather yours now) 'expectation' what you believe to be its fair price, meaning by 'fair price' merely the price which *you think* leaves neither side with a calculable advantage. People certainly can and do seem to make such estimates, at any rate to within certain spreads of values (we shall come to that later), quite independently of whether there is any objective way they can be grounded. Having taken the decision, however, that that question is no longer a profitable or constructive one to ask, we can focus instead on what constraints degrees of belief so measured should satisfy. Are there any, and if so what?

The answer, perhaps surprisingly (though not so much for those who have read Appendix 1 to Chapter 4) is that there are: the probability axioms themselves. So much already out of so little. This goes some way to explaining why, though adopting a subjective, or as

Savage called it *personal*, view of Bayesian probability might seem rather like throwing the baby out with the bathwater, the move will prove, as we shall see, a highly successful one. *Reculer pour mieux sauter* indeed. Of course, there still remains the problem of how a purely subjective basis for the theory of uncertainty can be at all useful, especially in the evaluation of scientific hypotheses. Many people still believe it cannot. They are wrong, though we shall postpone the discussion of exactly why to the next chapter. The programme for the remainder of this one is to show that the laws of subjective uncertainty are laws of logic. Bayes's derivation of the probability axioms shows in effect that they are indeed laws of subjective probability, regulating the consistent assignment of personal probabilities to propositions. The next stage will be to show that the probability axioms are themselves laws of logic. Onward ho.

'A New Species of Logic'

For the pioneers of epistemic probability there was little doubt that its rules were rules of logic; Leibniz called the new theory of formal probability 'une nouvelle espèce de logique'. The idea runs like a thread through the history of the subject, sometimes visible, sometimes not. It largely disappears in the phases of rapid technical development, where the richness of the results tends to move philosophical considerations into second place, and it never amounted to anything very much before the twentieth century because, in default of a better formal and philosophical development of deductive logic, there was no clear standard of exactly what it meant to be a logic against which to compare the theory. In the twentieth century it re-emerged clearly in the work of Ramsey, who saw in the axioms of probability an extension of what he called the logic of consistency (1931: 184). But then the idea languished yet again. Partly it was because Ramsey was writing in a good deal of ignorance of the revolutionary developments in formal deductive logic taking place in the early twentieth century, and partly because he himself also managed to steer epistemic probability into an apparently different course where its rules seemed to become rules, or a subset of the rules, for making rational choices. De Finetti, writing at about the same time, seemed just as equivocal about the way the laws of probability were to be classified, on the one hand claiming that they were rules for maintaining coherence in one's beliefs, thereby reflecting Ramsey's view of them as consistency constraints, but on the other justifying them in terms apparently of rules for making prudent bets. The approach to justifying probabilistic principles as rationality constraints, though not the way I believe that their true significance is best appreciated, is historically important; and because it will also introduce the apparatus of betting-quotients, odds, stakes, and bets which will come in handy a little later, a brief look at de Finetti's result will be useful.

The Dutch Book Argument

De Finetti gave an explicit proof of what has come to be called a *Dutch Book argument* for the probability axioms. This is a proof that any infringement of them could be penalized by making the violator vulnerable to a forced loss in a suitable system of bets (1964: section 1). Not that this property could have been completely unknown before de Finetti's proof appeared: Ramsey's remark that a bookmaker failing to observe the rules of the probability calculus 'could have a book made against him by a cunning bettor and would stand to lose in any event' (1931: 3) shows that he knew it even if he never publicly proved it. What neither of them seemed to realize, however, was that the first proof should be substantially credited to Bayes himself, for Bayes's own derivation of the probability axioms is a version of the Dutch Book argument. To see this requires a couple of easy steps. First, we note that bets just are the sorts of uncertain options Bayes discusses. For a bet is the option to receive (or give, depending on the standpoint) a specified positive amount S (the *stake*) in the event of an event A being true, sold by the bookie for the price Q. In betting terminology the ratio $Q/(S-Q)$ are the *odds*, and Q/S the *betting quotient* (betting quotients are therefore really just odds normalized so that they lie within the half-open interval [0,1); this is extended to the closed-unit interval [0,1] by allowing the odds to take the 'value' ∞).

In the notation that was introduced by de Finetti (1964) and has become canonical for discussions of this topic, a bet on A with non-zero stake S and betting quotient p is represented as a random quantity whose value is $S(1 - p)$ if A is true, $-pS$ if A is false (this is just setting $Q = pS$). Note that changing the sign of the stake S from positive to negative or vice versa merely reverses the role of the partners in the betting-contract. The odds are clearly $p/(1 - p)$. If these are deemed fair, in the sense above of equalizing advantage, by any person X, then p will be X's evaluation of the probability of A according to Bayes's definition. P is of course the constant of proportionality by which the value of N is reduced in Bayes's definition of the probability of A as the just price pN of the option 'N if A is true, 0 if not'. Betting quotients you consider fair are therefore your Bayesian probabilities. Bayes and de Finetti are discussing the same thing: the evaluation of uncertain options as a route to the numerical evaluation of uncertainty itself.

Bayes's derivation of the additivity principle exploits the fact that certain bets or combinations of them determine others. His proof, recall, shows that bets with the same stake on two mutually exclusive propositions A and B at betting rates p and q respectively determine a bet on the disjunction 'AvB' with betting rate $p + q$. A slightly improved notation, which will also come in useful later, shows this very simply. A bet on A at betting quotient p and stake S is a random variable of the form $X_A = S(I_A - p)$, where I_A, the so-called *indicator function* of A, takes the value 1 on those possible 'worlds' determined by A and 0 on the others. Noting that $I_{AvB} = I_A + I_B$, a little arithmetic shows that $S(I_A - p) + S(I_B - q) = S(I_{AvB} - (p + q))$. So if your fair betting rate on AvB is $r \neq p + q$ and you were to bet indifferently on or against A, B and AvB at betting rates p, q and r respectively you could in principle be Dutch Booked: if $r < p + q$ an opponent only has to have you betting on A and B and against AvB (if $r > p + q$ reverse all the bets).[1] It is easy to see how violating the other axioms makes you Dutch Bookable (see Howson and Urbach 1993: ch. 5).

But to see those axioms merely as assurances of financial safety in betting is to miss their real significance. Something deeper is going on. To see what it is it will be helpful to make a short digression into the nature of *logic* itself.

---

[1] Similarly, Bayes's proof (ch. 4, app. 1) that $P(A|B) = P(A\&B)/P(B)$, where $P(B) > 0$ and $P(A|B)$ is your fair price for a conditional bet on A, i.e. one called off if B is false, exploits the fact that there are non-zero k, m, n such that $k(I_{A\&B} - p) + m(I_B - q) = I_{Bn}(I_A - p/q)$: i.e. for suitable stakes a sum of bets on A&B, B with betting quotients p, q > 0, determines a conditional bet on A given B with betting quotient p/q (e.g. $k = q$, $m = -p$, $n = q$).

And So to Logic

A popular introductory text in formal deductive logic tells us that 'Logic is about consistency' (Hodges 1974: blurb). Should this just mean 'deductive consistency', or might there be other species of consistency closely kindred to the deductive variety entitling their ambient theories to the status of logic or logics? It may well be the case that logic is about consistency without foreclosing the possibility of there being logics other than deductive. To answer these questions we seem first to need an answer to the question 'What is logic?'

My own belief is that there is no fact of the matter about what entitles a theory of reasoning to logical status, and one has to proceed as one does in extending common law to new cases, by appeal to precedent and common sense. Here again, of course, one must be selective, but with modern deductive logic in mind I propose the following as necessary and sufficient conditions for a discipline to have the status of logic:

(*a*) It involves statements and relations between them.

(*b*) It adjudicates some mode of non-domain-specific reasoning.

(*c*) It is 'about consistency'. More specifically, it should incorporate a semantic notion of consistency which can be shown to be extensionally equivalent to one characterizable purely syntactically; this equivalence is the content of what are called *soundness and completeness theorems* for the corresponding system. First-order logic famously has a soundness and completeness theorem.

It may sound dogmatic to set out necessary and sufficient conditions in this way, and even more so to limit them to just three, but it must be remembered that if there really is no fact of the matter then we are only bestowing a title. That said, with a title come responsibilities ('noblesse oblige'), and one of them, especially where the title is already bestowed elsewhere, is that some explanatory purpose is served thereby: significant analogies with the other discipline already so honoured should cast light on things that are otherwise problematic and puzzling. And so it will turn out. First, let us see how Bayesian probability copes with (*a*)–(*c*).

Well, (*a*) and (*b*) are certainly satisfied: any proposition whatever can be in the domain of a probability function; even, as we shall see, statements assigning probabilities themselves. Less obviously, (*c*) is

satisfied as well: it just needs to be spelled out. Being deductively
inconsistent is usually taken to be manifested in the derivability of a
contradiction of the form A& – A for some statement A. But inferring A& – A is tantamount to assigning A different truth values: it is
implictly saying that A is both true and false. We can extend this idea
to that of an inconsistent assignment of truth-values to an arbitrary
set of statements, and tableau/tree systems of deduction, in particular trees whose initial sentences are 'signed' with truth-values
(Howson 1997c: 18, 19), show explicitly how an inconsistent assignment of truth-values to a set of statements results in some statement,
not necessarily a member of that set, being assigned the values both
'true' and 'false' simultaneously. Consider for example the assignment

$$A \qquad T$$
$$A{\rightarrow}B \quad T$$
$$B \qquad F$$

Appending beneath this the signed form of the tree rule for [A → B T]

$$/ \ \backslash$$
$$F \quad A \quad B \quad T$$

we see that on both available branches we have incompatible assignments: on the left branch we have A both true and false, and on the
right B both true and false. Thus the original assignment is an inconsistent one (for further information about these systems see Howson
1997: 18–21). The exhibition of deductive consistency for some
assignment τ to a subset X of the sentences in a language L by this or
indeed any suitable method consists in showing that there exists a
single-valued distribution of truth-values which extends τ to all the
sentences of L, subject to the general rules of truth supplied by the
standard Tarskian truth-definition, and which coincides with τ on X.
In other words, τ is consistent if there is a (propositional) *model*,
which we can call a model *of τ itself*.

We define a consistent assignment Q of fair betting quotients similarly, as one which can be extended to a single-valued function on all
the propositions of L (probabilities tend to get assigned to propositions, that is, to equivalence classes of sentences rather than directly
to the sentences themselves for historical reasons). But clearly, the
extension must be subject to some constraints, just as in the truth-
value case the extension was subject to the truth-table and other rules
of truth-in-general. By analogy, these should it seems be the rules of

fairness-in-general, that is, of the *general* criteria for assigning fair betting quotients. Call these (F). Pursuing the deductive analogy, an extension of Q to all the propositions in L which satisfies (F) will be called a *model* of Q.

What is the formal content of (F)? (F) says that fair betting quotients determine fair bets, that is, bets such that neither side has an advantage given the knowledge-state of the agent. This seems to subsume the following rules. Firstly, if p is a fair betting quotient then $0 \leq p \leq 1$, since it is easy to see that otherwise one side of the bet could make a certain gain come what may. Two others are that if A is a logical truth then P(A), the fair betting quotient for A, is 1, and that if A is a logical falsehood P(A) = 0, for the same reason. Secondly, fair bets must obviously be invariant under change of sign of the stake: if the bet on A has no advantage over the bet against A, the converse must hold too.

There is something else too, which will turn out to play a very important role. It is a closure principle of a type that is applied in deductive logic without any particular attention being drawn to it. Nevertheless it is there. Let me give an example. The truth-table rules give truth-conditions for a compound sentence in terms of the truth or falsity of its components. But the truth-conditions for atomic sentences are given by corresponding features of, or facts about, the interpretative structure itself (these are described in the basis clause in a standard inductive truth-definition). There seem therefore to be two quite distinct types of truth involved here: a substantive one, for the atomic sentences, and a formal one for the compounds. This is not a mythical story; even in this century philosophers have worried about the existence of negative facts. What of course happened was that the notion of 'real' truth simply got extended to a unitary notion of truth for all sentences, atomic and compound: it got closed off under truth-functional compounding. And as I said, the procedure is so natural that it passes without mention.

There is also a natural closure principle for fair betting quotients under compounding, this time compounding of bets. It is as follows: if a fair bet on some proposition A, or a sum of fair bets on some subset of propositions, determines a bet on some proposition B with stake S and betting quotient q, then it is natural, just as it was *mutatis mutandis* in the deductive case, to close off and call p the fair betting quotient on B.

We have now extracted the specific constraints implicit in (F), and are in a position to state the result that will form the basis of the claim that Bayesian probability is just logic:

Theorem: An assignment Q of betting quotients to a subset X of the propositions in L is consistent, in the sense defined above, if and only if Q satisfies the constraints of the (countably additive) probability calculus.

Proof

(i) (only if). Whatever L is we can minimally take it that it is closed under the operations 'and', 'or' and 'not'; in other words, the propositions determined by L form a Boolean algebra. Suppose that Q_L is a single-valued function which satisfies (F) and coincides on X with Q. We have seen that all the values assigned by Q_L must by (F) be in the closed unit interval, and that $Q_L(A) = 1$ if A is a logical truth and 0 if A is a logical falsehood. Now suppose that A and B are mutually inconsistent, and that p and q are fair betting quotients on each respectively. As we saw above, given the inconsistency of A and B, $I_A + I_B = I_{AvB}$, from which it follows that $S(I_A - p) + S(I_B - q) = S(I_{AvB} - (p + q))$. By the closure principle, therefore, $Q_L(A) + Q_L(B) = Q_L(AvB)$ if A and B are inconsistent with each other. In other words, we have the binary additivity principle of probability. A simple extension of the argument shows that we must also have countable additivity. For suppose $\{A_i\}$ is a denumerable family of mutually exclusive propositions with fair betting quotients p_i. It follows from finite additivity and the Bolzano-Weierstrass Theorem that Σp exists and does not exceed 1. We also have $I_{VA_i} = \Sigma I_{A_i}$, where V is the generalized disjunction operator (never mind that this disjunction is not in a standard language; in the present case it will be true when exactly one of the A_i is true). Thus $\Sigma S(I_{A_i} - p_i) = S(I_{VA_i} - \Sigma p_i)$, and by the closure principle Σp_i is the fair betting quotient on VA_i. In addition, it follows from the closure rule and the preceding footnote that if p is the fair betting quotient on A&B and q the fair betting quotient on B, where $q > 0$, then p/q is the fair betting quotient in a conditional bet on A given B, justifying the usual 'definition' of conditional probability.

Thus the assignments given by Q_L must satisfy the usual probability axioms, including countable additivity and the 'definition' of conditional probability. Hence they must satisfy all the deductive consequences of those axioms. Hence so must Q.

(ii) (if). Suppose all the rules of the countably additive probability calculus are obeyed by an assignment Q on some subset X of the propositions of L, whatever L is. Firstly, we need to show that this implies the existence of a single-valued assignment to all the propositions in L. We take this in two stages. First, suppose the language is a propositional language, with the propositions represented by equivalence classes of tautologically equivalent sentences. Then a well-known result about normal forms (Paris 1994: 13–15) shows that if Q satisfies all the constraints of the probability calculus then there is a probability *function* Q_L whose domain is all the propositions in L and which agrees with Q on X.

There are, of course, other ways of composing assertions out of less complex items than just by using the connectives (that is, Boolean operations on the corresponding propositions). For example, there are statements in ordinary discourse whose linguistic expression requires the universal quantifier 'For all individuals x', which when applied to the indefinite form 'x has property T' yields the definite true-or-false proposition 'For all x, x has T', symbolised $\forall xTx$, or 'Everything has T'; and dually there are existentially quantified assertions: 'there is an x such that x has T', symbolised $\exists xTx$, or 'Something has T'. Note also that consideration of quantified assertions establishes a relation with types of infinite Boolean operation, namely conjunction and disjunction existential quantification over a denumerably infinite set is 'equivalent' to a denumerably infinite disjunctions, and universal quantification over such sets is 'equivalent' to denumerable conjunctions.

Suppose that L contains not only the Boolean operations but also quantification. Assume that it contains also an infinite set of constants a_i, i.e. terms corresponding to names of individuals. Factoring logically equivalent sentences of L into corresponding equivalence classes generates a Boolean algebra |L|, the so-called Lindenbaum sentence algebra of L, of which the quantifier-free sentences form a propositional subalgebra. As before the equivalence class |A| of a sentence A in L will be regarded as the proposition that A. In |L| existentially and universally quantified propositions correspond directly to denumerable disjunctions and conjunctions of instantiations of those propositions with a distinct constant, independently of the domain L is interpreted in: $|\exists xQx|$ is the least upper bound of all finite disjunctions $|Q(a_i)v \ldots vQ(a_j)|$ (ordering by entailment; the universally quantified proposition is a greatest lower bound of the corresponding conjunctions). If the natural continuity condition that probabilities preserve suprema, called the Gaifman condition after Haim Gaifman who proved the result I am about to state, is imposed it can be shown that any probability function on the propositional subalgebra consisting of the quantifier-free sentences has a (unique) extension, again call it Q_L, to all the propositions of L (Paris 1994: 171).

The final stage is to show that Q_L satisfies (F). Trivially, $0 \leq Q_L(A) \leq 1$ and $Q_L(A) = 1$ where A is a logical truth and 0 where A is a logical falsehood. What about closure? Where $q = Q_L(A)$ the expected value, relative to Q_L, of any bet $S(I_A - q)$, is easily seen to be 0, as is the expected value of any countable sum of such bets, since expectations are linear functionals. Suppose that a sum of bets whose betting quotients are given by Q_L is equal to a bet on B with betting quotient p. Taking expectations, it follows that p must be equal to $Q_L(B)$ and closure is satisfied. QED.

We have in effect proved a soundness and completeness theorem. If Q is consistent, that is, has a model as defined earlier, then Q must satisfy the probability axioms including that of countable additivity, which is a purely syntactic criterion (the probability calculus is just a recursively enumerable theory which assigns numbers to elements of a Boolean algebra). Analogously with the deductive case, that is a soundness theorem. Conversely (completeness), if Q satisfies the probability axioms, including countable additivity, then Q is consistent (has a model).

Given that later we shall want to be able to consider probabilities of hypotheses which are denumerably infinite axiom systems not always reducible to any finite set and hence to a single statement (the conjunction of that set), we want to be able to consider probabilities defined on such sets and not simply on single sentences. For this purpose we move to the σ-algebra (in mathematical probability theory called a *Borel field*) obtained from |L| by closing under denumerably infinite disjunctions and conjunctions. It turns out that this algebra is isomorphic to, and hence only notationally distinct from, the σ-algebra generated by the algebra of sets of 'possible worlds' which make the corresponding sentences true, and which are just the things we called propositions in Chapter 4. We can now appeal again to the extension theorem mentioned above, which tells us that there is a countably additive probability on the Borel field generated by that algebra. It follows that if the probability axioms, including that of countable additivity, are satisfied then probabilities are uniquely determined not only on all propositions determined by L but all denumerably infinite sets as well. Such propositions can be expressed as single sentences in the infinitary languages which are like L except that denumerably infinite disjunctions and conjunctions are permitted, and the Lindenbaum algebras of these are isomorphic to the Borel fields generated by the sentences of the corresponding finitary languages (for a detailed study of probabilities defined on these languages see Scott and Krauss 1966).

'Soundness' and 'completeness' in the context of assignments of subjective probability are not just words. Just as in deductive logic, we see that a semantic property, consistency, is extensionally equivalent to a syntactic one, in this case the formal representation of P as a probability in the sense of the probability axioms, and according to the criteria (a)–(c) above, the Bayesian theory qualifies as a genuine *logic* (of consistent belief). However, the recent history of subjective probability has tended to neglect the logical aspect identified by Ramsey, favouring instead a rationality interpretation of the constraints as prudential criteria of one type or another. The trouble with adopting this line is that it is very difficult to *demonstrate* in any uncontroversial and non-question-begging way that violation of any of the constraints is positively irrational. The logical view, on the other hand, need not in principle be troubled by links with rationality of only doubtful strength, since logic is not *about* rational belief or action as such. Thus, deductive logic is about the conditions which sets of sentences must satisfy to be capable of being simultaneously true (deductive consistency), and the conditions in which the simultaneous truth of some set of sentences necessitates the truth of some given sentence (deductive consequence): in other words, it specifies the conditions regulating what might be called consistent truth-value assignments. This objectivism is nicely paralleled in the interpretation of the probability axioms as the conditions regulating the assignment of consistent fair betting quotients.

A logical interpretation of subjective probability casts illumination elsewhere too. Under the aspect of logic the probability axioms are as they stand *complete*: they are, with a qualification we shall discuss in Chapter 9, a complete set of constraints for consistency. Hence any extension of them—as in principles for determining 'objective' prior probabilities—goes beyond pure logic. This should come as something of a relief: the principles canvassed at one time or another for determining 'objective' priors have been the principle of indifference, symmetry principles including principles of invariance under various groups of transformations, simplicity, maximum entropy, and many others. We have discussed the principle of indifference and we shall discuss simplicity, but all these ideas have turned out to be more or less problematic: at one extreme inconsistent, at the other, empty. It is nice not to have to recommend any. Remarkably also, the logical view of the principles of subjective probability exhibits an extension of deductive logic which still manages to remain non-ampliative. It therefore also respects Hume's argument that there is no sound inductive argument from experiential data that does not incorporate an inductive premise, and it also tells us what the inductive premise will look like: *it will be a probability assignment that is not deducible from the probability axioms.*

Coherence versus Strict Coherence

Hume's argument has finally come home. Now we begin the constructive phase. I remarked earlier that bestowing the title of 'logic' should bring with it corresponding explanatory rewards. So it will turn out, and the remainder of the discussion in this chapter will present them, starting with a hitherto puzzling question posed first by Shimony (1955) and then repeated by Carnap (1971: 111–15), but easily answered once it is recognized that the probability axioms are laws of consistency. Consider a set of bets on n propositions $A_1, \ldots, A_n$ with corresponding betting quotients p_i. The classic Dutch Book argument shows that a necessary and sufficient condition for there being, for every set of stakes S_i, a distribution of truth-values over the A_i such that for that distribution there is a non-negative gain to the bettor (or loss: reverse the signs of the stakes), is obedience to the probability axioms. However, if we substitute 'positive' for 'non-negative' we also get an interesting result: the necessary and sufficient condition now becomes that the probability function is in addition *strictly positive*, that is, it takes the value 0 only on logical falsehoods. Which of these two Dutch Book arguments should we take to be the truly normative one: that we should always have the possibility of a positive gain, or that we should always have the possibility of a non-negative gain? It might seem that the second is the more worthwhile objective: what is the point of going to a lot of trouble computing and checking probability values just to break even? On the other hand, strictly positive probability functions are very restrictive. There can be no continuous distributions, for example, so a whole swathe of standard statistics seems to go out of the window. There does not seem to be a determinately correct or incorrect answer to the question of what to do, which is why it is a relief to learn that the problem is purely an artefact of the classic Dutch Book argument. Give up the idea that the probability laws are justified in terms of the pragmatic criterion of financial prudence and the problem vanishes. Instead, we now have a decisive objection to adding the condition of strict positivity of the measure: *the laws of probability as they stand are complete.*

Updating Rules

Nowhere is the illumination cast by the logical view more revealing, however, than in its clarification of the status, still subject to controversy, of the updating rule known as (Bayesian) *Conditionalization* whose passing acquaintance we have already made (Chapter 4, p. 68). An updating rule is a rule which tells you how you ought, if you ought, to change your belief function on receipt of new information. Discussion of updating rules has tended to dominate the Bayesian literature recently, not only because of the intrinsic interest and controversial nature of the topic, but also because of the keen interest in computer-implementable rules for use in machine-learning programs, the study of which has emerged as a fast-growing discipline in its own right. At any rate, several such candidate-rules have been proposed, of which conditionalization is the best known, and indeed is generally, but I shall argue wrongly, regarded as a core principle if the Bayesian theory.

Recall that conditionalization says that if your current belief function is the probability function P, and you learn that a proposition A is true, but no more, then you should update P to a new probability function Q according to the rule

$$Q(.) = P(. \,|A) = P(. \,\&A)/P(A) \qquad (1)$$

A is called the *conditioning proposition,* and Q said to be obtained by conditionalization on A. We have already noted (Chapter 4, p. 67) that Q is automatically also a probability function. It is implicit that P(A) > 0, for otherwise Q is not defined by this rule. We observed (Chapter 4, Appendix 3) that adopting a theory of learning from experience based on this rule leads to very serious problems; I refer the reader back to that discussion; on the other hand, it is known that not adopting the rule can result in a Dutch Book (Teller 1973, who, however, attributed it to David Lewis). Admittedly it is not a proof that anyone who infringes conditionalization at the time the new data are acquired (and who is willing to bet at their fair betting odds, etc.) can be Dutch Booked; it is not difficult to see that there can be no Dutch Book against such a person. It is a proof that there exists a Dutch Book against those who announce in advance that they will follow an updating rule different from conditionalization. Essentially the same Dutch Book argument for conditionalization is also alleged to establish the following identity, called by van Fraassen the 'Reflection Principle' (1984):

$$P(B|Q(B) = r) = r \text{ for all } r, 0 \leq r \leq 1 \qquad (2)$$

The Lewis–Teller Dutch Book argument for (1) (and (2)) is widely supposed to show that the only consistent updating strategy is that of conditionalization. This is not true, and demonstrably not true: on the contrary, *there are circumstances where conditionalization is an inconsistent strategy*. Here is a simple example. Suppose B is a proposition, e.g. '2 + 2 = 4', of whose truth you are P-certain; i.e. P(B) = 1. Suppose also that for whatever reason—you believe you may be visited by Descartes's Demon, for example—you think it distinctly P-possible that Q(B) will take some value q less than 1; i.e. P(Q(B) = q) > 0. Given the circumstances, it follows by the probability calculus that P(B|Q(B) = q) = 1. But suppose at the appropriate time you learn Q(B) = r by introspection; then Q(B) = q. But if you conditionalize on this information then you must set Q(B) = (B|Q(B)=q) = 1. By a nice parallel, though not a surprising one once it is realized that (2) is conditionalization in disguise (see Howson 1997*a*: 198), the counterexample to conditionalization is also a counterexample to this, for we know that P(B|Q(B) = r) = 1 by the probability calculus alone. It follows that conditionalization and its close relative (2) are not sound rules (though as the continued production of 'proofs' of conditionalization testifies, this conclusion is still implicitly resisted by some; see, for example, van Fraassen 1988: 183–96, and the discussion in Howson 1997*b*).

One objection that we can immediately foreclose is that 'second-order' probabilities, that is, probabilities like Q that appear as an argument of the function P, have not been and possibly cannot be formally justified. The objection fails because there is nothing *formally* second-order about Q, nor is there any need to provide a formal justification for allowing Q(B) = q as an argument. The justification already exists in the standard (Kolmogorov) mathematics, for Q is simply a random variable, with *parameter* B. defined in the possibility space generating the propositions/ events in the domain of P (it is assumed that these possibilities include information about the agent's future beliefs). It might be technically more accurate to write 'Q(B)' as 'Q$_B$', that is, explicitly as a random variable, but because it renders the discussion more easily intelligible I shall persist with the sloppier notation. I am assuming that Q(B) is limited to finitely many values; these, however, can determine a partition of [0,1] as fine as desired.

A natural enough question is how there could be a Dutch Book argument for an unsound principle. This certainly wasn't the case with the 'synchronic' probability axioms. Taking the logical view of Bayesian probability suggests that we should be able to use the deductive parallel to find the answer, and so we can. It is very simple. Consider two truth-valuations τ and σ, such that $\tau(A) = T$ and $\sigma(A) = F$. Is this an inconsistent assignment of truth-values? Certainly not. $\sigma(A) = T$ and $\sigma(A) = F$ would be, but that is not what was presented. *Mutatis mutandis*, the situation is the same in the conditionalization case. The derivation, in Appendix 1 of Chapter 4, of the equation P(B|A) = P(B&A)/P(A) where P(A) > 0, which we have taken as a definition of P(B|A), is based on interpeting P(B|A) as, in effect, a betting quotient in a bet that is called off if A is (discovered to be) false, but goes ahead with the betting quotient P(B|A) on B if A is true. This is an assignment based on the function P. The updating rule $P_A(B)$ is clearly obtained from a different probability function. These two functions correspond to the two different valuations σ and τ, and as we see there is no question of these being inconsistent. Similarly for the assignments P(B|A) = r and $P_B(A)$ = s where r and s are unequal.

We can put these rather spare logical points in a more informal context. If I accept a set of statements which is known to be deductively inconsistent, then the inconsistency becomes in an entirely natural way extendable to my belief state as well. But if that set is the union of two consistent sets, one of which represented my beliefs yesterday and the other my beliefs today, then it is not my state of belief at any time which is inconsistent. Indeed, I have in effect merely changed my mind about what I accept as true. Similar considerations apply in the probabilistic situation. The Lewis–Teller Dutch Book shows that a set of betting quotients can be penalized with sure loss (or equivalently rewarded with sure gain), but the betting quotients refer to both current and future belief states. Therein is no inconsistency.

Illustration: 'Dynamic Modus Ponens'

For dramatic emphasis of the rather trivial points above consider a parallel proposal of a deductive 'rule' which we shall call 'dynamic *modus ponens*', by analogy with what has come to be called (usually approvingly) the 'dynamic' rule of conditionalization. Dynamic *modus ponens* is the deductive 'updating rule' that if at time t I accept as true A→B (material conditional) and at time t' > t I increase my knowledge stock by just (the truth of) A then I should accept B as true at time t' also. This 'dynamic rule' is unsound for just the same reasons the dynamic rule of conditionalization is. Consider the following example. At time t I accept the material conditional A→B. But suppose that A is actually equivalent to the negation of B, and note that in this case A→B is equivalent to B. My acceptance of A→B might even be just a pedantic way of saying I accept B. But at time t + 1, for whatever reason, I decide to accept A as true. Clearly, it would result in inconsistency in my accepted beliefs at t + 1 if I were to invoke 'dynamic *modus ponens*' and accept B. To put it another way, deductive consistency requires you cannot simultaneously regard both A and A→B as true; decide to accept A and you must, to remain consistent, jettison A→B.

That is not all there is to be said about the spurious rule of conditionalization, however. Recall from our initial discussion (Chapter 4, p. 65) that a conditional probability function P(. |D) is the restriction of P to the sub-universe D; in other words, for any given C, P(C|D) measures your degree of belief in C on the additional supposition that D is true. As Ramsey pointed out, this does not have the implication that P(C|D) is what your degree of belief in C would be were you to learn D. Actually learning D might, as Ramsey observed, cause you to change your conditional degree of belief in C given D, just as learning A in the 'dynamic *modus ponens*' example positively demands the removal of A→B from the stock of things you accept as true. The reason why conditionalization sounds plausible is because *it is implicitly assumed that learning D causes no change in your probability of C conditional on D*. But then conditionalization would not only be plausible, but mandatory. For suppose that if, after learning D, and hence exogenously changing your old probability P(D) to a new one, Q(D) = 1, you still maintain the same conditional probability P(C|D). Consistency, in the form of the syntactical constraint of the probability axioms themselves, requires that your probability Q(C) of C is equal to P(C|D)! From the assumptions Q(D) = 1 and P(C|D) = Q(C|D) it is an easy exercise in the probability calculus to show that Q(C) = P(C|D). In other words, the conditions under which conditionalization is provably sound are just those under which *modus ponens* is provably sound: the acquisition of the new information does not change your judgements conditional on that information.

But we have seen that there are circumstances in which these conditional judgements cannot be maintained consistently, for example where D is the proposition Q(B) = q above, q < 1, and where P(Q(B) = q) > 0 and P(B) = 1. As we saw, consistency entails that P(B|Q(B) = q) = 1. And it is easy to see also that consistency requires that Q(B|Q(B) = q) be equal to q. For a conditional bet on B given Q(B) = q has the payoff table

B	Q(B) = q	gain
T	T	$1 - q$
F	T	$-q$
	F	0

Q is now of course your current betting rate. The payoff table is clearly that of a conditional bet on B given Q(B) = q at the betting rate q.

Conditionalization and Modus Ponens

We have pointed to some analogies between *modus ponens* and a sound, synchronic, form of conditionalization. It is interesting to see how far the analogy can be pushed. We shall now digress from the main discussion to look into this; the reader who isn't interested can just skip the next couple of sections.

It has sometimes been claimed that probabilistic reasoning permits no rule of detachment similar to *modus ponens*. This is incorrect. As we shall see, the rules are formally very similar, so similar that it is tempting to see one as merely a special case of the other. Unfortunately, that is not possible: though the logical distance between them diminishes, it never quite vanishes.

We saw in the previous section that a probabilistic rule of the form

$$\frac{Q(A) = 1 \qquad Q(B|A) = r}{Q(B) = r} \tag{3}$$

is demonstrably sound. Substituting P(B|A) for r, we obtain sound instances of the principle of conditionalization:

$$\frac{Q(A) = 1 \qquad Q(B|A) = P(B|A)}{Q(B) = P(B|A)} \tag{4}$$

It might be objected that (3), and hence (4), is trivial, since once you learn A then Q(B|A) just is Q(B). The objection is without merit. A parallel charge would be that the standard expression of *modus ponens*

$$\frac{A \qquad A{\rightarrow}B}{B} \tag{5}$$

is likewise trivial because, *given* that the truth-value of A is T, the truth-value of A→B is identical to that of B, that is, where $\models$ symbolizes semantic entailment A $\models$ B↔(A→B). This suggests that either both (3) and (4) are trivial or neither are (A and B here can be taken to refer to propositions or to sentences of a formal language; since the former can be regarded as equivalence classes of the latter the equivocation is harmless).

In fact, neither (3) nor (4) are trivial. Both are inference rules whose soundness is demonstrable by appeal to corresponding semantic criteria. *Modus ponens* is usually the sole inference rule in Hilbert-style axiomatizations of the propositional calculus, where its role is to generate the complete set of identically true sentences from a given proper subset of such sentences, the logical axioms. (3) generates the complete set of values of the new probability function Q from the set of identities $Q(B|A) = P(B|A)$, as in (4). These identities characterize the classic applications of the Bayesian theory where the learning of the conditioning proposition A is assumed not to change any of the probabilities conditional on A. For a long time these applications were regarded as so typical that conditionalization was not identified explicitly as an updating rule, being simply taken for granted. Only recently has it come to be appreciated that there are anomalous cases, typically involving conditioning propositions of a reflexive character like the example above, leading in effect to diagonal arguments somewhat analogous to those used by Gödel, Church, and Tarski to demonstrate various types of inbuilt limitation in deductive theories. The capacity for generating diagonalizable assertions is guaranteed once propositions like '$Q(C) = r$' are included in the domain of P: substituting B for C in '$P(B|Q(C) = r)$', where $P(B) = 1$, $P(Q(C) = r) > 0$, and $r < 1$, is a diagonalization implicitly asserting that Q cannot be obtained by conditionalizing on '$Q(C) = r$'.

(5) is of course sound relative to the semantic criterion of truth-transmission: if the two upper sentences are both satisfiable by a valuation τ, then so is the lower sentence. (3) is sound relative to the semantic criterion of coherence: that the value of $Q(B)$ is equal to the value of $Q(B|A)$ given $Q(A) = 1$ is a consequence of the probability axioms together with $Q(A) = 1$, a fact brought out clearly in the meta-rule which has an obvious formal similarity to (3):

$$\frac{\tau(A) = 1 \qquad \tau(A \rightarrow B) = r}{\tau(B) = r} \qquad (6)$$

where r is either 1 (true) or 0 (false). Observe that when $r = 1$ in the probabilistic rule of conditionalization (3) and in the general form (6) of *modus ponens,* we seem to have two models for reasoning about conditionals when both the conditional 'assertion' and its 'antecedent' are accepted (I use scare quotes because, as we shall see, it is is far from trivial that we are dealing with assertions *qua* elements of a propositional algebra).

The obvious formal similarity between (3) and (6) suggests, however, a systematic relationship between probabilities and truth-valuations on conditionals, a suggestion reinforced by the facts that τ in (6) is formally a probability function taking only the two extreme values 0 and 1 (clearly, τ adds over disjunctions of mutually inconsistent sentences), and that if the arrow is that of the material conditional then $Q(B|A)$ can be replaced by $Q(A \to B)$ in (4), since if $Q(A) = 1$ then $Q(B|A) = Q(A \to B)$. On the other hand, where $\to$ is material implication, $Q(A \to B) = Q(B|A)$ only in exceptional circumstances even where the latter is defined, since

$$Q(B|A) = Q(A \to B) - Q(-A).Q(-B|A)$$

giving equality between $Q(B|A)$ and $Q(A \to B)$ only where $Q(A) = 1$ or $Q(B|A) = 1$ (these are of course Lewis's assertibility conditions for the material conditional (1973: 306)). The force of this objection is reduced by the observations that (i) the material conditional is not the only or indeed necessarily the best representation of an indicative conditional, and indeed it is widely regarded as seriously defective in that role, and (ii), (6) should arguably be robust over any satisfactory account of a conditional assertion, since if the antecedent of such an assertion is true then intuitively the conditional, of whatever hue, is true or false according to whether its conclusion is true or false.

The two models of conditional reasoning, the probabilistic, expressed in the rule of conditionalization and the deductive, expressed in *modus ponens,* formally coincide when $P(B|A)$ is equal to 1 or 0. This is pleasing, but it is also suggestive. What it suggests is that conditionalization is a generalization of *modus ponens* with the term 'B|A' denoting some form of conditional *assertion.* The suggestion runs up sharply against Lewis's so-called trivialization theorems, which imply that it is not true that for each A, B in the domain of any probability function P there is a 'conditional' W such that $P(W) = P(B|A)$ (the proof, a fairly elementary exercise in the probability calculus, is given in Lewis 1973). The assertion so denied is usually referred to as *Adams's thesis* or *Adams's principle* (after Ernest Adams who proposed it in Adams 1975). Admittedly, and as Lewis himself was the first to point out, his theorems assume that the probability function satisfies the usual axioms and is defined on a Boolean algebra of events/propositions. There have been attempts to circumvent these assumptions consistently with maintaining Adams's principle. De Finetti himself proposed a three-valued logic of conditional assertions, which are suggestively written in the form B|A, with values 'true', 'false', and 'void', incorporating arbitrary composition with conjunction, disjunction, and negation. According to this alleged logic B|A is evaluated as true if A and B are both true, false if A is true and B false, and as *void* in all other cases. The Strong Kleene three-valued truth tables evaluate conjunctions, disjunctions, and negations (these rules are identical to Łukasiewicz's tables for those connectives). Though classical two-valued logic can be obtained by identifying sentences A not containing I with A|T, where T is a classical tautology, the full three-valued logic is not Boolean. Factored by truth-table equivalence it is a distributive lattice, with unique maximal element T|T and minimal element ⊥|T, where ⊥ is a classical contradiction (so neither contains the connective |). But it is not a complemented lattice: –(B|A) is equivalent to –B|A and is an involution only.

In a recent discussion of de Finetti's conditional logic Milne (1997) argues that the Kleene Strong rules are justified in the context of a conditional logic in terms of the notions of a complementary conditional bet (negation), and of infima and supreme relative to an ordering of bets according to which if the lesser is won so is the greater, and if the greater is lost so is the lesser. In effect, the truth-values of compounds are being identified with the notions of a compound bet's being won, lost, or called off, and this same identification underlies the 'truth-conditions' for the conditional events B|A themselves: 'A bet on B conditional on A is in effect a bet on the conditional assertion B|A, won when it is true, lost when it is false, called off when it is void' (Milne, 1997: 213). Thus it looks as if we have coherence again acting as a semantic underpinning for a logic, this time a non-Boolean logic of conditionals trivially satisfying Adams's principle when any probability function is defined on its sentences.

I think this view of what has been achieved should be resisted. First, it is gratuitous to identify the conditions for a conditional bet on B given A to be won, lost, or called off with corresponding truth-values for a conditional assertion B|A. Secondly, the identification has consequences that to my mind effectively deny these postulated assertions the status of conditionals in any legitimate sense. The most telling is this: *even when A does not contain |, A|A is not always true.* For if A is false then A|A is void. But the sentence 'If Bloggs is guilty then Bloggs is guilty' is surely true independently of whether Bloggs is in fact guilty. The principle of 'conditional introduction' in deductive logic is rightly regarded as fundamental: it tells us that if B is deducible from A then the conditional 'If A then B' must be true. Well, A is certainly deducible from A even in this strange logic, yet as we see we are precluded from assuming that the associated conditional is always true. A closely related objection is that these alleged conditionals violate the principle that conditional assertions should be genuinely *conditional,* that is, they should have no categorical implication. Yet the truth of B|A actually entails the truth of the antecedent A. Admittedly, the ordinary two-valued material conditional A→B has some anomalous properties too, but in contrast to B|A the truth of A→B has no categorical implication, while the universal truth of A→A is guaranteed. Moreover, some of the most counterintuitive properties of A→B are shared by B|A (Milne 1997: 224). Be all that as it may, reasoning with | is certainly not conditional reasoning as anybody would normally understand it. While it is true that a three-valued binary connective can consistently be introduced which satisfies Adams's principle, that connective is not a *conditional* operator in any ordinary sense of the word: it is just something that obeys Adams's principle.

Since the alternative conditional logics satisfying Adams's principle appear to be even less acceptable than this one (see Milne 1997 for a description of their salient features), Lewis's result seems reasonably robust. What then are conditional (Bayesian) probabilities P(B|A) probabilities of? This way of posing the question is misleading—literally, since it leads into the cul-de-sac of conditional assertions. It is better to ask simply what is the best way of interpreting Bayesian conditional probabilities. Well, we know how they are to be interpeted: P(B|A) is your probability of B on the supposition that A is true, without any parallel commitment to degrees of belief in the truth of conditional *assertions.* Indeed, on this understanding the expression 'B|A' is a *term* of the *metalanguage* of A and B as opposed to an *object-language sentence* (or equivalence class of sentences). We are in effect in the situation, familiar from discussions of modelling truth and the modal 'necessary', of deciding whether a type of reasoning is best modelled by an expansion of an object language, or by a restriction to a metalanguage. In all cases there is a loss entailed by going object-linguistically. In the case of 'is true' and 'is necessary', a simple Liar-type argument shows that the intuitively obvious conditions TA→A' and NA→A' cannot consistently be maintained if truth (T) and necessity (N) are modelled as object-linguistically definable predicates. In the case of truth this bullet is bitten and truth is now standardly taken to be an irreduceably metalinguistic predicate, whereas in modal logic necessity becomes a unary object-language operator, foreclosing the formulation of reflexive sentences like 'This sentence is necessary' (for an extended discussion, see McGee 1988: ch. 1). In the present context, expanding the object language by incorporating B|A as a sentence satisfying Adams's principle merely results in the failure of B|A to behave like an acceptable conditional.

Ramsey's Views

I have mentioned that Ramsey's views on how conditional probabilities are interpreted do not support a view of conditionalization as a uniformly sound rule. But inspection of the relevant passages in Ramsey's paper also reveals the following remarks:

Obviously if p is the fact observed, my degree of belief in q after the observation should be equal to my degree of belief in q given p before, or by the multiplication rule to the quotient of my degree of belief in pq by my degree of belief in p. When my degrees of belief change in this way we can say that they have been changed consistently by my observation. (1931: 192; italics added)

Contrast this with the remark earlier in the same paper:

'the degree of belief in p given q' . . . does not mean the degree of belief . . . which the subject would have in p if he knew q (p.180)

These two statements taken together appear to contradict each other. But Ramsey also has an answer why they do not:

for knowledge of q might for psychological reasons profoundly alter his whole system of beliefs. (ibid.)

That as a matter of psychological fact knowledge of q might act as an external shock disrupting one's conditional degrees of belief given q does not conflict with Ramsey's view that the result is still an inconsistent belief-change. What, however, in a rare slip, he fails to appreciate is that knowledge of q might, not merely for psychological but for *logical* reasons, for reasons of *consistency* itself, force the rescission of the relevant conditional probabilities. In our counterexample of the mind-changing drug the agent had a non-zero degree of belief in the proposition q that their degree of belief in p would change, and prior to learning q was certain, to degree 1, that p was true. Consistency, in the form of the rules of the probability calculus itself, demands that the degree of belief in p given q is also 1. But learning q means knowing that the degree of belief in p is now less than 1; to equate that new degree of belief with that in p given q before learning q is therefore to be inconsistent.

'Probability Kinematics'

The objections to the rule of dynamic conditionalization are necessarily objections also to a generalization of it known variously as Jeffrey's rule, Jeffrey conditionalization, and probability kinematics. Jeffrey introduced this rule to cope with what he saw as an undue restrictiveness on the part of 'standard' conditionalization, which we shall henceforward call Bayesian conditionalization, namely that it could accommodate only the learning of the truth of a proposition, the conditioning proposition, with probability one. Jeffrey's rule is a rule for redistributing probability over the entire domain of your (consistent) belief function after an exogenous shift in the probability of one or (subject to a qualification I shall mention) more propositions, maybe due to some unarticulated and possible inarticulable sense impression, like forming successive impressions of the colour of some fabric seen at first in dim and then in stronger light (Jeffrey's own example). Suppose that A is the unique proposition on which such a shift occurs, from p to q. Let your redistributed probability be given by the function Q, where your old function is P. Then Jeffrey's rule is this:

$$Q(\,.\,) = P(\,.\,|A)q + P(\,.\,|-A)(1-q)$$

Clearly Jeffrey's rule tends continuously to Bayesian conditionalization as q tends to 1 or 0.

A technical problem with Jeffrey's rule is that it can only deal with exogenous shifts on partitions, that is, exclusive and exhaustive sets of propositions. Above we see it applied to the partition $\{A,-A\}$, and the generalization to any countable partition A_1, A_2, . . . is clear. What is not clear, and indeed appears not to be tractable, is how to amend it to the case where some arbitrary set of propositions suffers an exogenous shift. But technical problems are not the principal issue. Dynamic rules are not sound. In fact, there is a dynamic Dutch

Book for Jeffrey's rule, which proceeds from noting that a necessary and sufficient condition for Jeffrey's rule is that $P(\; . \; |A) = Q(\; . \; |A)$ and $P(\; . \; | - A) = Q(\; . \; | - A)$, and then showing that anyone who announced any departure from these equations as a planned mode of updating can be dynamically Dutch Booked (Armendt 1980). And there are other 'proofs' besides (see Howson 1997a: for a discussion). But because Jeffrey's rule is a generalization of Bayesian condition-alization the sorts of counterexample we have looked at in connec-tion with Bayesian conditionalization are counterexamples also to Jeffrey's rule. According to the view argued for here the two families of equations $P(\; . \; |A) = Q(\; . \; |A)$ and $P(\; . \; | - A) = Q(\; . \; | - A)$ are to be viewed, as is the single family $Q(\; . \; |A) = P(\; . \; |A)$ in Bayesian condi-tionalization, not as unconditionally valid principles but merely as conditions of the (synchronic) validity of Jeffrey's rule. Jeffrey's rule itself is therefore like Bayesian conditionalization a rule of only con-ditional validity, valid just when those pairs of equations are satis-fied—which, of course, they may not be. It is time to move on.

Mathematics and Logic

Deductive logic, as we know, is capable of adjudicating a much greater class of inferences than those merely involving empirical-factual statements. One of its most conspicuous successes is its appli-cation to mathematics and even logic itself, where very deep results have been obtained (in the work of Gödel, Church, Tarski, Skolem, Cohen, and others). The principal application of Bayesian logic has been to the problem of induction in empirical science, but its scope certainly exceeds that and is in fact no less wide than that of deduc-tive logic itself. For example, in the discussion of conditionalization we have seen that propositions about the agent's probabilities can appear in the argument-place of his or her own probability function. *Any well-formed assertion can have a probability predicated of it*, even the propositions of mathematics and of meta-logic, like the state-ment that such and such a statement is a truth of logic. All that con-sistency requires is that such statements obey the probability axioms.

And thereby hangs a problem, or so it seems. In presenting the probability calculus in Chapter 4 we did so in the conceptual context of a state-space S and a class of propositions defined in that space: in other words, to each such proposition A there corresponded a

determinate class of possibilities in S which 'made' A true. But suppose A is a statement of mathematics. Then, according to a hallowed
tradition in analytic philosophy A is *necessarily* true or *necessarily*
false, and hence should presumably be true in all possible states of
affairs or in none. Hence A is representable as one of only two subsets of S: the empty set $\varnothing$ or S itself. It is thereby to all intents and
purposes equivalent to a logical truth or a logical falsehood. Hence
by the probability calculus the probability assigned to A must be 0 or
1. At least A does get assigned a probability, but a trivial one, rendering the Bayesian logic completely useless as an account of how
ordinary sublunary mortals can have consistent non-trivial degrees
of belief in the propositions of mathematics or logic—hence the fre-
quent charge that the Bayesian theory presupposes that agents are
logically and mathematically omniscient.

Perhaps surprisingly, none of this is true. For the last seventy or so
years, and for reasons which are widely held to be very good ones,
mathematics has not been thought to be a system of logical truths.
Even set theory, the most abstract mathematical theory to date,
which is still also regarded as a more or less acceptable foundation
for all mathematics, does not consist of logical truths. On the contrary, in its standard formalization (known as ZFC, Zermelo-
Fraenkel set theory with the Axiom of Choice) there is an
uncountable infinity of possible structures interpreting the same formal language in which the axioms of ZFC are not all jointly true; and
none of the so-called proper axioms of ZFC is a logical truth. In
other words, the state-space of mathematical statements is a class of
mathematical structures, in some of which, if it is not a contradiction, such a statement will not be true. Formally, the situation is no
different from the one we have been facing for so-called factual statements.

Nor is that all. Even if A is a logical truth, *the statement that A is
a logical truth is not itself in general a logical truth*. If true, that statement is a synthetic consequence of ZFC and also, by the completeness theorem for first-order logic, and after a suitable coding à la
Gödel of formulas into the natural numbers, of a suitable subtheory
of the standard axioms of number theory, Peano's axioms ('Being a
logical truth' is coded as an arithmetical formula defining what is
called a Σ_1^0 property of numbers; these are certainly not logical
truths). In other words, statements of meta-logic, statements like 'A
is a logical truth', 'A is a consequence of the set Π of assumptions',

and so on, are synthetic *mathematical* statements, true or false in the standard model of the appropriate mathematical theory.

It might be queried whether merely having the *form* of fact-stating assertions—which all that has been shown—is enough to permit the assimilation of mathematical assertions to empirical-factual ones. After all, it is a contingent matter whether a statement of *empirical* fact is true or not, but it is not presumably a contingent matter whether 'there is an infinite number of twin-primes' is true. Even Kant, who agreed that mathematics is synthetic, still denied that it was contingent. But contingency in any real sense (whatever that might be) is beside the point. We are not talking here of chances of things being as they are in some presumed indeterministic context; and anyway, as we shall see later, it is quite possible to have chance distributions where there is no such presumption. We are talking of the possibility of consistently being able to entertain doubt about the truth of a proposition that is not logically true. The natural fear is that in trying to distribute degrees of belief with the same freedom that you would over empirical statements, inconsistency might arise because logical relations already constrain the distribution of probabilities according to the probability axioms. For example, the probability axioms tell us that if any proposition A is a deductive consequence of another B, and $P(B) > 0$, then $P(A|B)$ must be equal to 1. Can we consistently assign a probability less than 1 to the statement that B entails A, even when it does? The answer is 'yes': there is no more danger of inconsistency than in assigning a probability less than one to any statement which is factually true. Similarly, the statement 'A is a logical truth' may be true, but we can consistently assign a probability less than 1 to it nevertheless. For it is false as a matter of fact, not empirical fact, to be sure, but fact for all that, for there are certainly 'worlds' or structures in which it is true.

And that is really the fundamental point. The probability axioms do not discriminate between different sorts of non-logical truth and falsity, and because they do not no inconsistency can arise through treating meta-logical and mathematical statements generally no differently from statements of empirical fact. Indeed, it is probably better, at any rate for our purposes, to regard the distinction between mathematical and 'ordinary' factual truth as wholly artificial. *From the point of view of being able consistently to assign non-trivial probabilities, they amount to the same thing.* This is not to endorse a view that mathematics by itself 'says anything' about matters of empirical fact. It does not. When interpreted in the terms of a physical theory it is of course a different matter. Indeed, in apportioning credit for the empirical success of theories in the mathematical empirical sciences it has turned out to be very difficult to factor out the contribution of the mathematics itself. The problem is obviously not trivial, since the fundamental principles of such theories are actually mathematical equations. Attempts like that of Field (1980) to show that the pure mathematics is a conservative extension of the real empirical theory have foundered on the way that mathematics, and rather refined mathematics to boot, is employed to deliver the theorems (so-called representation theorems) that he thinks establish the case. It may well be that we shall eventually come to believe that mathematics is not conservative at all in this way: for what it is worth I myself think this not at all improbable.

But this is to digress. Allowing intermediate probabilities to mathematical hypotheses brings with it some interesting possibilities. For example, if we don't know that B entails A, and assign a correspondingly non-unit probability to the proposition 'B entails A', then we might also be inclined to set P(A|B) at less than 1. Since we have not so far made it a condition that P is a total function on a field of propositions, merely that it is extendable to one, we do not have to assign any value to the conditional probability: we have the luxury of being able to be agnostic occasionally. Actually to assign a value to the conditional probability of A given B less than 1 would be inconsistent, of course; but the possibility of inconsistency is like that of death, a condition of life, an omni-present hazard. We have to live with it. When we find that we are in peril we adjust our behaviour accordingly. So when we discover that B entails A we adjust P(A|B) to 1. At any rate, there is no reason to believe that we cannot have a Bayesian theory of mathematical and logical discovery just as much as we can have one of scientific discovery. We shall return to this point in the next chapter.

A formal theory of Bayesian logical learning was proposed in 1983 by Garber, and subsequently excited a great deal of discussion (a great deal of the interest in Garber's theory arose because it seemed to offer a solution to the problem of 'old evidence', a problem—or alleged problem—which we shall discuss in Chapter 8). In Garber's theory a probability function P is defined on a formal logical language containing sentences like 'A deductively entails B', 'A is a logical truth', etc., in addition to a set of sentential 'atoms' A, B, C, etc., and certain constraints are imposed on P additionally to those of the probability axioms, while one of the latter is dropped. The principal additional constraint is a representation of the deductive rule of *modus ponens*: P('A entails B'&A) = P('A entails B'&A&B), and the discarded probability axiom is that if A is a logical truth then P(A) = 1. The reason for discarding this axiom is precisely to accommodate the possibility of an agent's remaining a rational reasoner and failing to assign A the maximal probability even when A is a logical truth, because he or she simply does not know that logical fact; and ditto, when A is a logical falsehood.

Rational or not, I do not think that such an abridgement serves any useful purpose, or is even permissible, in a theory of consistent reasoning. Nor do I think that the additions are justified either. As we have seen, meta-logic is mathematics, and according to the view adopted not only here but by most logicians, mathematics is synthetic, not itself logic. On the other hand, it might still be thought that there should be *some* systematic relation, to be registered in an explicit constraint, between P(A) and the agent *believing* that A is/is not a logical truth: if you are far from certain that A is a logical truth then surely consistency in a broad sense requires that you should set P(A) at less than 1. But to grant that clearly runs the risk, actually a near-certainty, of a conflict with the condition that P(A) = 1 if A is a logical truth. It would seem that dropping that condition really is the only way to obtain a realistic, 'humanized Bayesianism' (Earman 1992: 124): the condition of logical omniscience implicit in that probability axiom is neither 'humanized' nor realistic, and the axiom must go.

No. This line of criticism (it informs Earman's own otherwise excellent discussion) rests on a mistaken view of the nature of formal models of reasoning. Nobody presumably charges formal deductive logic with assuming that agents are logically omniscient. So why do so with a theory of sound probabilistic reasoning? A set of constraints determining consistency does not by itself assume that anyone does or even can satisfy them in every instance. To weaken them so that they are all humanly achievable is a misguided enterprise, rather like weakening the deductive principle that a contradiction implies everything to one stating merely that known contradictions imply everything.

There is one final objection to treating the hypotheses of mathematics as just like ordinary factual hypotheses. When we conjecture that a mathematical statement is true—the objection proceeds—we are not really conjecturing that it is *true*; what we are really conjecturing is that it is a deductive consequence of the appropriate mathematical theory, or axiom system, that is taken to characterize that particular field of investigation. We might even be conjecturing that it follows from ZFC itself, the foundational theory, as it is still often regarded, for all mathematics.

This is badly wrong. For a start, as we have seen asking whether A follows from B *is* asking a factual question: we are asking whether it is *true* that A follows from B, and that is a mathematical question. But there is even more wrong than that. Gödel showed that no axiom system for any interesting class of mathematical statements is complete if it is consistent, and one of the most interesting questions is whether our current systems, like Peano arithmetic or ZFC itself, are consistent. It is certainly a question that has preoccupied many mathematicians (including, of course, Hilbert: to prove consistency in some absolute way was one of his famous list of outstanding unsolved problems). But as we know, the question of consistency can be formulated as a strictly mathematical question. Gödel showed that it is even a question that has a purely arithmetical formulation, and that it could not be proved in any system for which the enquiry is made if that system is consistent. But this fact does not prevent people asking the question. They want to know the answer, even for ZFC, but they do not, or should not, want to know if ZFC can prove that ZFC is consistent. If it can, then by Gödel's second incompleteness theorem ZFC is inconsistent. Might it be the case that they are looking for some acceptable extension of ZFC in which it can be proved that ZFC is consistent? Possibly, but that would also not prevent them from wondering whether that extension itself was consistent. It is simply not realistic to say that they are looking for a sequence of extensions of ZFC in which each can be proved consistent by all its successors. They want to know whether *in fact* ZFC is consistent. And once it is allowed that some mathematical statements are factual, the objection is fatally undermined. For why should they not all be? After all, that is what (most) people think. But that is enough on this topic for now. In Chapter 8 we shall look at some of the applications of the Bayesian logic in logical, or rather meta-logical, contexts.

Utility: Ramsey and Others

Nothing worthwhile is gained without some cost (this could be the (–1)th law of thermodynamics), and to do its job satisfactorily Bayes's definition must be accompanied by some qualifications. To the most important of these I now turn. Let us go back to that definition again. Suitably modulated into a measure of *subjective* probability Bayes's 'definition' makes your (personal) probability of A your personal estimate of the fair amount by which the value of an option 'N if A' should be discounted to compensate for the uncertainty of A; the 'fair amount' we can take to mean 'the quantity which you believe would give no calculable advantage to either side of the transaction'. I have put 'definition' in quotes because the fact is that we have some informal idea of probability; Bayes's definition is a definition only for the purposes of developing a mathematical theory of uncertainty based on a formally precise notion. As we saw from Appendix 1 to Chapter 4, Bayes is able to show that, subject to some simple consistency constraints, probability so defined is formally a probability in the sense of the probability axioms.

As a way of eliciting your degree of belief in A Bayes's definition will only be successful if the proportional amount of the discount reflects *only* your estimate of A's uncertainty. This discounted value should therefore not depend on the reference currency used, and in particular p must not depend on the quantity N. But here we have to confront the familiar phenomenon of the 'diminishing marginal utility of money', that is, the fact that the value of an amount N of currency is not proportional to N but such that its marginal value (rate of increase) decreases with increasing N, a fact first noted by another member of the famous Bernoulli family, Daniel Bernoulli, writing shortly before Hume, who employed a marginally diminishing function of N as the 'utility' of N to solve the notorious St Petersburg problem (see below, p. 157).

A way often suggested out of this alleged difficulty (to what extent it is a difficulty will be assessed later) is to restrict consideration to the interval of values of N in which N is roughly proportional to utility. That is all very well, but what is utility and how is it measured? Until those questions are answered the proposal seems too vague, if not actually question-begging, to be acted on. So at any rate it seemed to Ramsey, whose response in his seminal paper (1931) was to develop from as unexceptionable postulates as possible a general *theory of utility* within which the problem of the value of uncertain options could be attacked systematically. In so doing he set a trend for the foundations of Bayesian probability that flourishes to the present. In view of both this and the inherent interest and importance of Ramsey's and his successors' achievements, a brief account of their work over the last half-decade is in order.

Ramsey did not give a detailed presentation of his theory; only proof-sketches of his main results accompany the principal definitions and postulates. The postulates, apart from those there for purely mathematical reasons, provided the model for all later work, imposing consistency constraints on a binary *preference relation*, defined on possible states of affairs, or 'worlds' as Ramsey called them, and also on options whose payoffs are such 'worlds' (it is also implicitly assumed by Ramsey that the domain of the preference relation is closed under the formation of binary options whose payoffs are already in it). These 'worlds' are to be thought of as the various possible states of affairs that have *value* in some sense to an agent; namely that the agent conceives as more or less desirable. Ramsey showed that his postulates implied three main results. The first is the existence of a family F of functions, now usually called *utility functions*, defined on a domain including the class G of possible worlds, such that for all u in F, and all X, Y in G, X is preferred to Y if and only if u(X) > u(Y), and for any u,u′ in F and Z in G, there are real numbers a and b, a > 0, such that u(Z) = au′(Z) + b. This implies that for all V,W,X,Y in G

$$\frac{u(Y) - u(V)}{u(W) - u(X)} = \frac{u'(Y) - u'(V)}{u'(W) - u'(X)}$$

that is, ratios of utility differences are the same whichever utility function is used to measure them. The most significant feature of this result is that utility is not a primitive notion, but 'emerges' as an epiphenomenal property of the preference relation itself, giving an 'almost unique' numerical representation of the preference ordering.

Ramsey's second result follows immediately from the invariance of ratios of utility differences. It is that we can define a unique probability function P in the manner of Bayes's own definition but where the options are measured in utility units. Ramsey's actual procedure is as follows. If you are indifferent between Z for sure and the option

'W if A, X if not', then your probability P(A) of A is defined to be the ratio

$$\frac{u(Z) - u(X)}{u(W) - u(X)}$$

(it is simply assumed by Ramsey that this will be independent of the reference quantities W, X, Z). Note that since we can always find a u in F such that $u(X) = 0$, we have here in effect Bayes's definition with $u(Z)$ the discounted price of 'W if A'. It is straightforward to show from Ramsey's postulates for a consistent preference ordering that, so defined, P satisfies the probability axioms I–III. Thus one's preferences if consistent determine a unique probability function according to the ratio above. *In other words, not only is an almost unique utility function an epiphenomenon of a consistent preference ordering: so too is a unique probability function.*

Ramsey's final result extends the way in which utility is merely a numerical reflection of the preference ordering. He supposed that this ordering was not merely over states of affairs in G, but also over options of the form 'X if A, Y if –A', for any proposition A. Ramsey's third result follows almost immediately from the way in which P(.) is defined. Suppose that you are indifferent between Z for certain and the option 'W if A, X if not'. Then from the definition of $p = P(A)$ we have after some simplification

$$u(Z) = pu(W) + u(X)(1-p).$$

But we also have

$$u(Z) = u[W \text{ if } A, X \text{ if not}].$$

Hence

$$u[W \text{ if } A, X \text{ if not}] = pu(W) + (1-p)u(X); \qquad (7)$$

that is, the utility of a binary option is its expected utility. By considering suitably compounded binary options this result can be generalized to the case of options involving n exclusive and exhaustive propositions $A_1, \ldots, A_n$, with respective payoffs $X_1, \ldots, X_n$, and we obtain

$$U[X_1 \text{ if } A_1, X_2 \text{ if } A_2, \ldots, X_n \text{ if } A_n] = p_1u_1 + p_2u_2 + \ldots + p_nu_n$$

where $p_i = P(A_i)$ and $u_i = u(X_i)$. It follows that one such n-fold option is preferred to another if and only if the expected utility of the first is greater than that of the second. It can also be shown that if such an inequality holds for one utility function in F then it holds for all. This result is perhaps less remarkable when it is realized that the expected utility principle (7) is *equivalent* to defining P(A) in the way Ramsey does; it is easy to see that that definition is implied by it. So to some extent the principle is covertly being assumed in the definition of P(A).

To appreciate the significance of these results we have to go back to the very beginnings of the mathematical theory of probability itself. For some time after the initial developments, in the second half of the seventeenth century, there were two notions, *probability* and *expectation*, which, though not independent of each other, seemed equally fundamental. The expectation of an uncertain option was regarded as the fair price to pay for it, and probability was often defined in terms of this fair price, in the manner of Bayes's own definition which explicitly calls the price the expectation of the option. Alternatively, the expectation, or expected value, of an option of the form 'N if A, M if not' was also regarded as definable in terms of probability, equal by definition to the quantity $NP(A) + M[1-P(A)]$. More general options, of the form 'N_1 if A_1, N_2 if A_2, . . . , N_k if A_k, . . .', where the A_i are a set of mutually inconsistent and exhaustive propositions, possibly infinite in number, were also considered, whose expectations were, by extension, equal to $\Sigma N_i P(A_i)$ (in contemporary terminology any such option is called a *random variable* taking the value N_i for all outcomes making A_i true). Clearly, the probability P(A) of a proposition A can be recovered from the knowledge of the expectation of 'N if A', that is, of 'M if A, 0 if not', defined in this way, since the expected value is just $NP(A)$, and hence P(A) is the ratio of this expectation divided by N, à la Bayes.

Gradually through the eighteenth century probability began to be identified as the more basic concept, and expectation as the derivative one, with expectations still retaining their earlier interpretation as fair prices for uncertain options, expressed in the appropriate units. This procedure implicitly posed two questions: (i) what are the appropriate units? and (ii), exactly why is the fair price equal to the expected value defined as the sum of the products of the probabilities with the respective payoffs in these 'appropriate' units? Is this an independent axiom or is it derivable from more fundamental assumptions?

We have mentioned the St Petersburg paradox. It was this that suggested to Daniel Bernoulli that the units in question (i) must be utility, or 'value', units and not currency (Bernoulli's paper, (1738) is in Latin; Martin-Löf (1985) provides a critical modern commentary). The 'paradox' concerns the following gambling game. A fair coin is repeatedly tossed until a head occurs, when the game stops. The payoff is 2^n ducats if the head occurs at the nth toss. That the coin is fair means that the 'correct' view of the probability of a head at the nth toss is 2^{-n} (you can justify this by regarding the probabilities as implicitly conditional on the coin being fair; I shall discuss this procedure in more detail in the next chapter). Assume that the fair price for receiving this payoff is the expected cash value of the option, '2 ducats if the first toss is a head, 4 ducats if the second is a head, . . . , 2^n ducats if the nth toss is a head, . . .'. This expectation is equal to $1 + 1 + 1 + 1 + \ldots$, i.e. to infinitely many, ducats. But (so it seemed to Daniel Bernoulli, and indeed to virtually everyone else) no rational person would ever contemplate paying more than a finite amount, and not even an especially large one, for the option.

Bernoulli's solution to the problem was not to dispense with the idea that expectations determine fair prices, but to claim that expected *utility* not expected cash-value was the relevant expectation, where the utility u(x) of an additional x ducats (or any other currency) over an additional fortune of a ducats increases increasingly slowly compared with x. Bernoulli's suggestion was that the rate of increase of u(x) was actually proportional to $1/(x + a)$, which implies that u(x) is itself proportional to $\log(x + a)$. It is actually a linear function of $\log(x + a)$ but the constant can be taken to be 0, and so by adjusting the base of the logarithm we can take u(x) to be just $\log(x + a)$. This seems to solve the St Petersburg problem. To make the calculation simple suppose $a = 0$. Substituting $\log(x)$ for x in the expected value calculation (assuming a zero initial fortune) yields not infinity but a finite quantity of the order of $\Sigma i/2^i$ (= 2).

An obvious problem with Daniel Bernoulli's solution, which, however, he did not seem to have noticed, is that suitably readjusting the payoffs brings the problem back again, even with the payoffs measured in his utility units. Thus, instead of paying 2^i ducats on the appearance of the first head at the ith toss (if a head appears at all), now pay 2^i itself raised to the power of 2: using Bernoulli's logarithmic utility function the problem now reappears in virtually its original form (exactly its original form if the logarithms are to the base 2), with an expected utility of infinity. The problem with logarithmic measures of utility is that they are unbounded above, and the St Petersburg problem shows that this should not be a feature of any account which is to explain how individuals rank their preferences for gambles with large enough payoffs. So Bernoulli's theory did not satisfactorily answer question (i). It did not answer (ii) at all: Bernoulli simply took over the expected utility principle, but completely failed to explain why it should be adopted.

However, these questions seem at any rate to some extent answered with Ramsey's demonstration that utility itself is merely the projection onto a suitable numerical scale of one's qualitative preference ordering, and that, so long as they satisfy minimal consistency constraints, the subject's preferences among uncertain options are reflected on the utility scale in terms of the corresponding numerical ordering of their expected utilities. Ramsey's work was not fully recognized in the wider mathematical community until much later, and before it did the American statistician L. J. Savage had more or less independently proved Ramsey's results, giving systematic proofs where Ramsey had only given proof-sketches, and in a mathematical setting both more general and more closely related to the formal development of probability theory that by that time had become standard (Savage 1954). Also, Ramsey's system depends crucially on the existence of what he called an 'ethically neutral' proposition, that is, one whose truth-value is not regarded as having independent value in itself, and, as we noted, his explicit definition of probability is merely a reformulation of the expected utility principle. Savage's system does not need an ethically neutral proposition to exist, and it generates in a more organic way both the expected utility principle and a unique probability function that is shown to be determined implicitly by the agent's preference relation (this, like the existence of a utility function unique up to positive affine transformations, is proved by means of a so-called representation theorem).

As a result, it was Savage's axiomatization of subjective utility and probability that became canonical. These results were not the end of the story about utility, however: that is still far from over. Savage's theory has itself come in for a good deal of criticism. Empirical work seems to show fairly entrenched violations of one in particular of

Savage's postulates, the so-called Sure Thing principle,[2] while the conceptual distinction between acts and states independent of those acts, which underlies Savage's theory, has also been sharply questioned. Jeffrey (1965), Anscombe and Aumann (1963), and others have developed alternative accounts, and the work still goes on to develop a theory that answers all objections. Discussion of these developments, interesting though they are, is beyond the scope of this book, and for further information the reader is advised to consult the collection of Gärdenfors and Sahlin (1988).

Despite the fact that a wholly satisfactory account of utility has yet to be given, many continue to prefer to develop subjective probability entirely within a utility framework. On the other hand, it is easy to exaggerate the force of the objections, diminishing marginal utility of money etc., to a non-utility based account like the one I have given, in terms of betting odds fair in the sense of giving neither side an advantage. To evade the standard objections one only has to think of a notion of advantage that does not fall prey to them, and there is more than one. For example, there is long run gain. It is perfectly sensible to consider whether you believe that at the given odds one party would be likely to enjoy a long run gain were the bet to be repeated over and over again in the same circumstances. That may not be physically possible but there is nothing to stop you considering the counterfactual possibility, just as you can consider the possibility of the coin which just landed heads having instead landed tails. Indeed, were there an appropriate probability distribution, for the sort of two-valued bet considered here with a finite stake, the expected value is not infinite. Neither is the variance. That being the case, there is a very high chance that in uncorrelated repetitions with the same probability eventually the long-run net gain of both bettors would approach its expected value zero. Of course there can be no presumption that these conditions are met with in the general case of an arbitrary bet, but that doesn't really matter. If one analyses the way one does in fact prescribe fair odds, and people do this all the time without worrying about the sorts of objections above, it is nearly always in such pseudo-objective terms.

As Hellman has pointed out, we can make the divorce between value and your fair odds complete by making the stake any quantity

<hr/>

[2] This states that if one act is preferred to another on the assumption some proposition B is true, and they have the same consequences if B is false, then the same preference ranking holds overall, whether B is true or false.

which has no connotation of value whatever, just so long as there is a natural quantitative measure of it which is suitably divisible: sand or manure, he suggests, would do just as well as money (1997: 195) if we construe null advantage simply as a zero expected gain. Here I shall just assume that people are accustomed to registering uncertainties as fair odds in bets, whatever the stake or its constitution, and take these odds to be indicators of their degrees of belief.

Undecidable Truth-Values

There are a few other loose ends to be tied. One is the way the Bayesian theory is to apply to the general hypotheses of science, particularly physics. Since we are developing this theory with the problem of induction ultimately in mind, one of the most important applications of this machinery from our point of view is going to be to such hypotheses. But now we have a problem. For the truth of general scientific hypotheses will typically transcend any finite set of observations; yet if the proposition A is such a hypothesis, how can we meaningfully speak of a probability for A determined by Bayes's discounting method? If A is true its truth will never be known, and so the promise to receive N units of currency, or utility, on A's truth becoming known is an empty one, for which nobody in their right mind would pay anything at all. On the other hand, your degree of belief in a general scientific hypothesis is not necessarily zero: such hypotheses are not contradictions, and any theory proposing to measure actual uncertainty should be able to accommodate non-zero degrees of belief in them. But this seems to imply that Bayes's definition of probability will not, as it was intended to, reveal your true estimate of the probability of such a hypothesis.

Some people have seen in this a fundamental if not insuperable obstacle to the application of Bayes's machinery to the evaluation of scientific hypotheses (e.g. Gillies 1998: 154); perhaps surprisingly, there is no problem at all. To see why, or rather why not, bear in mind that the betting scenario is merely what is called an *elicitation procedure*, a convenient imaginary exercise whose function is to calibrate a scale for uncertainty in the unit interval, one which will be useful for subsequently testing the consistency of its degrees so measured. I should stress that you yourself are not being asked to engage in any such transaction, or indeed perform any action at all. It is actually rather important that you are not an actor in this drama, since we do not want to confuse your evaluations with irrelevant considerations of how much you can afford to lose, whether you have some principled objection to betting, or whatever. The price-discounting scenario, in other words, is merely a thought-experiment with which to measure your uncertainty.[3] Obviously possibilities which by their nature may remain forever undecided do not fit well in this model. What can be done about them? There are a number of possibilities. One is just to add a mythical Decider to the dramatis personae. There is nothing in principle wrong in doing this, since the whole exercise is imaginary anyway. Another is to compare your degree of belief in such an undecidable hypothesis to your degrees of belief in a suitable comparison set of decidable possibilities, for example in those of drawing a white ball from an urn containing black and white balls in various different proportions. And there are other methods as well.

Diffuse Probabilities

There seems to be yet another problematic feature of any procedure for eliciting subjective probabilities, one mentioned earlier in passing and not dwelt on. It is time to dwell on it a little now. In reality, as we noted earlier (Appendix 1, Chapter 4), we seldom if ever have personal probabilities, defined by Bayes's procedure of evaluating uncertain options, which can be expressed by an exact real number. My value for the probability that it will rain some time today is rather vague, and the value 0.7, say, is no more than a very rough approximation. In the Bayesian model the probability function takes real-number values. But if we are trying to use the model to understand agents' actual cognitive decisions, it would seem useful if not mandatory to assume that they have more or less diffuse probabilities—because they mostly if not invariably do in the real world.

---

[3] It is a thought-experiment which there is a great deal of anecdotal and documentary evidence that scientists themselves engage in; compare, for example, Haldane's comment that while he did not believe in the absolute truth of Marxism, 'I only believe that it is near enough to the truth to make it worth while betting my life on it as against any rival theories' (1939). Nor were these empty words: Haldane had distinguished himself as an officer in the Black Watch in the 1914–18 war by feats of conspicuous bravery, and later in his life he frequently performed dangerous scientific experiments on himself.

A parallel objection can be brought, equally successfully (how successfully is something the reader can ponder after reading the rest of this section), against current models of deductive reasoning. This chapter is principally an attempt to show that probabilistic and deductive models are intimately related, suggesting if successful that considerations which prove illuminating in one can be profitably transferred, *mutatis mutandis*, to the other. So ask: what corresponds in deductive models to consistent probability-values? Answer: truth-values. Well, deductive models, or at any rate the standard ones, equally fail to be realistic through incorporating 'sharp' truth-values, or what comes to the same thing, predicates having sharp 'yes'/'no' boundaries. Thus, it is assumed in standard deductive logic that for each predicate Q and individual a in the domain, a definitely has Q or it definitely does not. An equivalent way of stating the assumption is in terms of *characteristic functions*: the characteristic function of Q is a function f_Q on the domain of individuals such that for each a, $f_Q(a) = 1$ (i.e. a has Q) or $f_Q(a) = 0$ (a does not have Q). No intermediate values are permitted. And this apparatus is used to model reasoning in natural languages which by nature are highly unsharp, except in the very special circumstances when technical vocabularies are employed. There are actually good functional reasons why natural predicates are not sharp: their flexibility in extending beyond known cases is an indispensable feature of their adaptive success. Not surprisingly the modelling of these languages by artificially sharp ones results in 'paradoxes' of the Sorites type (whose classic exemplar is the paradox of the Heap: one grain of sand does not constitute a heap, and if any given number of grains do not constitute a heap then neither would the addition of one more grain; hence by mathematical induction no finite number of grains of sand can ever form a heap, which is absurd since there certainly are heaps of sand and all of them contain only finitely many grains).

Such unpalatable results have prompted the investigation of more accurate methods of modelling informal deductive reasoning by means of 'vague' predicates, and in particular the use of so-called fuzzy ones, where $\{0,1\}$-valued characteristic functions are replaced by continuous functions, with appropriate rules for their use (for a comprehensive survey see Dubois and Prade 1989). The analogue for humanizing (so to speak) 'sharp' probability values is to replace them with unsharp, interval-valued ones. It is at first sight not obvious that the point-valued model *can* be weakened to an interval-valued one without losing all its structure. For example: the Dutch Book argument for the probability axioms presupposes that the agent has point-valued degrees of belief. If instead it is merely supposed that the agent's estimate is an interval which only in special cases degenerates into a point, then it may not seem obvious what sort of constraints should apply, if any should at all.

That question was convincingly and comprehensively answered in a paper by the statistician C. A. B. Smith (1961). Suppose the agent specifies only the end-points of an interval for their fair betting quotient. Denote the upper end-point by P^* and the lower by P_*; these respectively are called the agent's *upper and lower probabilities* for the proposition in question. Smith showed by a natural modification of de Finetti's original Dutch Book argument that, where only such intervals are specified, the condition for invulnerability to a Dutch Book is that among others the following constraints must be satisfied:

If $P^* = P_*$ then the function is an ordinary probability function.
$0 \le P_*(A) \le P^*(A) \le 1$.
$P_*(A) = 1 - P^*(-A)$.

If A and B are mutually inconsistent then

$$P_*(A) + P_*(B) \le P_*(A \lor B) \le P^*(A \lor B) \le P^*(A) + P^*(B).$$

So we get a formal theory which reduces naturally to the Bayesian one when the end-points of the intervals coincide. Walley (1991) gives a detailed and comprehensive discussion.

To proceed further let us consider the probabilistic and deductive cases in tandem. In each, given that there is a respectable formal theory closer to the reality to be modelled, are there grounds for adopting a more distant theory when the facts do not seem to warrant one? The answer is one familiar from scientific modelling: getting closer to the reality can lead to a loss of useful information (it is then called *overfitting*). In the probabilistic case the stronger theory can tell us something interesting which the weak theory cannot, namely what the impact of evidence *would be* on a particular prior probability. And this is important because, as I hope the reader will recall, the problem we have been facing all the way through is whether and how evidence in the form of reports of observations should affect estimates of the credibility of hypotheses. In the context of a probabilistic model of uncertain reasoning it is very difficult to answer this and questions like it without using a theory that can say things like 'Suppose the prior value of the probability is x', and then use the machinery of the point-valued probability calculus (in particular Bayes's theorem, as we shall see in the next chapter) to calculate that the posterior value is y. Also one often wants to see just how sensitive y is to x where the data are particularly numerous or varied or both. So we need a fairly strong theory which will tell us things like this; and in the standard mathematical theory of probability we have a very rich theory indeed. At the same time, the model is not too distant from reality; it is quite possible to regard it as a not-unreasonable approximation in many applications, for example where the results obtained are robust across a considerable range of variation in the probability parameters. Many of the limiting theorems, in particular those just mentioned, have this property, as do the sorts of applications we shall consider, in Chapter 8, in the application of the model to informal patterns of scientific reasoning where almost by definition no sharp results would anyway be appropriate or expected.

Very similar considerations apply to the usual formal models of deductive reasoning. There are non-sharp models, considerably investigated, but it is partly the sharpness itself of the more familiar models that explains why they still dominate logical investigations: nearly all the deep results of modern logic, like the completeness theorem for the various formulations of first-order logic, and the limitative theorems of Church, Gödel, Tarski, etc, are derived within 'sharp' models. Much more could be written on this subject, but space and time are limited and enough has, I hope, now been said to convey why sharp models are not the unacceptable departures from a more equivocal reality that at first sight they might seem to be.

Bounded Rationality

Consideration of significant parallels with deductive logic is, the reader has probably gathered by now, one of the *Leitmotive*, if not *the Leitmotiv*, of this book. So many of the allegedly unrealistic features of the Bayesian model which have provoked critical comment are features also possessed by the familiar deductive models, but there they are not thought to merit such a similarly critical response. And that of course is because the deductive models are recognized to depict a formal structure, and not, at any rate straightforwardly, to be descriptive of any empirical reality. So too the Bayesian model depicts another formal structure, that of sound *probabilistic* reasoning, and equally is not intended to describe in any straightforward way what agents actually do.

Another much criticized alleged piece of unrealism in the Bayesian model of uncertain logical reasoning is the fact that the application of some of its rules, like the additivity principle and the axiom that logical truths have probability 1, depend on certain deductive conditions being satisfied. But, so the objection runs, real-world individuals are not logically omniscient. Nor are they all good enough computers to perform all the calculations, which may be very complex, completely or even fairly accurately. Indeed, in principle there is no upper bound to the complexity of the arithmetical calculations that may have to be made in any derivation of a final probability. If this is supposed to be a model of rational behaviour then on the face of it it is a model of perfect logico-mathematical reasoners rather than of us limited sublunary beings. At any rate, we can assume that, if people are rational agents at all, they are only *boundedly rational*; and they frequently make mistakes. So why develop a theory that seems to implicitly deny this?

The answer should need little prompting. To see in the fact that people are only boundedly rational while the model is not a defect of the latter is to misunderstand the function of formal theories like this one. Deductive models are not, for example, charged with assuming infinite memory, though they incorporate a principle of infinite composition: they all assume a class of sentences closed under composition by truth-functional operations and quantification. Or take another formal discipline that also has something to do with correct reasoning: mathematics. When people add and multiply and perform other operations on numbers they do not always do so correctly (nor is this just a human failing: Church's Theorem implies that not even the most superhuman computer can answer every arithmetical question). Nor, for example, can ordinary people usually multiply multi-digit numbers by each other, at any rate correctly. But of course none of this undermines mathematics as a discipline. And logic is a discipline very like mathematics, where by logic I mean both deductive logic and the probabilistic variety of deductive logic we have developed here. These disciplines are simply not intended to model human behaviour in any purely descriptive sense, any more than mathematics is. On the other hand, they can and do appear in explanations of human behaviour, just as it is a reasonable assumption that people are using mathematics, at a higher or lower level, when they make calculations involving numbers. It is logically possible that they might not be, of course: they might be doing something completely different. But it's a good bet that they are using mathematics, or trying to. And there is an additional and very important reason to suppose this over and above noting that the assumption broadly seems to fit the facts: mathematics supplies a canon of correct reasoning about numbers, and these agents know it. We shall return to this point in Chapter 8.

Similarly, deductive and probabilistic logic supply canons of correct deductive and uncertain reasoning. Human beings do not and indeed in principle cannot reproduce all sound deductive or probabilistic reasoning. Human reason, like the human physique, is frail. But human frailty, at any rate in its reasoning faculty, far from invalidating the development of theories of correct reasoning, makes them all the more necessary, as props for the infirm; to err, after all, is human. Perfect reasoners don't need theories of correct reasoning, any more than perfect mathematicians would develop theories of mathematics, except as a recreation.

Conclusion

The rules of Bayesian probability are rules of logic. The idea that there is a logical way of looking at probability is of course hardly new; we saw that Leibniz called the nascent mathematical theory of probability 'a new species of logic'. The work of Ramsey and de Finetti has, I believe, finally brought the programme to fruition. The delay can largely be attributed to the principle of indifference and its gradual discrediting. But there were other reasons. Prominent among these was what turned out to be a fairly long—in time terms—blind alley, involving a quite different logical interpretation of probability initiated by J. M. Keynes (1973), elaborately developed by Carnap (1950, 1952, 1971), and endorsed by Popper (1970), according to which there is some probability *function*, specifically a conditional probability function P, such that where A and B are propositions P(A|B) measures the 'degree to which B entails A'. Despite Carnap's best efforts over twenty or more years, however, no such function could be uncontroversially identified, nor does it seem likely that one ever will. At any rate, the programme has now been largely abandoned, leaving by default chances and subjective probabilities as the only internally coherent and systematic notions which are formally (classical) probabilities.

8

The Logic of Scientific Discovery

Introduction

In 1935 R. A. Fisher published one of his most influential works on scientific methodology, *The Design of Experiments*, intended to inaugurate a revolution—and succeeding—in which the Bayesian ideas which had until recently provided the orthodox account of scientific inference would be finally swept away and replaced with his own falsificationist theory of randomization and significance tests. It was in that book that the tea-tasting lady made her appearance. Fisher's revolution was successful because the Bayesian theory seemed either inconsistent, if it incorporated the principle of indifference, or merely subjective if it didn't, while Fisher's own theory seemed by contrast objective, logical, and widely and straightforwardly applicable. The tea-tasting lady became the Marianne of the Fisher revolution, another emblematic female personifying the austerer virtues of the new regime against the decadence of the old (the greatest spokesman of Bayesianism up to the turn of the nineteenth century was, appropriately, a French nobleman, the Marquis de Laplace[1]).

A year earlier than the publication of Fisher's tract there had appeared another book, *Logik der Forschung*, published by a young Austrian philosopher, Karl Popper, proposing the same sort of methodology, and in very much the same terms (see Chapter 5, pp. 94–100), as had Fisher, though Fisher implicitly restricted his proposals to statistics, whereas Popper's were applied principally to deterministic science. Popper is usually credited as the sole author of the doctrine of falsificationism, but Fisher, as we noted earlier, deserves equality of status on this point (we can also note that falsificationism outside statistics never achieved the monolithic authority it achieved within).

---

[1] His noble pedigree was not *ancien régime* though; it was created by Napoleon.

Like Fisher, Popper was also a scourge of inductive probability, namely nineteenth-century Bayesianism. They had an easy target. However, Bayesianism has since been shorn of the particular feature—the principle of indifference—which had made it such a fertile producer of paradox, and reborn as a theory of consistent reasoning equipped, as any good logic should be, with its own soundness and completeness theorems. And the falsificationist revolution has not withstood destructive criticism: even its stronghold in statistics finally seems to be crumbling. The main concern of this book is less to promote the counter-revolution, however, than to see how the New Bayesianism established by Ramsey and de Finetti bears on Hume's Problem. Hume's Problem at bottom is that of evaluating uncertainty in a sound way. In Bayesian probability we now have at least the machinery for doing this: it supplies the logic of consistent reasoning involving a numerical measure of uncertainty—but *no more*. The rider is of the utmost importance. If the part of Hume's argument about the limitations of 'probable reasoning' is correct, then any satisfactory theory of uncertainty must satisfy an important *weakness* constraint (a weakness constraint sounds odd but there it is): it must not tell us what the uncertainties of contingent propositions are. And indeed this one does not: unconditional probability distributions are exogenous to the theory. For so long seen as a problem for the Bayesian theory, *this indeterminacy can now be seen as natural and inevitable*, entirely appropriate in a theory of uncertainty which respects Hume's sceptical argument. Matthews puts the point nicely:

the axioms of probability, via Bayes's Theorem, show that subjectivity cannot be wrung out of the scientific process for the simple reason that it is mathematically *ineluctable*. Much as we might want to, it is *impossible* to obtain the value of Prob(theory|data) without having some value for the prior probability Prob(theory). (1998: 19; italics in original)

That's the bad news. The good news is that we are not deluding ourselves when we think we can still make sound inductive inferences. This is a solution of the problem of induction which is analogous to—in their different forms—Kant's and Hume's revolutionary solutions of the problem of causation: both proceed by taking causation out of objects, so to speak, and putting it into people: in Kant's theory it is a condition of coherent thought and in Hume's it reflects a propensity to form expectations. In the theory I shall propose here, sound induction has nothing to do with coming to a correct understanding of the way the world is structured, but is merely the result of applying a constraint on beliefs which maintains their internal consistency. But in so doing it supplies the foundation for inductive reasoning in science.

It might be objected (and indeed it has been) that science is not about people's beliefs. It is about truth; so a theory of consistent belief cannot in principle provide an account of scientific inference. Powerful and highly influential advocacy for this view was supplied by Fisher himself: 'advocates of inverse probability [Bayesian probability] seem forced to regard mathematical probability . . . as measuring merely psychological tendencies, theorems respecting which are useless for scientific purposes' (Fisher 1947: 6–7). But Fisher's inference is a non sequitur: Bayesian probabilities might be subjective objects, but the rules they must obey to be consistent are anything but subjective; and so far from being 'useless for scientific purposes' these supply a wholly *objective* theory of inductive inference; so objective, indeed, that they are infringed on pain of making genuine and possibly costly mistakes. The sanction is not just the (usually remote) theoretical possibility of being Dutch Booked were you to bet indiscriminately at your fair betting quotients (there is no presumption in the earlier discussion that you will and certainly not that you ought to do this), but those arising in general from accepting fallacious arguments with probabilities: we have only to look at the Harvard Medical School test to see what these might be. Moreover, probabilistic inconsistency is as self-stultifying as deductive: as we saw in the previous chapter, inconsistency means that you differ *from yourself* in the uncertainty value you attach to propositions, just as deductive inconsistency means that you differ from yourself in the truth-values you attach to them.

These considerations answer an objection of Max Albert. Commenting on the attempt by some (including myself) to find instructive parallels with deductive logic, Albert finds what he thinks is a telling *disanalogy*, precisely on this question of sanctions:

Logical [deductive] consistency serves a purpose: theories cannot possibly be true if they are inconsistent . . . ; thus, if one wants truth, logical consistency is necessary (but not, of course, sufficient). An analogous argument in favor of Bayesianism would have to point out some advantage of Bayesianism unavailable to those relying on non-probabilistic beliefs and deductive logic alone. Such an argument is missing. (Albert 1997: 29)

This is fairly thoroughly wrong. The two principal assertions here are both incorrect. First, logical consistency is *not* necessary for truth. False statements are well known to have true consequences, lots of them, and inconsistent statements the most of all since every statement follows from a contradiction. Current science may well be inconsistent (many distinguished scientists think it is), but it has nevertheless provided a rich bounty of truths. So much for deductive inconsistency. Secondly, arguments for trying to maintain probabilistic inconsistency have been produced many times (and not just by me here). But mine, I think, will do.

It is conceivable (anything consistent is conceivable) that even these considerations still may not be enough to change attitudes formed in ways which find it difficult to stomach an account of scientific method founded on anything at all to do with mere *belief*. But those attitudes are misinformed. For ultimately we are talking about *credibility*, the credibility of accounts of what there is in the universe and how it behaves, and how and according to what criteria observational evidence increases or decreases that credibility. It is no good saying that it is not credibility that is the goal of science but truth (as does Miller 1994). That is true but beside the point, for it does not argue that considerations of credibility are redundant. Indeed, on the contrary, they are indispensable. Only if truth-values were revealed unequivocally would criteria of credibility be redundant. But truth-values are seldom if ever revealed unequivocally: we can generally only conjecture them. We therefore need to know how credible our various conjectures are, and for that we need a theory of credibility.

This is where we came in. Hume showed that such a theory could not without circularity hope to make justified assertions of the form 'this conjecture has such and such credibility given the observational data', where the conjecture is consistent with but transcends the data. Hume has shown us that a successful theory of credibility should *not* be strong enough to make such categorical assertions without equally strong assumptions. It is a situation we should anyway be familiar with in a theory that purports to be a theory of sound reasoning, for there is already an extant well-known such theory, one of ancient pedigree, whose failure to deliver categorical assertions we are familiar and even happy with: deductive logic. By general agreement arrived at long ago, the valid arguments of deductive logic are all representable in the *conditional* form 'if such and such statements are true then necessarily so is this'. As Ramsey, emphasizing the similarly conditional nature of probabilistic inferences, clearly puts it: 'This is simply bringing probability into line with ordinary formal logic, which does not criticize premises but merely declares that certain conclusions are the only ones consistent with them' (1926: 91).

It might be replied that deduction has not for a long time pretended to be a theory of discovery. Science does discover, and yet we are told (by me) that the inferences it makes, and which have yielded such a rich harvest of empirical knowledge, are inferences made according to a logic whose only criterion of soundness is the purely internal one of consistency. We come back to Miller's question: Where does, for that matter *can*, truth come into this? And if it doesn't, what is the point of such a logic of science: doesn't it, indeed, miss the point of science? One is reminded (to be precise an anonymous referee was reminded who reminded me) of the following celebrated passage from Hume's *Treatise*:

Let us chase our imagination to the heavens, or to the utmost limits of the universe; we never really advance a step beyond ourselves, nor can conceive any kind of existence, but those perceptions, which have appear'd in that narrow compass. This is the universe of the imagination, nor have we any idea but what is there produc'd. (I. ii. vi)

This is, however, Humean *metaphysics*, certainly not licensed by the position which elsewhere he advances with such dexterity. It is quite possible that we do 'advance a step beyond ourselves', even many steps, merely that we shall never have warrant to claim that we do. More generally, it doesn't follow that because the logic of inductive reasoning is bound by internal criteria of consistency anyone who applies it is doomed to remain in a Wittgensteinian fly-bottle of his or her own construction. Probabilities may be, and usually will be in these applications, probabilities *of truth*. So there you are: truth has reassuringly got back in (though it was never really out). Hume's other point was that inductive inferences require inductive assumptions, and it is quite possible that the ones we habitually employ are reliable assumptions. Darwin's theory, whose possible truth is not in any way impugned by Hume's argument, suggests that in the main they are.

The justification for obedience to an essentially non-ampliative logic for scientific inference is one we have already made. It prevents inconsistency, and we know—from a page or so back—why that is to be avoided. It is now high time to see how this particular logic bears on inductive reasoning.

A Model of Inductive Reasoning

The Bayesian theory supplies a *model* of inductive reasoning. When we want to theorize about a domain we often do so by constructing suitable models of it. There seems no good reason to prohibit *sound reasoning* itself from being the subject of this activity. Indeed, there are already such models, and familiar ones. Systems of deductive logic are models of sound deductive reasoning. This does not mean that they are models of deductive reasoning as people actually do it, soundly or not, but of sound deductive reasoning *in itself*. What is that? It is what all deductively valid inferences have in common by virtue of being deductively valid, whether anybody ever made or could make them. It is also what all deductively consistent sets of sentences, sets thought of and sets not thought of, and sets that in principle never could be thought of, have in common by virtue of being deductively consistent. What makes the theories we have of these things models is that they are constructed in a mathematically rather idealized way, over 'languages' that people would not generally think of as languages in any ordinary way. In the previous chapter I have tried to construct, or possibly reconstruct, the Bayesian theory as a model of sound uncertain reasoning in a similar way, and in this chapter shall try to show that that model also provides a good model of sound inductive reasoning, that is, a model of how the credibility of conjectures is enhanced, diminished, or unaffected by evidence, good both in the sense of providing an illuminating explanatory model of scientific reasoning, and in showing how it is possible to make sound inductive inferences.

In fact, we should strictly be talking of Bayesian *models* in the plural, since for different purposes there are different ways of specifying the model. In some cases, where the mathematics is more subtle (as in the convergence-of-opinion theorems we shall talk about later), the precise mathematical specification is important; in others, we can safely take the rather rough-and-ready approach to the mathematics taken in Chapter 4. There are also large-scale and small-scale models, the latter corresponding to what economists call 'small worlds', and analogous to what physicists call closed systems: in these, attention is confined to a class of possibilities describable within some restricted vocabulary, for example that describing the possible outcomes of an experiment, which in the extreme case can be just the labels '1' and '0' (standing for 'as predicted' and 'other than as predicted'), or sequences, possibly infinite sequences of these, corresponding to sequences of repetitions of such an experiment (we have already looked at restricted state-spaces of this form in Chapter 4, and shall look at some more later). There is no assumption in such restrictions that the situation modelled is completely independent of features external to it (as it is never assumed that closed systems are ever truly closed), merely that it is independent enough according to whatever background information is being assumed; and in general some non-empty background information is assumed. For convenience I shall nevertheless continue to talk of *the* Bayesian model; this can be regarded as defined in context.

These remarks might seem to add up to an endorsement of the view about the nature of scientific theories called *the semantic view*. According to this, scientific theories are best not looked at as sets of statements, but as collections of models (Suppe 1989, van Fraassen 1980: ch. 3) are extended defences of the semantic view). Fortunately, we need not enter into a discussion of the often tortuous byways of this controversy, since the observations above are entirely neutral on the issue. I have merely described the collection of all Bayesian models as collectively the Bayesian model, and that is simply a matter of terminology. I do not myself subscribe to the semantic view, preferring to believe instead that, to adapt Kant's famous aphorism, theories without models are empty and models without theories are blind: that is to say, the constitution of the class of models tends to be constrained, though not of course determined, by the theory, and not vice versa, though there are cases where the model may well suggest an extension of the theory.

The present case is a good example. The theory/models distinction roughly corresponds to the intension/extension one. The Bayesian theory is—again, roughly—the intension whose corresponding extension is the class of Bayesian models. The latter are no more than a certain class of real-valued functions on suitably extensive classes of propositions. The theory can be identified with the entire process of reasoning that proposes a notion of consistency for evaluations of uncertainty, at any rate when these are measured in an appropriate scale, and proceeds to explain why these evaluations must obey the axioms of probability, and why these axioms are complete in an important sense. The class of Bayesian models is this theory *in extenso*, and includes those which no person's belief-system even in principle could ever exemplify, for they would have to be able to decide purely deductive problems that are known to be beyond the capacity of any digital computer, even one equipped with infinite memory and with no upper bound on the time given it to complete any task.

Nevertheless these caveats do not prevent the models functioning, in some interesting and useful way, in explanatory contexts. Again we turn for enlightenment to the deductive analogy. The formal languages of deductive logic are usually infinite (false for any natural language); they allow composition to an arbitrary degree (false for any natural language); they obey universally strict bivalence (false for any natural language); they assume truth-functional definitions of all the connectives (false for any natural language); and so on. Perhaps paradoxically in view of all this, often these models were the result of observing some form of 'best practice'. For example, the German mathematician and logician Gentzen arrived at one very influential such model, natural deduction, now a standard feature of textbooks of formal logic, by analysing the structure of Euclid's reasoning in the *Elements*. But there is only the appearance of paradox, for many of these features arise merely through following the fruitful methodological rule of striving for generality. The cases arising in practice are then merely suitable restrictions of the model. Other departures from the limitations of practical reality are permitted for not dissimilar reasons: extreme precision, for example, on the ground that practice is akin to seeing 'through a glass darkly', as the Platonizing apostle Paul put it via the translators of the King James Bible, the attempt by imperfect minds to mimic something more perfect. The fact that the model embodies additional structure that the field of application doesn't, or doesn't embody some of the structure that it does, is excused on the ground that the features the model attempts to capture—for both deductive and probabilistic models this is some underlying criterion of soundness—are broadly invariant under their addition or subtraction: the additions or subtractions are there (or not) to facilitate a theoretical treatment.

Given the disclaimers, the target of Bayesian explanations is emphatically not what goes on in people's heads when they are doing what they might call inductive reasoning. Having said that, however, we do want the model to explain, if it can, why appropriate samples of human reasoning are, or are approximately, samples of sound inductive reasoning. If a piece of actual reasoning is representable in the model as consistent, that is, sound probabilistic reasoning, then it is explained as such in much the same way that we can sometimes explain as sound deductive reasoning samples of allegedly deductive reasoning when we can represent them in a corresponding model, like that of first-order logic. This of course means that the model has to be *applicable*, which correspondingly means that it has to have a suitable amount of representative capacity—it has to be able to represent the sorts of *things* that human beings reason about, like data, hypotheses, etc. This we know it can do. It can also do other things, in particular one thing we have been concerned about: given suitable initial conditions (I shall specify what these are shortly), not only can inductive reasoning be represented as sound reasoning, but *the model(s) tells us that to reason soundly in those circumstances is necessarily to reason inductively.*

Since the previous chapters of this book have in their various ways been a defence of Humean inductive scepticism, and in particular Chapter 4 was an extended denial that there is any probabilistic solution of the traditional problem of induction, this pronouncement might sound somewhat strange if not downright paradoxical. How can Humean inductive scepticism be maintained simultaneously with the claim not only that there are sound inductive inferences, but that to reason soundly in a wide variety of circumstances one *must* reason inductively? It all sounds very puzzling, at best. It may come as a surprise therefore to learn that we are already in possession of all the pieces required to construct an answer to the conundrum; all that remains is to assemble them correctly.

We can make a start right now. Recall Theorem 1, in Chapter 4, that if $1 > P(H) > 0$, $0 < P(E) < 1$ and H entails E modulo some initial conditions assigned probability 1 by P then $P(H|E) > P(H)$, i.e. H is inductively confirmed by E. And recall Theorem 2 from the same chapter. These theorems state that, given suitable initial conditions, in this case distributions of prior belief, the Bayesian model explains inductive reasoning as a condition of maintaining the internal consistency of an agent's beliefs. Consistency with Humean inductive scepticism is maintained by noting that the inferences are sound, but also that they depend on a premisses describing suitable belief-distributions. The situation is, *mutatis mutandis*, the same as that in deductive logic: you only get out some transformation of what you put in. Bacon notoriously castigated the contemporary version of deductive logic, Aristotelian syllogistic, for what he perceived as a crucial failing: deductive inference does not enlarge the stock of factual knowledge. But Bacon's condemnation has with the passage of centuries become modulated into a recognition of what is now regarded as a if not the fundamental property of logically sound inferences which, as we see, probabilistic reasoning shares, and in virtue of which it is an authentic logic: *sound inference does not beget new factual content.*

This is by no means all there is to inductive reasoning in the Bayesian model: fortunately, since there is a rich variety of inferential principles and strategies usually regarded as falling under that heading. We shall see in very general terms how these are modelled, and where any problematic issues are located. More detailed treatments exist in what has grown over the last quarter-century into a very extensive literature (consisting of legion discussions and articles in statistics and philosophy of science journals, together with extended book-length discussions, for example Good 1950, Horwich 1982, Howson and Urbach 1993, Jeffrey 1992, Maher 1993). In addition, a variety of results has been proved which both extend the scope of the model (for example, building on earlier work by Levi, Maher 1993 constructs a theory of expected epistemic utility on the basis of which he defines a notion of the verisimilitude of a false theory) and advance our understanding of the phenomena the theory deals with. Needless to say, this is reassuring both from the point of view of endorsing intuitively compelling strategies and from that of giving some indirect support to the model itself.

A noteworthy feature of all these model-explanations is that the assumptions which have to be made to generate the results figure explicitly in the reasoning. In Bayesian, that is, probabilistic, logic assumptions which figure in an inference are signified somewhat differently than in the deductive case. There they simply figure as undischarged lines in a proof. The canonical form of an inductive assumption, on the other hand, is the assignment of an initial probability to a corresponding proposition or propositions, which will characteristically be employed with other such assumptions in the computation of some target probability. For example, the decision to consider just a few explanatory accounts as serious contenders figures in the Bayesian model as the decision, which must be made if the answers are to be forthcoming, to assign just these appreciable prior probability. Readers of non-Bayesian methodological texts will appreciate characteristic transitions from the statement that some reasonably abstract hypotheses are to be tested, to model-assumptions whose adoption is usually defended in a more or less hand-waving way, leaving the questioning reader puzzled about the epistemic status of results obtained on their basis. This seems especially noticeable in statistics, where statistical models, and data distributions based on them, are frequently introduced with the minimum of justification—or none at all:

Where do probability-models come from? To judge by the resounding silence over this question on the part of most statisticians, it seems highly embarrassing. In general the theoretician is happy to accept that his abstract probability triple $(S, \mathfrak{F}, P(\,.\,))$ was found under a gooseberry bush, while the applied statistician's model 'just growed'. (Dawid 1982)

In a Bayesian inference there is, of course, also plenty of scope for hand-waving: the difference is that, since the inferences drawn appear in the form of calculations, crucial assumptions tend to appear explicitly, and, most importantly, in a way that makes it evident exactly how the final probability depends on these: Bayesian inferences are *epistemically transparent*. But that is enough by way of general preamble. We should now look at the principal features of the Bayesian model of inductive reasoning, usually called *Bayesian confirmation theory*.

A Beginner's Guide to Bayesian Confirmation Theory

According to the Bayesian theory the probability axioms express a complete *logic* of credibility judgements. They become a model of inductive inference in so far as they determine in what conditions the credibility of H is affected by the assumption that E is true. As we saw in Chapter 4, in a probabilistic theory the credibility of H on the assumption that E is true is rendered by the conditional probability $P(H|E)$, where H can in principle be any meaningful hypothesis; it might, for example, even be a hypothesis saying that some scientific theory T is true only within certain limits, or for a certain time, or that T will continue to be empirically adequate, etc. In the model P is not any particular person's personal probability: it is a generic, consistent degree-of-belief function. In fact, for the reasons we have noted above, it will not be any person's belief function.

Nevertheless the model must be able to represent in some adequate way a notion of evidence and the way evidence can support or undermine a hypothesis. To the extent that any factual report is evidence for or against a hypothesis depends on the informational context in which it is situated.[2] A large book found in a street is by itself not evidence that Jones killed Smith, but given the further information that Smith was killed by a blow to the head with a large object, in that particular street, and that the book was damaged and had Smith's blood and Jones's fingerprints on it, it is. Evidence issues in the enhancement or diminution of the credibility of a hypothesis,[3] and this capacity will be determined only in the context of some specified ambient body of information. This rather trivial observation will nevertheless turn out to be very important, for it contains the solution to a problem that has adorned the literature for some time: the so-called 'problem of old evidence', which we shall discuss in due course.

Independently of particular context, the model also of course incorporates a set of general, logical, laws—that is to say, the probability axioms—governing the behaviour of the function $P(H|E)$; indeed, Bayesian confirmation theory is little more than the examination of its properties for various 'interesting' instances of H and E. The most famous tool for analysing its behaviour of is contained in the eponymous consequence of the probability axioms, *Bayes's theorem*, whose acquaintance we have already made. Here we shall be more interested in a particular rewriting of that theorem which displays $P(H|E)$ explicitly as a function of $P(H)$ and a term $P(E|-H)/P(E|H)$ depending on E, H and –H, the so-called *Bayes Factor in favour of –H against H*,[4] call it f:

$$P(H|E) = \frac{P(H)}{P(H) + f P(-H)} \qquad (1)$$

(see Chapter 3, p. 57). $P(-H)$ of course is equal to $1 - P(H)$.

The evident dependence of $P(H|E)$ on the prior factor $P(H)$, though a simple and elementary property of the Bayesian model, is

---

[2] This is rather analogous to Frege's well-known context principle: a word has meaning only in the context of a sentence.

[3] This is not intended to be a definition of 'evidence'; drugs can do the same thing.

[4] Good (1950) tells us that this quantity was called 'the factor in favour of –H' by the eminent logician, mathematician, and code-breaker of the Second World War, Alan Turing. 'Bayes factor' seems to have been Good's own contribution.

one whose importance cannot be exaggerated, since it implies that *evidential data cannot alone determine the credibility of a hypothesis.* This feature distinguishes the Bayesian account from practically every other model of scientific reasoning—to the detriment of the latter. Because these accounts fail to take the prior factor explicitly into account, concentrating instead only on functions of the likelihoods P(E|H) and P(E| – H), they cannot cope even with such a simple problems as the grue problem, which is why I laid such stress on it in the earlier chapters.

Now we shall turn up the resolution a little. (1) shows that as long as P(H) is greater than zero, the posterior probability of H is sensitive to the evidence E through the Bayes factor, and will in general change with changing E. Of course, as we saw earlier, in the discussion of 'dogmatic' versus 'non-dogmatic' prior probabilities (Chapter 4, p. 70), if P(H) is zero then P(H|E) will not be sensitive to *f* at all, for P(H|E) itself will be zero if P(E) is non-zero. Nevertheless, just so long as P(H) is non-zero (1) asserts that, as a *condition of consistency*, the evidence be allowed some weight in determining H's credibility. How it does so depends on the Bayes factor, *f*. This is non-negative but unbounded above. A little experimentation shows that P(H|E) increases as P(H) increases and as *f* decreases. This implies that, other things being equal, you will be more confident about H the more confident you were initially—which seems like common sense (the great Laplace remarked that the Bayesian theory—though he did not call it that—was just 'good sense reduced to a calculus', *le bon sens réduit au calcul*. Also, other things being equal, the less likely E would have been if H were false, the smaller *f* is and the larger the posterior probability, while the larger P(E|H) is, and, other things being equal, the smaller *f* is, and the larger the posterior probability.

To get a better grasp of the significance of all this, suppose E would have been just as likely to be observed had H been false as had it been true. Does the occurrence of E in those circumstances tell us anything about H? Intuitively nothing at all: if H is neutral on the subject of E then E's occurrence tells us nothing about H. This is just what (1) tells us too: if P(E| – H) = P(E|H) then *f* = 1, and since P(H) + P(–H) = 1, we infer from (1) that P(H|E) = P(H), that is, E has not changed the credibility of H from what it was before. Now suppose that the probability of E's truth if H is false is zero but that E has some non-zero probability of being true if H is true. Intuitively, in this case the truth of H must be certain given the truth of E (assuming, as before, that its and E's prior probability are non-zero). Going over to formal probabilities this means that $P(E| - H) = 0$ and $P(E|H) > 0$, and so $f = 0$. It immediately follows from (1) that $P(H|E) = 1$.

The case where the Bayes factor f is not zero or one or infinity is the most interesting, and the one most likely to arise in practice (all that is meant by this is that it is this case that most closely mirrors the situations in working science), and it is now the relative magnitudes of the two factors, Bayes factor and prior, that will determine $P(H|E)$. A very small Bayes factor can be dominated by a sufficiently small prior to leave the posterior probability small; we have already seen evidence of this in the Harvard Medical School test where the criteria of small f were admirably fulfilled but nevertheless H ('the subject has the disease') was still most unlikely to be true, because its prior probability was so extremely small that the smallness of f was insufficient to raise the posterior probability to anything appreciable. All this is not to say that the Bayes factor is unimportant, however. Quite the contrary: other things being equal, the farther from unity f is, the more informative is E. In particular, if f is infinite then, supposing $P(H) > 0$, $P(H|E) = 0$ and H is in effect refuted by E, while if f is zero then $P(H|E) = 1$. In other words, a principle of good experimental design means creating conditions in which these extremes can be best approached, if they can be approached at all. To a great extent that will depend on the hypothesis H and also on what we take as acceptable background information, but we can use the model to give some general indications that correspond with our intuitive criteria. One rather obvious consideration is that if H is deterministic we could make a useful start by looking for experimental situations in which there is a possible outcome E such that $P(E|H)$ is fairly close to 1, that is, where H makes more or less definite predictions. Such an outcome should not be too a priori unlikely either, but this is automatically taken care of by the fact that we have assumed that $P(H)$ is not too small, for if H entails E we know that $P(E) \geq P(H)$.

Suppose we want to construct the experiment in such a way that we can be sure beforehand that $P(E| - H)$ will be small, that is that, in the terminology of diagnostic tests, the likelihood of getting a false-positive result is minimized. How do we do this? To look at the matter informally at first, we try to see whether we can translate the informal reasoning into constraints we can build into the model. To conclude that E is very unlikely to be true if H is false intuitively means that every possible factor that might cause E to be true other than H is eliminated in advance by the experimental design. Well, we can't set out to eliminate every possible factor, since we may not and generally will not know how to identify all of them. But we can set out to try to minimize the influence of the ones we either do know about, or suspect. So, looking at these known or suspected factors unrelated to the truth of H, call them $\{C_i\}$, we want the design to be such that if H_i says that the positive E of the experiment would also have been expected as a consequence of factor C_i, then the probability of H_i being true is to be as small as possible. So, if $P(E|H_i)$ is itself fairly considerable, we want $P(H_i)$, the probability that C_i could have caused the outcome, to be very small. Equivalently, the experiment should be such that the product $P(E|H_i)P(H_i)$ is very small for all H_i other than H. Now a little juggling with the probability axioms shows that $P(E|-H)$ is equal to a constant times the sum of the factors $P(E|H_i)P(H_i)$ over all the mutually exclusive H_i such that $P(H_i) > 0$; i.e. $P(E|-H)$ is proportional to just that same sum of products $P(E|H_i)P(H_i)$! Hence we have shown that, given the body of background information we have accepted which describes the class of plausible alternative explanations of a positive result, designing a test so that the result if it occurs cannot plausibly be attributed to any of them *just is* to design a test with as small a $P(E|-H)$ as possible. Recall from Chapter 3 that this is the intuition behind the No-Miracles argument, and from Chapter 5 that it is the principle which the Neyman-Pearson theory of powerful tests attempted to embody—but unsuccessfully.

We can summarize these observations in an elegant formula. The Bayes factor in favour of $-H$ against H is $P(E|-H)/P(E|H)$, which we can write as $f(-H)$; the reason for omitting explicit reference to H will become apparent shortly. We know from the foregoing discussion that we can also write the posterior probability as

$$P(H|E) = \frac{P(H)}{P(H) + \Sigma \dfrac{P(E|H_i)}{P(E|H)} P(H_i)}$$

where $\{H_i\}$ is some exclusive and exhaustive set of alternatives to H. If we now take H itself to be some H_j, the set $\{H_i\}$ is what is called a partition, that is to say a decomposition of the space of possibilities into cells determined by the H_i. Noting that $P(H) = P(H_j)P(E|H_j)/P(E|H_j)$, we can write

$$P(H|E) = \frac{P(H)}{\Sigma f_i P(H_i)}$$

where $f_i = P(E|H_i)/P(E|H_j)$. But $\Sigma f_i P(H_i)$ is the expected value $E(F_{|E})$, relative to the partition $\{H_i\}$, of the random variable $F_{|E}$ which takes the constant value f_i on those possibilities consistent with H_i. So we can write $P(H|E)$ compactly as

$$P(H|E) = \frac{P(H)}{E(F_{|E})}$$

In words, the posterior probability of H is the prior probability of H is inversely proportional to the expected value of Bayes factors against H, with $P(H)$ as the constant of proportionality. It is now immediately apparent that $P(H|E)$ is large if this expected value is small, and that the expected value will be small if and only if, for each alternative H_i to H of non-negligible prior probability, $P(E|H_i)$ is small compared with $P(E|H)$.

That completes the outline structure of the Bayesian model. More detail can be obtained by using principles of the probability calculus to adapt the model to specific problems, and in what follows we shall see what happens when it is applied to some. Before we do so we must exorcize an old demon, though rather less of a demon now than a nuisance: degree of confirmation.

Degree of Confirmation

A question that much exercised some people forty or so years ago, and which we have already briefly touched on, was how to provide a numerical definition of *degree of confirmation*, using some 'appropriate' probability function. Out of this arose disputes some of which generated a good deal of heat if not light. In the 1960s Carnap and Popper were engaged in a particularly acrimonious dispute about whether any of Carnap's allegedly 'logical' probability functions c(h,e) (Carnap's notation; c is formally a conditional probability) could be identified with the degree to which e confirms h. Carnap had after all called c(h,e) a formal explication of degree of confirmation. Popper claimed that various considerations showed that degree of confirmation, or in his terminology degree of corroboration (see above, p. 96), is not a probability at all (Carnap 1950; Popper 1959: 394). Carnap pointed out that c(h,e) was primarily an explication of 'rational degree of belief', and that what Popper was talking about was incremental confirmation. Carnap also believed that the latter was not a probability, but a function of probabilities, and proposed the difference between the posterior and prior probability c(h,e) – c(h,t) where t is a tautology. In our notation here the latter is $P(H|E)$ – $P(H)$. Popper's degree of corroboration function is essentially $P(E|H)$ – $P(E)$, which is not identical to Carnap's function. The situation was further confused by the appearance of alternative explications, notably by Good and Cohen. Good himself considered various possible definitions, all in terms of some suitable probability function (1968).

So which is the 'correct' measure out of these three, or is perhaps some other measure the correct one? It is difficult to say, because there are few transparently essential properties that degree of confirmation should have, though Popper's measure seems immediately ruled out nevertheless because of its incapacity to handle the grue problem. It might be a better strategy to try to fix on some clear desiderata first, and see if these determine the resulting notion anything like uniquely. Good himself employs this strategy, as does Milne (1997) and Howson (1983), all of these people however choosing rather different basic desiderata: perhaps surprisingly, the same function $\log[P(E|H)/P(E)] = \log[P(H|E)/P(H)]$ is uniquely determined by each (unique up to the choice of base of the logarithm). Note that this function is superficially similar to both Popper's and Carnap's simple difference functions, obtained from each or either of them by taking logarithms of the terms in the respective differences.

Does the uniqueness mean that this function is the correct one? That is still far from clear. It might, for example, be regarded as a plausible principle that 'independent' chunks of evidence should be additive in their contribution to the confirmation of H. This condition is not satisfied by $\log[P(E|H)/P(E)]$, but it is by so-called Shafer–Dempster belief functions, which are not even functions of probabilities (Shafer–Dempster functions are based on Shafer's non-additive belief-functions,[5] to which are adjoined Dempster's rule for combining independent pieces of evidence), and also by Turing's 'weight of evidence which E provides for H', which is. This is the

[5] See above, p. 78.

function $W(H,E) = \log[P(E|H)/P(E|-H)]$, where again the base of the logarithm is inessential. It is not difficult to show that pieces of data probabilistically independent of both H and of –H do contribute additively to W; i.e. if $P(E_1 \& \ldots \& E_k|H) = P(E_1|H) \ldots P(E_k|H)$, and ditto for –H, then $W(H,E_1 \& \ldots \& E_k) = W(H,E_1) + \ldots + W(H,E_k)$ (Good 1950: 64). In addition, $W(H,E)$ is just the logarithm of the Bayes factor in favour of H (the reciprocal of what earlier we simply called the Bayes factor, which is the Bayes factor in favour of –H). This means that weight of evidence relates very directly to the evidential component in Bayes's theorem; in a sense, since it is a strictly increasing function of it, it just is that component. Thus W itself might look a promising candidate to explicate 'degree of confirmation'.

The trouble is that there are too many candidate explications, satisfying too many distinct sets of criteria all of which sound 'sensible'. I think that the most we can conclude is that 'degree of confirmation' is a highly underdetermined concept. The real problem is that as far as the Bayesian or indeed any other probabilistic model, even Carnap's, is concerned, degree of confirmation plays no obvious role. There is an obvious function for the probabilities themselves, since they are interpreted as degrees of belief and thus fit directly and centrally into a model of uncertain reasoning. In addition, in the decision-theoretic extension of the Bayesian model (caveat: for some Bayesians the Bayesian model is from the outset decision-theoretic) they combine in a direct manner (multiplicatively) with utilities in the computation of best decisions, that is, those with the largest expected utility. Regrettably for those with a nostalgia for some of the fiercest intellectual battles of not-so-long ago, it seems that 'degrees of confirmation' can simply be dispensed with without loss of model function.

Popper–Miller

If *degree* of confirmation as such has no significant role to play, that evidence confirms a hypothesis as it increases its probability most certainly does, and indeed is fundamental to the Bayesian theory of evidence. It is that very idea that is attacked by one of the protagonists of the degree of confirmation debate, Popper, assisted by David Miller. In several joint papers (see particularly 1983, 1987), Popper and Miller claim to be able to demonstrate that any increase in the probability of H by E merely reflects the verification of that part of H's content deductively entailed by E, and represents no evidence *for the content of H net of E*. On the contrary, they claim to show that the probability of the excess content of H over E is not merely not increased but actually *decreased* given the truth of E.

At first sight this seems obviously wrong. Theorem 2 of Chapter 4 tells us, for example, that the probability of future predictions of H is enhanced, to the point eventually of unity, given the truth of sufficiently many past predictions (and given a non-zero prior probability for H). And future predictions are surely in the excess content of H over E. Or are they? It is a consequence of Popper's and Miller's view of what an inequality $P(A|B) > P(A)$ conveys that they can deny this. For them the inequality merely reflects the deductive verification of the common content of A and B. In the context of Theorem 2, this means that the enhancement in probability of E_{i+1} given by the truth of $E = E_1 \& \ldots \& E_i$ is no enhancement in the probability of the content of E_{i+1} *additional to* its common content with E. All probabilistic confirmation, they claim, is merely disguised deductive confirmation.

These claims clearly depend on there actually being some well-defined thing signified by 'excess content', and, granted that, on Popper and Miller's having correctly identified it. According to them, the excess content of H over E is exactly represented by a single sentence, $-EvH$ (for simplicity we shall use the logician's symbols v, – and → for 'or', 'not' and 'if . . . then __' respectively; to see how they are defined logically, see Howson 1997c: 7–13). They base their identification on the ground that $-EvH$ is the logically weakest sentence which conjoined with E yields H as a consequence. This last claim is true. For suppose B is any sentence which together with E implies H. Then by the so-called rule of →-introduction (also known as the deduction theorem) B implies '$E \rightarrow H$', which is equivalent to $-EvH$. They then show that although $P(H|E)$ may exceed $P(H)$, $P(-EvH|E)$ is necessarily less than $P(-EvH)$, that is, the excess content of H over E is actually decreased if we are assuming E to be true.

Few commentators have pointed out that it is strange that two avowed anti-inductivists should happily accept that the content of H going beyond E could be *countersupported* by E. Nevertheless, it is as anomalous as if they had shown that it was supported by E, for neither possibility seems to square with the sceptical tenet that E only informs us about E and *nothing beyond it*, and suggests that Popper's and Miller's result is merely an artefact of an incorrect way of characterizing excess content. And so it turns out. For their choice of –EvH to represent the excess content of H over E is driven by a self-imposed requirement that the excess content must itself be expressed by a *sentence* (for the background to this requirement in Tarski's 'calculus of deductive systems' see Howson and Urbach 1993: 396–8). Given that requirement, the choice of –EvH is virtually inescapable. But the requirement is a gratuitous one. Intuitively, the excess content is the *set* C of all the consequences of H not implied by E, and it is not difficult to see that C in general *exceeds* the class of consequences of –EvH. Characterising the excess content by C also clearly endorses the intuitive idea that E_{i+1} is in the content of H going beyond E (and note that E_{n+1} is not a consequence of –EvH).

Popper's and Miller's analysis of what information can be conveyed by one quantity, E, about another, H, is faulty. It is interesting to see what mathematical information theory itself tells us; in addition it will also cast light on why a numerical measure of excess content that Popper and Miller also deploy is also faulty. First, a little background. Shannon in his pioneering work (1948) proved that a small set of intuitively plausible constraints on an acceptable measure U(X) of the uncertainty attaching to a random variable X, taking n different values with probability $P(X = x_i) = p_i$, determines U(X) to be $\Sigma - p_i \log p_i$, where the base of the logarithm is arbitrary (the base 2 gives the 'bit', or **bi**nary digit, unit). The definition can be extended to the joint uncertainty of any number of random variables (though the extension to the case of continuous variables, joint or single, is more problematic; but this is not the place to go into that). This leads naturally to a definition of quantity of information in terms of the uncertainty eliminated by information about the value of a random variable. Since U(X) is the expected value of the quantity $-\log p_i$, $-\log(X = x_i)$ can be plausibly identified with the information obtained in learning that $X = x_i$. Let us accordingly denote $-\log P(X = x_i)$ by $\text{Inf}(X = x_i)$.

We can relate Shannon's measure to the present discussion by noting that, given a probability distribution over its truth-values, a hypothesis H is a two-valued random variable taking the value 'true' with probability p and 'false' with probability $1 - p$. Continuing as before to write H as shorthand for 'H is true', Inf(H) is the information contained in the statement that H is true. Because of the fundamental property of logarithms that they transform products into sums, Inf is additive over probabilistically independent propositions: if A and B are probabilistically independent, that is, P(A&B) = P(A)P(B), then the information contained in A&B is the sum of the uncertainties of A and B. The quantity of residual uncertain information in H once E is assumed true, where we assume that H entails E, is equal to Inf(H) − Inf(E), i.e. −logP(H) + logP(E), which is equal to −log[P(H)/P(E)], which is also equal to −logP(H|E) (since H entails E) which we can write Inf(H|E). Note that Inf(H|E) is *not* equal to the information contained in the proposition −EvH, as Popper and Miller maintain, and is not equal in general to the information contained in any proposition.

Popper and Miller themselves employ a measure Ct(H) of the content of H which, like Inf(H), is a function of P(H). But they define Ct(H) to be a linear function of P(H), and a particularly simple one, 1 − P(H); i.e. P(−H). it is easy to prove that Ct(E) + Ct(−EvH) = Ct(H). Thus according to Ct, −EvH is the excess content in H over E, as Popper and Miller claimed. However, it is also easy to verify that for any two propositions A and B, Ct(A&B) *is never greater* than Ct(A) + Ct(B), and is equal only where P(AvB) = 1. Conversely, it is possible to show that any mathematical structure in which contents can be added and subtracted (minimally, it must be what algebraists call a monoid, that is, a semigroup with an identity element) and which identifies −EvH as the excess content of H over E *must* have this property (Howson and Franklin 1985: 427). But intuitively the measure of the information conveyed by conjoining two propositions should in certain circumstances *exceed* the sum of their separate informational contents, for example when the truth of B indicates that A is very unlikely to be true. On the other hand, if A entails B then we should not be surprised if the information conveyed by conjoining them is less than the sum of their informational contents separately. It is not difficult to see that both these considerations are faithfully reflected by the measure Inf, since logP(A&B) = logP(A|B) + logP(B). Thus if P(A|B) < P(A) then Inf(A&B) > Inf(A) + Inf(B), while if B entails A and the probabilities of A and B are both between 0 and 1 exclusive, then it follows immediately from Theorem 1 that Inf(A&B) < Inf(A) + Inf(B) (for a more extended discussion of Ct and Inf see Howson and Franklin 1986).

Note that P(H) = 0 if and only if Inf(H) is infinite: the information you would obtain on learning the truth of a statement you have assimilated in probability to a contradiction is infinite. This should mean that learning the truth of any statement containing a finite amount of information will not be capable of reducing the overall information in H. The implication is proved formally by the fact that P(H|E) remains 0 for all E such that P(E) > 0, i.e. Inf(H|E) remains infinite. This gives us another way to appreciate just what is involved in assigning a 'dogmatic' prior. It means that the amount of uncertain information conveyed in H is so *immeasurably* large that no amount of finite data can achieve any reduction in it. It is difficult to see how such a judgement about any hypothesis could be proved a priori. It is certainly not enough to note that where H is a universal hypothesis it makes in principle infinitely many distinct predictions. This does not entail that Inf(H) = infinity, as we have seen. Nor is it even intuitively correct: 'Every natural number has a successor' is a universal hypothesis which is not a logical truth yet most people take as being certain. Indeed, nearly all the axioms used to generate currently accepted mathematics are universal propositions, and are not logical truths.

Let us come back again to the problem which started this discussion, namely what is going on when successful prediction raises the prior probability of a hypothesis, as in Theorem 1. The answer is actually very simple and unremarkable. By the definition of conditional probability P(H|E) = P(H&E)/P(E) = P(H)/P(E) since H entails E. Recall the remarks about the intended meaning of P(H|E) at the beginning of this chapter: conditioning on E means restricting the universe of discourse to the space of possibilities making E true. Since H entails E by assumption, the possibilities making H true in this new space are just those making H true in the original space; but their original probability now has to be renormalized, that is, proportionately increased by a factor of 1/P(E). That is all that the equation P(H|E) = P(H)/P(E) says. But the increment of probability is spread over all the possibilities consistent with H: there is nothing whatever implied in this account about the augmented probability reflecting a 'purely deductive confirmation' of the E-part of H's content. Indeed, as Cussens points out (1996: 7–9), that claim is rather trivially refuted by the fact that there are (infinitely many pairs of) probability functions P and P' such that the quantity P(H|E) − P(H) differs from P'(H|E) − P'(H) by an arbitrary amount subject to the constraint that both differences must lie in the interval [−1,1].

Accommodation and Prediction

I believe that we can safely conclude that Popper and Miller have not been able to refute the idea that an increase in probability due to the acceptance of the truth of E reflects on the whole of what H says and not just that part of it which is entailed by E. In most of the remainder of this chapter we shall apply the Bayesian model to some issues in the philosophy of science, starting with a very old problem. Bacon asserted that the power to anticipate the outcomes of experiments that had never before been made is a telling sign in favour of a hypothesis's truth. Recall from Chapter 1 his remark in *Novum Organum* that 'we must look to see whether it confirms its largeness and wideness by indicating new particulars, as a kind of collateral security' (1994: 1, 106). Bacon calls hypotheses that do this 'interpretations of nature', reserving the term 'anticipatio', oddly enough to our ears, for just the sort of hypotheses that are modified always to agree with the data; see Bacon 1994, pp. xvi–xvii).

In the nineteenth century, the same view was strongly endorsed by Pierce and Whewell. A further, apparently even more compelling, converse has recently been added by Giere, Worrall, and others: any hypothesis constructed after the facts to explain them will not only not do so, but those facts will have no evidential value *vis-à-vis* the hypothesis:

If the known facts were used in constructing the model and were thus built into the resulting hypotheses . . . then the fit between these facts and the hypothesis [sic] provides no evidence that the hypothesis is true [since] these facts had no *chance* of refuting the hypothesis. (Giere 1984: 161; my italics)

Perhaps surprisingly, Giere, a non-Bayesian, seems to be expounding a Bayesian criterion: that if the Bayes factor is unity then E is not evidence for H. For if E is predicted by H (there is agreement between the data—here E—and the hypothesis H) then $P(E|H) = 1$ or is close to 1. But if H was deliberately engineered to agree then we know that there is no chance of disagreement even if H should in fact be false. Thus we appear to have $P(-E|-H) = 0$ and hence $P(E|-H) = 1$. Hence we have a Bayes factor of unity, which as we know implies that $P(H|E) = P(H)$. So it appears that the Bayesian model explains the depreciation of merely accommodating theories.

Unfortunately that explanation cannot be correct. Here is a simple counterexample. I happen to know that this barrel contains some apples, but I do not know how many. I plan a simple but effective experiment to find out how many: I look in the barrel and count the apples. There are ten. Having performed my experiment I employ its data to advance the hypothesis H(10) that there are ten apples in the barrel. This explains the data perfectly well and indeed the data are the best possible evidence that the hypothesis is true. So the thesis that data explained *post hoc* have no evidential value is simply wrong. The Bayesian model immediately endorses this judgement too, for $P(H(10)|E) = 1$, whereas the probability of H(10) was not unity before I performed the experiment. Is the model inconsistent? No. Can you see what has gone wrong? If you can't, here is the answer. The wrong move was to infer that if the agreement between E and H was engineered deliberately then this means that $P(-E|-H) = 0$. This may seem surprising but a little reflection will show that it really is a mistake. For if $P(-E|-H) = 0$ then as we saw $P(E|-H) = 1$. But if $P(E|H)$ is also 1 then it follows from the probability calculus that $P(E) = 1$; i.e. E is true with probability 1. But the observation(s) did not *have to* produce the outcome E. They did as a matter of contingent fact, but the facts could have been otherwise. The fallacy, then, is in the inference that because H was engineered to agree with the data, the data stood no chance of refuting H. As we saw earlier in Chapter 3, this is simply not true: the data had every chance of disagreeing with H.

So the inference to $P(-E|-H) = 0$ must be wrong. To complete the discussion we need to explain why it is wrong. The explanation is that it is obtained by performing an illicit substitution. Just about everybody who writes on this subject makes the same mistake, so it is worth taking a little time to explain why it is a mistake. Suppose we have a physical experiment EXP. Depending on how exactly the world is structured EXP could in principle generate different possible outcomes. For example, in the world as it is, or as we believe it is, dropping a brick results in accelerated downward motion. But if gravity decided to act in the reverse direction the brick would move upwards (and a lot more would be different besides, but never mind that). Let X stand for 'the outcome generated by EXP'. X is, with inessential qualifications that need not concern us, what is called a *random variable*: something that takes different 'values' in different possible worlds. Now let f(X) be the result of applying some strategy to X which, whatever X in fact is, will yield a hypothesis guaranteed to agree with X. For example, f(X) might be obtained by waiting until the value of X is known and constructing the hypothesis in a way that depends on this knowledge to agree with that value, as in using data to evaluate free parameters. At any rate, we can certainly say that the chance of f(X) disagreeing with X is zero; that is, P(X agrees with f(X)) = 1. That is entirely in order. But what we cannot do is substitute joint values for X and f(X), like E and H, *inside the scope of the probability operator P.*

Different disciplines have different names for the fallacy. A mathematician sees it as substituting a scalar (a fixed object) for a function. A logician can show that it involves substituting a variable into a context in which it becomes bound (Howson and Oddie 1979: 257). Philosophers call it 'substitution into opaque contexts'. Whatever you call it, it's wrong, and will lead to contradictions. A fuller discussion is contained in Howson and Oddie (1979), but here is a simple counterexample. Suppose that the probability that the outcome of the next toss of this coin is heads is ½. Letting the random variable Y signify 'the outcome of the next toss' we can write the probability in the standard formula as P(Y = heads) = ½. Suppose that the outcome of the next toss of this coin is in fact tails. Well, we obviously cannot use the factually true identity 'the outcome of the next toss of this coin is tails' to substitute 'tails' for Y in the formula. Apart from anything else it would give the absurd result that the probability that tails is heads is ½. Giere's fallacious inference arises from such a substitution. *That* is why we are not entitled to conclude P(–E|–H) = 0 from a premiss stating that, given the way the data are employed to generate a corresponding hypothesis, the chance of the hypothesis agreeing with the data is unity. No valid Bayesian explanation can proceed from such an inference; which is just as well, for as we saw it would explain something that is not in general true.

What the Bayesian model does truly explain is why the prediction of highly novel facts is evidentially meritorious, and the explanation is a very straightforward application of the earlier formulas: if the data E are predicted by H and by no other plausible hypothesis we should expect P(E|–H) to be correspondingly small while P(E|H) is close to 1. In that case, of course, the Bayes factor is small and if P(H) is not too small, E will raise the probability of H considerably.

Old Evidence

I said that $P(E) = 1$ does not follow from the fact, if it is a fact, that H is engineered to fit E. On the other hand, since E was by assumption known before H was constructed—to fit E or not as the case may be—then surely $P(E)$ *must be* 1, since we know E and P measures degree of belief. Yet this appears to entail (as was noted first in Glymour 1980: 86) that *no already-known evidence* can confirm any hypothesis according to the Bayesian model, since if $P(E) = 1$ then $P(E|H)$ and $P(E|\text{-}H)$ are also both equal to 1, and as we observed above the Bayes factor is therefore 1 and so $P(H|E) = P(H)$. But this seems to imply that the Bayesian model must necessarily fail to fit well-established inductive practice, and practice that seems intuitively well-justified. For it is sometimes the case that empirical data which have been known for some time are very strongly thought to support a newly developed hypothesis: a much-discussed example is the discovery (by Adams and Leverrier) that Mercury's perihelion precesses, a fact that Newtonian gravitational theory could not explain in any very successful way, but which was a straightforward, and justly celebrated, consequence of General Relativity. Even Earman, an otherwise sympathetic commentator on the Bayesian theory, regards this as a profound difficulty for it (a 'black eye'; 1992: 135) in so far as it claims to provide a model for scientific inference.

And the discussion continues, with a consensus that the problem is at the very least a serious one for the Bayesian model, with no obvious solution. It may come as a surprise, therefore, to be told that there is a very simple solution, or, rather more accurately, that *there is no problem*. For that is indeed the case. Recall the observation earlier that the extent to which a body of data counts as evidence relative to a hypothesis, that is, its power to enhance or otherwise the credibility (probability) of the hypothesis, depends on the informational context in which it is situated: of other factual reports, of background theory, the extent to which other plausible hypotheses exist, etc. This apparently obvious remark is enough to dissolve the old-evidence problem. To prepare the mind, go back again to the Mercury-perihelion problem. The differential evidential impact of the known value for the precession of Mercury's perihelion on the two rival theories, classical gravitational theory and Einstein's solution to the field equations of General Relativity (GR henceforth), is assessed by the posterior probability relative to what was, say in 1916, regarded as the available credible background information about the structure of the solar system, that is, about the larger massive bodies, including known dust clouds etc., and the distances between them. By assumption that background information obviously does not contain the data for the perihelion-precession itself, for it is those very data which are being assessed against the background of whatever else is known.

The old-evidence problem is now dissolved. For what these otherwise-trite points tell us is that the evidential value of any item E is assessed relative to the *remainder* of the contemporary body of background information, should E be already known, *for the very notion of being evidence just means being assessed against the background provided by that residual body*. All this carries over smoothly to the model. Let E be the data for the precession of Mercury's perihelion, let H be GR and H′ Newtonian gravitational theory. Simplifying greatly, suppose that the prior probabilities of both H and H′ are equal, and for the sake of argument ½. Relative to the residual known or likely information about the disposition of masses in the solar system, we have $P(E|H) = 1$ (again, approximately) and $P(E|H')$ very small; again for the sake of argument 1/100. These figures are supposed to be only what a contemporary might conceivably assign; whether they are accurate even in this we can ignore. But they enable us to compute $P(H|E)$ and $P(H'|E)$, as approximately 1 and 1 per cent respectively. Also, since $P(H) = P(H') = \frac{1}{2} P(E) = P(E|H)P(H) + P(E|H')P(H')$, they determine $P(E)$, *and determine it moreover to be a number less than one even though we 'know' E*: approximately one half.

A quite different Bayesian analysis of the role of old evidence has been developed by Garber, following a suggestion of Glymour. Glymour (1980) remarked that possibly the power of old evidence E to give inductive support to a new hypothesis H predicting E was due not to any increase of the probability of H in the light of E itself, but an increase in the probability of H in the light of the knowledge that H was found to predict E. Thus the idea that old evidence cannot directly confirm is sustained in this theory; according to it what confirms is the new evidence that H predicts E. The other novel twist to standard Bayesian theory is that this new evidence is not empirical: it is the report of the discovery of a *logical* fact. We saw in Chapter 7 that Garber developed a theory in which the domain of the probability function is extended to include statements of the form 'H deductively entails E'. In fact, Garber developed this theory explicitly to develop Glymour's suggestion into a systematic theory of the confirmation of factual hypotheses by evidence about logical relations.

As we saw, Garber's theory is also a radical break with classical Bayesianism, in that it relaxes at least one of the probability axioms, that logical truths are uniformly assigned unit probability. Whether that is desirable or not (and I argued that it is not), there are cases of hypotheses constructed precisely to explain the data which show that, however adequate in itself, Garber's theory cannot be an adequate explanation of the role of old evidence. For as we have seen, at least some of these hypotheses, like H(10) in the earlier discussion, contrived to fit the data would on any sensible view be regarded as maximally supported by it, since they are virtually entailed by it. Here the logical relation between E and H is known, indeed exploited, but E none the less confirms H. These considerations show that it is not the discovery of the deductive relation that is doing the confirming, *but the content of E itself*. Concede that and you are back with the classical Bayesian theory. But that doesn't matter, because as we know there is no problem of old evidence for classical Bayesianism.

Diverse Data

Here is another short exercise in the use of Bayes factors. We are frequently told that experiments should be not only repeatable, but that when repeated they should give the same result if they are to be regarded as conveying reliable information. The reason is intuitively clear: the first result might have been a fluke, the result of some malfunction in the apparatus or its interpretation rather than the record of a genuine effect. In other words, the observed outcome E, predicted by H, may be caused by some cause other than that described in H. Suppose H_C is the hypothesis that the observed outcome is due to some cause C other than that described in H. If the experiment is well designed, then a repeat of it under tight control will make it unlikely that there is any plausible H_C playing this role a second time. Hence, if E_1 and E_2 are the two outcomes and they record the same event, and $H_{C,1}$ and $H_{C,2}$ are the statements that E_1 and E_2 respectively are due to C, then $P(E_1\&E_2|H_{C,1}\&H_{C,2})$ will still be large but the factor $P(H_{C,1}\&H_{C,2})$ will not. This means that the priors multiplying the Bayes factor for $H_{C,1}\&H_{C,2}$ will be small. Hence the posterior probability of H with respect to the joint outcome will be higher than for a single one.

We can generalize this reasoning in the following interesting way. A repeated experiment is never exactly the same in all details as the first; apart from anything else the time at which it was performed will have changed. So what we have seen above is an instance of the more general phenomenon of the value of *diverse evidence*. And now another factor comes into play. Suppose a hypothesis makes a variety of experimental predictions. These will be perfectly positively correlated if H is true, but in the absence of any other plausible unifying hypothesis not particularly well-correlated if not. In other words, if E_1 and E_2 are predictions in hitherto remote domains, then we should put $P(E_2|E_1\&H) = 1$ and $P(E_2|E_1\&-H)$ much less than one. A little manipulation of the Bayes factor shows that in such a case $f = P(E_2|E_1\& - H)P(E_1| - H)$. Hence the smaller the correlation between E_2 and E_1 were H not true, the greater the confirming power of $E_2\&E_1$ with respect to H. So the ability to characterize diverse evidence as effects predicted by a single explanatory hypothesis in general tells in favour of that hypothesis.

Once May be Enough

We have seen that we can model a variety of 'classic' inductive inferences in a way that seems both faithful and immune to Humean objections in the sense that the inductive premises are *explicit*. Commonly these premises take the form of delimiting a class of 'seriously considered' hypotheses, modelled as those with appreciable prior probability. As we know, in suitable circumstances (generally meaning the absence of plausible alternatives that can equally well explain the data), such theories can attain probabilities close to 1 with suitable evidence in well-designed experiments. If the ambient circumstances are propitious very little evidence may suffice, a fact that has been noted by many commentators but which has equally resisted their attempts to explain. One such was Hume himself, whose own attempt was perfunctory:

the mind, having form'd another observation concerning the connexion of causes and effects, gives new force to its reasoning from that observation; and by means of it can build an argument on one single experiment, when duly prepar'd and examin'd. (1739: I. III. xii)

The explanation famously eluded Mill:

Why is a single instance, in some cases, sufficient for a complete induction, while, in others, myriads of concurring instances, without a single exception known or presumed, go such a very little way toward establishing a universal proposition? Whoever can answer this question knows more of the philosophy of logic than the wisest of the ancients and has solved the problem of induction. (1891, bk. III, ch. III, section 3)

There's a challenge. The doctrine of natural kinds is frequently invoked to answer it: we feel confident in generalizing from the 'single instance' when we observe that the property in question belongs to an otherwise 'arbitrary' member of a natural kind. Since the observed exemplar was 'arbitrary', then, if the property belongs to it, it must belong to every member of that kind. But this explanation is entirely question-begging (see the discussion in Chapter 2, pp. 31–2) and does nothing to illuminate the inferential processes involved. It is also often claimed that these cannot be probabilistic in nature, precisely because of the readiness in appropriate circumstances to generalize immediately:

It is a matter of historical fact that many of the fundamental principles classical mechanics, electricity, magnetism, chemistry, biology and physiology were discovered without recourse to probability theory. The scientists who made these discoveries proceeded from a small number of observations to a general conclusion. Of course, the conclusion sometimes proved wrong or incomplete. Nevertheless, from the standard position of the philosophy of science, the physicist who establishes a figure for the conductivity of copper is like a man who draws one marble from a bag and, finding it to be red, stakes his all that all marbles are red. This indicates that the model of the marble-drawer is not appropriate to large areas of scientific reasoning. This point has been made forcefully by Popper. (Macnamara 1991: 22)

The marble-drawing model certainly isn't appropriate, but then it has not been the basis of the probabilistic theory of evidence for a long time—certainly not since the advent of the neo-Bayesian theory, identified as a logic rather than a body of substantive truths, founded by Ramsey and de Finetti. Also, whether agents actually engage in formal probabilistic reasoning is, as I warned earlier, quite beside the point in judging the adequacy of the model of reasoning the Bayesian logic does provide, as beside the point as observing that people do not formalize inferences in first-order languages when they argue deductively.

And as it happens, of course, there is nothing essentially unprobabilistic about generalizing from a small sample in appropriate circumstances. On the contrary, to see such an inference as probabilistic solves the problem completely: as we can easily see, it has a natural probabilistic interpretation as one from a small Bayes factor to a high posterior probability. That *is* the solution: we believe we have a minuscule Bayes factor combined with a non-negligible prior. Suppose, for example, we have a causal hypothesis, H, attributing the phenomenon, E, to some causal property of the object or objects under investigation. We are confident that H is the true explanation because the experiment, 'duly prepar'd and examin'd', is so constructed that it would be highly implausible to hold any adventitious factor responsible. In terms of the equations above, this simply means that all the explanations H_i which might in principle attribute the result to alternative causal factors (i.e. such that $P(|H_i)$ is considerable) are such that the experimental design makes them highly unlikely if not impossible ($P(H_i)$ is very small). In that case, as we saw, the Bayes factor (of H against –H) will be very small and, given a non-negligible prior (assumed), $P(H|E)$ will be close to 1. In the case where we do not feel confident in extrapolating beyond what we have observed it will be because we have feel that we have observed merely some accidental collocation of properties; that is, it is not at all implausible that some extraneous factor is responsible. But this means that for some alternative H_i, both $P(H_i)$ and $P(E|H_i)$ are considerable. This is of course, not 'solving the problem of induction': it is just what the model describes as consistent behaviour subject to the initial constraints. It does not tell us, nor should it, that these are correct.

A Sounder Argument for Realism[6]

We saw earlier that attempts to found scientific realism (henceforward simply 'realism') on the No-Miracles argument fail because

---

[6] The argument of this section with minor changes follows Dorling 1992.

that argument is unsound. Moreover, if Hume is correct then there can be no argument for realism that does not somewhere beg the question. I shall simply assume that this is the case. But scientists markedly tend to be realists: virtually all the texts on particle physics start by classifying these particles and describing their properties. Moreover, it seems intuitively right that any empirical support for the empirical adequacy of a general theory T, whose content vastly transends current observational data, must be support to some extent also for the realistic claims made by the theory.

This is an almost trivial consequence of the Bayesian model. Let TR assert the truth of the fully realistic version of T, and TE merely assert T's empirical adequacy. We can assume that TE follows from TR. It follows immediately from the very simple but very important Theorem 1, Chapter 4, p. 71, that if E is a consequence of TE and $P(TR) > 0$ and $P(E) < 1$, then $P(TR|E) > P(TR)$. Hence, given that the realistic version had *some* positive prior probability, that probability will be positively augmented by any successful prediction. We are of course making some assumptions here. One is that (as seems always assumed in the instrumentalism vs. realism debate) some method can be employed to discriminate observational from non-observational consequences. This is not of course a distinction that can be made sharply or considered as once-for-all; what are observational consequences of a theory today might well not have been three hundred years ago. Not just the empirical content but the total content of a theory depends very much on its ambient theoretical environment as well as on the development of suitable technology. So we must certainly take the empirical content of any theory as time-indexed. Granted that, another assumption is that TE is actually a determinate hypothesis to which probabilities can be assigned. But that is all right: TE is a denumerable set of sentences and can be represented as a single proposition within the possibility-space (it is a denumerable intersection, and we have allowed for the set of propositions to be a σ-algebra of subsets of this space).

Finally, we are assuming a non-zero prior for TR, and it may be objected that this is the very point at issue. Of course, from the Humean point of view any non-zero prior is already an inductive premiss, but we are not really in that sort of discussion now: we are talking about the adequacy of a model of inference in which it is assumed as an initial condition that people do various things whether justified or not according to the austerer Humean canon. In the

Bayesian theory a non-zero prior is intended to model a state of mind that is prepared, even minimally, to be changed with the reception of suitable information, and we know from Chapter 4 that a zero prior will not model such a state of mind. Practically everything in the Bayesian model is premissed on the assumption that scientific theories are taken minimally seriously in this way. If they are not, it is not science that is being modelled but some dogmatic faith. It is no accident that instrumentalism initially arose as the response of the Catholic Church to the threat of a secular explanation of the universe, and that two of its most prominent advocates, Berkeley and Duhem, were devout believers. It is true that there may also be theories that appear to resist any consistent realistic interpretation. The prominent feature of modern science that has reopened what is a very old debate is, of course, the difficulty of regarding quantum mechanics as anything other than a superb black-box predicting machine. Attempts to embed the theory into one in which quantum systems can be said to possess real properties in any intelligible way continue, of course, and with interesting consequences for the way we regard the 'fundamental' notions of logic and probability in the context of physical theory.

The next question is by how much the probability of the realistic version of T can be increased. We can answer this too, at least up to an interesting inequality. It is a consequence of the model that the ratio of the posterior probabilities of a weaker and a stronger version of a theory that each predict the data is proportional to the ratio of their priors (the reader might like to try this as a simple exercise). It follows that being a 'pure' instrumentalist is as difficult in principle as it is in practice. To see this, let us assume that both TR and TI are assigned positive prior probabilities (the usual Bayesian explanatory initial condition), and let these be p and q respectively. By construction, the predictions deducible from TR are identical to those deducible from TI. It follows by the result mentioned that

$$P(TR|E)/P(TE|E) = p/q.$$

It follows that if P(TE|E) increases, then so too must P(TR|E) in proportion to P(TE|E). Whether TR ever becomes more probable than not a posteriori will, of course, depend on its prior probability. For a positivist, which in this context we shall take to mean one who denies the realist claims of a theory, this will be small, but Dorling provides an example in which the prior is 0.2 but is nevertheless sufficiently dominated by E that 'conversion' to realism occurs, in the sense of the agent determining that TR is more probable than not (1992: 368–9).

Evaluating Logico-Mathematical Hypotheses

It was remarked in Chapter 7 that there is nothing in principle against considering the posterior probability of logico-mathematical hypotheses. Consider the problem of (deductive) consistency which we also discussed there. Every mathematician believes that Peano arithmetic, a set of axioms for natural number arithmetic attributed to Peano but actually due to Dedekind, is consistent. But it is a consequence of Gödel's second incompleteness theorem that any proof of this fact, if it is a fact, requires a stronger system, thereby rendering the epistemological value of the proof doubtful if not entirely nugatory. Similar remarks are valid for any axiomatized theory. So proof is a luxury denied us. Can we nevertheless justify a belief in the consistency of Peano arithmetic—henceforward we shall call it PA—falling short of that corresponding to deductive certainty? The reader should by now be aware that *justified* belief is not something in the gift of Bayesian—or any other—logic. But what that logic can do is represent consistent reasoning about consistency. Well, let us see. There is, first of all, for most people aware of the problem, a very high degree of belief in the consistency of PA. It arises from a variety of sources: from the fact that we seem to clearly discern as a structure visualizable clearly in the mind's eye the intended model, the natural number system itself; from the fact that a vast number of deductions using those axioms, even if informally, has failed to reveal a contradiction; and from the fact that we can prove the consistency of PA in a variety of systems which, while admittedly stronger, have each an independent, and very high, plausibility. For example, there is an almost trivial proof of consistency within ZFC, where the so-called finite von Neumann ordinals are provably—provably within ZFC, that is—a model of PA; and Gödel himself and Gentzen gave proofs within weaker systems than ZFC. For these reasons, and perhaps others, we feel that it is almost certain that PA is consistent. But how do we represent that reasoning within the Bayesian model?

Part of the answer is very straightforward. The consistency of PA follows deductively from each of the following: the consistency of ZFC; the consistency of the weaker systems used by Gödel and Gentzen; and (trivially) the assertion that PA has a model. Assuming that we assign to each a large probability (an assumption that functions here merely as an initial condition in the reasoning; we just do think this way), the probability of the consistency of PA must be at least as great. So far so good, though we have of course unearthed nothing new. In effect that fixes the prior probability. But what about the 'inductive' evidence, that no contradiction has so far been forthcoming? Now we can reason more in the spirit of Bayes's theorem. Here we are in effect appealing to a large variety of data ('no contradiction discovered in this application', 'no contradiction discovered in that application', etc.) all predicted by the hypothesis of the consistency of PA. There is of course the possibility that there might have been errors in these deductions, but it is very unlikely that there have been in the vast majority, which like repeatable empirical experiments are open to cross-checking. But for anything firm to come out of this we need a low Bayes factor, and that is obtained only if the probability of all that data if PA is inconsistent is very small. Is that the case? There is no determinate answer, but we do believe, again as a matter of fact, that the Bayes factor is small because we believe that in the time-scale of applications of these principles of arithmetical reasoning some contradiction would by now have been discovered were those principles inconsistent. There is no way of proving this, but it is certainly what many people feel. Plugging that 'feeling' in, we obtain the requisite small Bayes factor and hence an even higher posterior probability than the prior. It may not be wholly justifiable, but it is (probabilistically) consistent reasoning; and that is all we asked. Admittedly, we have dealt only with one problem, that of explaining why we are as confident as we are of the consistency of PA, but it is not an atypical problem. At any rate, we must leave the discussion there, because it is time to move on to one of the most controversial of questions, discussed by Bayesian and non-Bayesians alike, the role which *simplicity* should be accorded in inductive reasoning.

Simplicity

The characteristic and fundamental feature of the Bayesian model, that evidential evaluation is a function of two variables, one indicating how 'good' the data are (the Bayes factor) and the other the independent plausibility (prior probability) of the hypothesis, is both itself very intuitively obvious and hence not surprisingly echoed in the informal observations of scientists themselves (Laplace's 'good sense reduced to a calculus' again). As a well-known statistician has remarked

this provides a qualitatively correct picture of the way in which opinion is formed. One may believe a theory either because one's initial prejudices are strong, and observation does not provide enough evidence to shake them, or because the observational evidence is strong enough to overcome any prejudice, or perhaps one's initial opinions and observational evidence reinforce one another. (Smith 1961: 4)

Admittedly Smith is explicitly a Bayesian. Einstein wasn't, of course, but consider the following comment (brought to my attention by Robert Matthews) on Kaufmann's and Planck's experimental results concerning the velocity-dependence of the energy of a moving electron. These results appeared to agree with Abraham's theory (according to which the dynamics of electrons are based on purely electromagnetic considerations) and to be in conflict with the predictions of Special Relativity. But Einstein was not impressed:

Herr Kaufmann has determined the relation between [electric and magnetic deflection] of β-rays with admirable care. . . . Using an independent method, Herr Planck obtained results which fully agree with [the computations of] Kaufmann. . . . It is further to be noted that the theories of Abraham and Bucherer yield curves which fit the observed curve considerably better than the curve obtained from relativity theory. However, in my opinion, these theories should be ascribed a *rather small probability* because their basic postulates concerning the mass of the moving electron are not *made plausible* by theoretical systems which encompass wider complexes of phenomena. (translated and quoted by Pais 1982: 159; my italics)

Never mind Einstein's reasons for regarding Abraham's and Bucherer's theories as 'implausible'; it is the form of the inference *from* that implausibility which is important here, for it translates naturally and directly into the Bayesian one that a small prior probability counters the effect of a large Bayes factor to yield an overall small posterior probability.

It is nevertheless an interesting question what if anything of value can be said about the factors that scientists regard as promoting a high prior probability. Einstein in the quotation above suggests largeness of scope of a theory, the extent to which it can 'encompass wider complexes of phenomena'. Einstein is also on record as elevating more aesthetic considerations, of simplicity and even beauty, to a very high status. In this no one, of course, surpasses another great twentieth-century physicist, Dirac. Undoubtedly such considerations have played and do play a large role, though more with some people than with others.

But *simplicity* has always been regarded with a special favour. A good many people's idea of simplicity is that it is not merely a rather nebulous quality of 'elegance', but an avoidance of unnecessary complication in structure, and particularly that part of the structure that is held responsible for generating the remainder. In other words, a judicious wielding of Occam's razor results in simple explanations. Newton captured the idea in a well-known observation: 'To this purpose the philosophers say that Nature does nothing in vain, and more is in vain when less will serve; for Nature is pleased with simplicity, and affects not the pomp of superfluous causes.' One way of explicating avoidance of 'the pomp of superfluous causes' in the mathematical sciences is in terms of minimizing the number of adjustable parameters which appear in explanatory hypotheses. The pioneering Bayesian Harold Jeffreys went so far as to make the goal of simplicity in this sense a fundamental postulate of his theory of probabilistic inference: simpler hypotheses, he proposed, should be regarded as a priori more probable. This is Jeffreys's so-called *simplicity postulate* (1961: 47). Popper adopted Jeffreys's analysis of simplicity in terms of paucity of undetermined parameters while, however, denying that simplicity in that sense could, for logical reasons, vary in the same direction as prior probability. Other people (most recently Forster and Sober 1994) have followed Popper in taking this view. The charge is based on the mathematical fact that any hypothesis with k free parameters, $k > 0$, determines a hypothesis with $k - 1$ free parameters by setting one of the original k parameters equal to some fixed number. For example, the hypothesis that an orbit is some circle centred at the origin of the coordinate system (this has one free parameter, the length of the radius) implies the hypothesis that the orbit is some ellipse (two free parameters), but one with eccentricity 0 (now one free parameter). The logical form of a hypothesis with k adjustable or free parameters is

$$\exists a_1 \exists a_2 \ldots \exists a_k \forall x A(a_1, a_2, \ldots, a_k, x)$$

where x may be an m-dimensional variable, and the reason the defender of a Simplicity Postulate appears to be in trouble is that the simpler hypothesis implies by existential specification the less simple, from which it follows by the probability calculus that its probability can be no greater, *contradicting* the simplicity postulate.

While all this is true, it ignores Jeffreys's own qualifications which preserve the consistency of the postulate. Jeffreys wanted to model the behaviour of those scientists who, to get a better fit to the data, reluctantly complicate a simpler hypothesis, say a linear hypothesis, call it H, by adding a small quadratic term, whose coefficient is to be determined by further observations. The point is that the new coefficient is to be adjustable, *subject to its being non-zero*.[7] But now it is clearly consistent to assign H a larger prior probability than the hypothesis, call it H^2, that the functional form is quadratic with some non-zero leading coefficient, for H and H^2 are now mutually exclusive alternatives. Specifying some non-zero value b to H^2 will yield another hypothesis, $H^2(b)$. By the probability calculus $P(H^2) \geq P(H^2(b))$, and $P(H) > P(H^2)$ by the simplicity postulate. H and $H^2(b)$ have the same number of free parameters, namely two, but they have different prior probabilities. This might seem to conflict with the simplicity postulate but Jeffreys regards it as quite acceptable to assign $H^2(b)$ the prior probability 0 (1961: 247)! In fact, there is no conflict with the Simplicity Postulate as Jeffreys himself intended it to be understood, and given that understanding he supplies a perfectly coherent rationale for these assignments. This is not the place here to go into the matter; the interested reader can consult Jeffreys (1961) himself, or the discussion in Howson (1988).

---

[7] Forster and Sober's response to this is misguided: 'we note that this *ad hoc* manoeuvre does not address the problem of comparing LIN [the family of linear curves] versus PAR [parabolas] but *merely changes the subject*' (1994: 23). Not so: it is not an *ad hoc* manoeuvre, nor does it change the subject. On the contrary, more than anything Forster and Sober themselves say, it expresses accurately the fact that scientists are interested in comparing linear curves with *nonlinear* quadratic ones, not linear curves with quadratic-or-linear ones. Nor (finally) is the comparison between LIN and PAR a problem for Bayesians, for these same reasons.

Not everybody accepts Jeffreys's theory of simplicity (though it still has supporters), though most physicists agree with the importance he attached to theoretical determinacy: a standard objection to the so-called Standard Model—the current theory of strong, weak, and electromagnetic interactions—is that it contains no fewer than seventeen independent adjustable parameters (the ideal of physicists appears to be a theory which contains none). But unfortunately simplicity is a far from univocal concept: a glance at the literature reveals almost as many non-equivalent analyses of simplicity as there are advocates of it. Bunge's admirable critical survey (1963) looks at a good number of them, though the currently fashionable approach based on minimum description length (see Rissanen 1982) occurred too late to be included.

Different Bayesians commend different versions of the simplicity postulate (see e.g. Swinburne 1979). But whatever notion of simplicity one thinks fits a simplicity postulate best, assigning priors in accordance with it goes beyond the bounds of Bayesian inference construed as logically sound inference. The fact that simplicity, whatever in any particular context it may be required to mean, is widely valued no more entitles it to the status of a part of the *logic* of inference than does the fact that the current set-theoretical axioms are almost universally adopted entitle them to the status of logical principles, a principle which is general acknowledged. But a preference for simplicity, in whatever form it might take, can certainly be modelled within the Bayesian theory as a suitable constraint on prior probabilities.

Explanatory Emptiness?

The fact that prior probabilities are exogenous to the Bayesian model is one of the conditions for consistency with the Humean position that no sound inductive solely from the observed facts themselves exists. This means that a variety of possible non-logical constraints, of which simplicity is only one, could in principle be modelled by a suitable choice of priors. However, this very plasticity of the Bayesian theory has been held up as criticism, for a reason we have already discussed in Chapter 7. Since it does not in general fix the priors, the Bayesian model would seem to be consistent with any way of responding to evidence at all. Indeed, we shall see that this is largely true. It is a common charge that models that can model anything by a suitable choice of parameters are to be despised, because the ability to model anything implies the inability to explain anything, at any rate in any authentic way. Thus the Bayesian theory has been charged with being explanatorily empty.

Albert, whom we have already encountered in the role of scourge, makes just this charge, supporting it with the following remarkable theorem (I give a slightly simplified statement of it). Suppose one's hypothesis space can be parametrized by an interval Z of real numbers (this is very often the case in statistics); that is, the hypotheses can be represented by the members of the set $\{t:t\in Z\}$. Suppose also that each of these hypotheses determines a different infinite sequence s of possible data, represented as a sequence of 0s and 1s (this is no restriction in principle because almost any data can be represented in binary code). In fact, as Albert points out, if we take Z to be the unit interval we can regard the sequences simply as the binary representations of the numbers between 0 and 1. Let Ω be the set of all such sequences s. Thus any prior probability distribution over Z induces a corresponding distribution P over Ω. Let $(s)_i$ be the ith member of s, and s_n be the data collected up to and including epoch n. Shorn of technicalities Albert's theorem (proved in Albert 1999) states that the posterior probability $P((s)_{n+1}|s_n)$ can be consistently chosen in any way whatever! In particular, any choice of posterior probabilities will determine some prior probability measure on (a sigma algebra of subsets of) Z. Relative to extensive enough possibility spaces, therefore, the Bayesian model is consistent with *any* way of adjusting predictions about the future to what has been observed to happen in the past. Albert rightly points out that possibility spaces at least as rich as Ω, which includes all the possible ways in which the course of Nature might evolve (here a Nature restricted to emitting 0s and 1s), are implicit in the problem of induction, and concludes that the Bayesian model is explanatorily empty and therefore useless even as a normative theory of rational behaviour, let alone a descriptive one (1997: 5).

But this is not the correct conclusion. One might as well charge much of physical theory with being explanatorily deficient because it can be used to model a vast range of possible different properties of physical systems, depending on suitable choices of initial conditions. The fact is that the free parameters of *any* model, Bayesian or physical, need to be appropriately fixed in order for the model to apply to anything at all. It is no objection to say that nevertheless the usual physical models will forbid some logical possibilities independently of initial conditions (in classical physics, particles disappearing or appearing spontaneously; modern particle physics rules out much less), *because exactly the same is true of the Bayesian model of the situation above.* For example, any event A assigned prior probability 0 in that model will have posterior probability 0 with respect to *any* evidence sequence. Such 'pathological' possibilities are frequently excluded at the outset, as is the case in the precise formulation of Albert's own theorem, where it is a condition that the prior probability assigned the proposition that the data will contain only a finite number of 0s is 0. And that of course is precisely to restrict the initial conditions appropriately.

It is not an objection that models of the evolution of physical systems are often robust in the sense that the model predicts that in *nearly all cases* a particular general pattern will be exemplified, as statistical mechanical models characteristically do (it is the main reason why they are so valued). So are Bayesian models. Many of the classical results of statistical physics are what is called 'almost surely' or 'almost always' results; that is to say, they say that a particular feature proved to characterize the relevant system does so on a set of probability-measure 1 (the 'almost' in 'almost surely' or 'almost always' has come to acquire this purely technical meaning). But as we shall now see, a similar, if not even stronger, robustness holds for the evolution of posterior probabilities on increasing data, *and in exactly the same sense, that the systems that do not evolve this way constitute a set of negligible probability.* These 'almost surely' Bayesian theorems, called 'convergence-of opinion-theorems', are worth a brief discussion.

Convergence-of-Opinion Theorems

To prove these theorems the mathematical details of the model have to be elaborated rather carefully. Typically there will be a state-space S, called an infinite product-space, consisting of all denumerably infinite sequences s of elements of some set A. These sequences model all the possible records of an unending sequence of observations, whose individual outcomes are registered as appropriate members of A. A might be a set of numbers, for example. There is nothing particularly restrictive in the use of numbers for this purpose, since as Godel famously showed even the natural numbers are capable of encoding arbitrarily large amounts of information. A complete set of propositions about the data-source is taken for the domain of the probability function, complete in the sense that it is represented extensionally by a sigma-field of subsets of S; that is to say it is closed under binary union (binary disjunction), complement (negation), and countable union (countable disjunctions). The probability function is 'predictive' (the word is due to Blackwell and Dubins 1961, who prove there a 'typical' convergence theorem), in the sense that it determines, for every positive integer and every s, a sequence $P_n(s_n)$ of conditional probability functions defined for each element s of S, where s_n is the initial segment of s up to n, and which assigns probabilities to all the events which might occur after n. In thoroughly Humean language Blackwell and Dubins describe such a function as assigning probabilities to the future given the past (1961: 883). Suppose P and Q are two such probability functions absolutely continuous with respect to each other (i.e. they assign probability 0 to exactly the same events). The theorem which Blackwell and Dubins proves states that the variation-distance between $P_n(s_n)$ and $Q_n(s_n)$ as n tends to infinity itself tends to 0, except at most for a set of possible 'histories' s to which which P and Q both assign probability 0 (p.883). Another well-known result, due to Halmos, for the same sort of state-space of infinite possible data streams, states that the posterior probability of *any* such hypothesis H about the future, that is, the probability of H conditional on s_n, will tend to one if H is true, and to 0 if not, again except for a set of sequences s of probability 0 (Halmos 1950: 213, theorem B; see also Savage 1954: 46–50).

In Chapter 2 we discussed reliable learning programs, and the work of the formal learning theorists. Recall that among things they consider in an abstract and formal way is the existence of 'inductive methods', that is, algorithms, into which are fed as inputs increasing initial segments s_n, which have the ability to identify truth-values of hypotheses defined in the set of infinite histories as n tends to infinity. As Kelly remarks, Hume's argument effectively rules out the existence of a method which will identify the truth of such a hypothesis at any finite stage across all possible sequences s (in all 'possible worlds'), and the results obtained are mostly technical theorems, interesting in themselves but of little epistemological significance. They are often rather restrictive. One of them (Kelly 1996, proposition 4.10), for example, shows that the hypotheses verifiable in the limit of increasing data occupy a place very low in the relevant topological hierarchy (in Baire space); very roughly, the ranks in this hierarchy, the Borel hierarchy, indicate increasing complexity. By contrast, the probabilistic convergence-of-opinion theorems place no such restriction on the complexity of what can be 'learned' from experience in this probabilistic sense (for a discussion of this point see Earman 1992, chs. 6, 9), because that is only 'with probability one'.

For the same reason, it should be clear that these convergence results do not conflict in any way with the claim that Hume's Problem is unsolvable. Convergence to the truth is definitely not guaranteed. For a simple counterexample, suppose the data source can emit only 1s and 0s, and you assign prior probability 0 to the hypothesis H: Only 1s are emitted. Then whatever your sample evidence s_n at epoch n, the probability calculus requires that $P(H|s_n) = 0$, and hence $\lim P(H|s_n) = 0$. Remarkably, it is not even necessary that your prior probability takes the value zero on any hypothesis: there are hypotheses with positive prior probability whose posterior probability never exceeds $\frac{1}{2}$ even on data streams for which they are true (Kelly, 1996: 308, proposition 13.5). And as we saw above, for any time-evolution of any posterior probability on a big enough space there is some prior distribution which will generate it. The convergence of opinion theorems claim only that *according to the agent's own belief function* (always countably additive, incidentally) there is a probability of one of convergence to the truth or whatever. In other words, they state a property not of your posterior probabilities but on your *prior* probabilities, for they prescribe what value your *prior* probability must take on the proposition that your posterior probability converges to the real truth-value of the hypothesis (the posterior probability relative to an n-fold sample s_n is actually a random variable defined on the space).

I said that these theorems are the formal analogues of a similar constellation of theorems of statistical mechanics where the evolution of a system is determined only with probability one. Thus Khinchin:

> The most important problem of general dynamics is the investigation of the character of the motion of an arbitrary mechanical system on the initial data, or more precisely the determination of such characteristics of the motion which in one sense or another 'almost do not depend' on these initial data. (1949: 10; 'almost' is the probabilist's technical shorthand for 'with probability one')

If anything the Bayesian results are stronger, because the physics theorems usually apply only to one type of measure, Lebesgue measure, while the Bayesian theorems apply to any measure satisfying some usually very weak conditions. It is perfectly possible for there to be system-evolutions which are exceptions to the 'rule', but such exceptions are collectively of probability zero in the set of initial conditions (a perfectly elastic sphere traversing a box exactly parallel to one wall would be an exception to the 'law' of increasing entropy). I also said that the probability model to prove these results required countable additivity. In fact, what is used to prove all these theorems is the full theory of measure, an extremely powerful mathematical tool developed in the nineteenth century to achieve results of the greatest generality, and in particular to provide a theory of what should be meant by there being sufficiently 'few' exceptions to a rule as indeed to prove it in some sufficiently strong sense. In refining our understanding of the very notion of generality in this way the development of measure-theoretical probability must count as one of the most important conceptual innovations of the twentieth century.

The generality of the Bayesian convergence-of-opinion theorems is of course a generality in what is necessitated ('almost') *as a condition of consistency in the agent's own belief structure*. To this extent these results might appear to take the Kantian revolution, in which man is placed firmly at the centre of things, a bit too far. Thus another remarkable theorem, due to Dawid, asserts that with probability one in the limit of increasing sample-data the agent's posterior probabilities will be 'calibrated', in the sense (roughly) that they match observed frequencies (Dawid 1982). But what I must believe 'with probability one' need bear no relation to the truth of the matter: the fact that I must be certain that I will be calibrated in Dawid's sense does not imply that I actually am. In fact, the theorem allows me to be uncalibrated on infinitely many data streams. But theorems like these do allow us to answer in an interesting way the question posed in Chapter 6: why are we so certain that our beliefs correspond in some sufficiently good way to the facts? The usual answer, as we noted, is a not-terribly-satisfactory appeal to natural selection, not terribly satisfactory because even if the theory of natural selection is correct, the use of to explain social and cognitive aspects of human behaviour notoriously requires a good deal—many people think far too much—by way of untested additional assumptions. Here we have another explanation: *we are often consistent uncertain reasoners*.

These convergence-of-opinion results seem to present again, however, the paradox discussed in Chapter 6: they tell us that even though we may appreciate the force of the Humean argument that induction is invalid, if we have suitably non-vanishing priors we should still be inductive reasoners. Of course, the resolution is in the non-vanishing priors, which we now know to be the classic inductive premiss. Note also that grue has had its teeth drawn as well: we must believe in the limit that with suitable evidence even a grue hypothesis will be correct. We noted in Chapter 2 that we do believe all sorts of sudden-change-of-phase hypotheses, and in Chapter 3 that inconsistency is avoided because the convergence to the truth-value is non-uniform across the class of competing hypotheses.

Must Bayesian Agents Accept the Most Probable Theory?

Ironically, most of the criticisms of the Bayesian model charge it with being *insufficiently* plastic to accommodate established patterns of empirical reasoning, and on the contrary embodying patterns of inference that are not only not exemplified in practice but which it would be insane to demand exemplified. For example, one of the most persistent charges of Popper's against inductive probability is that the model it supplies implies that scientists should value always the most probable hypotheses, and in the limit necessary truths:

> In one way or another the various probability theories of induction establish too much, and in most cases more than is intended; they do not merely give an estimate of the degree to which a theory has been tested, *but they dictate in every case which theory we ought to accept as the best theory, that is to say, the most probable theory.* (1983: 335; my italics)

At first sight it will probably appear astonishing that a mere theory of consistent assignment of probabilities could be viewed in this light. But there is something interesting in this absurd charge none the less, for in most people's minds there is a link between high probability and acceptance. Intuitively, acceptance of a hypothesis, in the sense of using it as a basis for action etc., is consequent on a certain probability-threshold being exceeded (this value may of course depend on the individual involved, and his or her taste or distaste for risk). The most likely explanation, which seems supported by the italicized part of the quotation, of Popper's otherwise puzzling charge is that it results from the following inference: acceptance of H as an explanation of the facts requires a high enough probability; *therefore* the most acceptable explanation is that which has the highest probability.

That inference is clearly invalid. We could leave matters there except for a well-known problem, or alleged problem, with this account of acceptance, which is commonly held to be vulnerable to the so-called *lottery-paradox*. Due to Kyburg (1983), this goes as follows. Suppose the threshold probability for acceptance is x, where x is sufficiently close to but strictly less than 1 (if x were 1 very little would ever get accepted). Let n be any positive integer such that (n − 1)/n exceeds x; clearly for any choice of x short of 1 itself there must be such an n. Now consider a fair lottery with n tickets numbered 1 to n. The probability that any given ticket will win is 1/n, and hence that it will not win is (n − 1)/n. (n − 1)/n exceeds x and so it is accepted that the ticket will not win. Hence for each ticket j it is accepted that j will not win. But equally, since there is probability 1 that some ticket will win, it is accepted that one of these tickets will win. In other words, defining acceptance in terms of exceeding some threshold probability less than 1 entails that the set of propositions accepted is potentially inconsistent.

However, it does not follow that if the set of propositions accepted is inconsistent then an inconsistent set is also accepted. That genuinely pathological state of affairs would only arise from the additional adoption of the following closure principle, that if C is the class of accepted propositions then C is deductively closed, that is, the set of all logical consequences of C, including of course the *conjunction* of those elements, is in C. But such a closure principle is most certainly not a necessary one, and indeed, as Kyburg pointed out, we can regard the present case as a counterexample to it: each of n propositions may be accepted, in the sense of each having a probability in excess of x, but as we saw above their conjunction certainly need not have a probability in excess of x.

Defining acceptance in terms of a threshold probability has the virtue of simplicity, but it also may be too simple. Maher, himself a Bayesian, has argued that a sufficiently high probability does not seem historically to have counted either as a necessary or a sufficient condition for acceptance (1993: 133–52). Maher takes the plausible view that acceptance is a species of decision and so should be treated decision-theoretically, which in Bayesian terms means in terms of maximizing an expected utility, in this case a type of epistemic or cognitive utility. He even constructs, by means of a representation theorem à la Savage, a restricted family of utility functions. It becomes theoretically possible to accept in this sense a hypothesis firmly believed to be false, because, though believed false, it has a sufficiently large expected cognitive utility. In general, measures of verisimilitude can be constructed, though there is nothing like consensus on which is correct, or even whether there is an unambiguously correct measure (see Niiniluoto 1998), which rank *false* theories in terms of truth-likeness.[8] This fact is of considerable importance in view of the phenomenon emphasized in the writings of Cartwright, that science habitually uses models of phenomena which are 'known' to be false (the scare quotes are a nod in the direction of the general fallibilism in all things epistemological that most people now take for granted).

People Are Just Not Bayesian Reasoners

Empirical research into the psychology of reasoning carried out in the 1960s and 1970s by Kahneman, Tversky, and others seems to show rather conclusively that the Bayesian model isn't a model of the way people actually reason at all. Not only that: individuals seem to reason in ways that cannot even be reconstructed as Bayesian. For example, they persistently fall into the base-rate fallacy (see above, p. 54), and, if cued in an appropriate way, even believe that a conjunction can be strictly more probable than one of its conjuncts (the well-known 'Lindy the Bank-Teller Problem' is a nice way of showing this). And, of course, there is the fact that people, even highly educated people, are systematically prone to give far too large an estimate of the probability of disease in the Harvard Medical School test.

Kahneman and Tversky's work excited a good deal of discussion. But I took pains to point out earlier that the Bayesian model is *not* intended to be one of how people actually reason. It is a model of sound probabilistic reasoning, which can be as distant as you like, or don't like, from the way people actually reason. There would be

---

[8] Maher himself defines a measure of verisimilitude in terms of a normalized cognitive utility function, in a manner formally very similar to Ramsey's definition of probability (Maher 1993: 228).

cause for concern if people denied that certain patterns of reasoning identified by the model as sound were sound, and one would then want to know why. But that is not the case: in the main, the patterns of deviance identified by Kahneman *et al.* are seen as being incorrect (even by the respondents, when given time to reflect). The fact that the respondents kept getting the wrong answer in the Harvard Medical School test justifiably caused concern, and raised the demand for some sort of remedial education.

I have been using deductive analogies a great deal. Here is another one. The following experiment, due originally to the psychologist P. C. Wason and called after him the Wason selection task, is designed to test people's grasp of a simple type of deductive relationship. Respondents are presented with four cards, face down, and told that on one side of each card is a positive whole number, and on the other side a letter of the Roman alphabet. The cards exhibit numbers and letters on their visible upper faces as follows:

$$A \quad 3 \quad J \quad 4$$

The respondents are asked to indicate those cards which need to be turned over to evaluate the hypothesis H: 'If a card has an even number on one side it will have a vowel on the other'. The experiment has been performed over and over again, always with very similar results: a large majority of respondents indicate the cards with 4 and A on them. But this is incorrect, as far as the usual canons of deductive reasoning are concerned. The correct answer is 4 and J, since if on the other side of the 4 card there is a consonant H is false, and if on the other side of the J card there is an even number H is false also. Should neither counterexample be found, H is true. But turning over the A card will yield no information about the truth-value of H.

Wason's experiment has generated an enormous literature attempting, I believe as yet rather inconclusively, to explain the entrenched response (for a current assessment see Evans and Over 1996). Whatever that explanation will turn out to be, however, it is beside the point of this discussion. The fact that people systematically disobey some rules in certain contexts does not mean that those rules do not provide a good account of the correct performance of an intellectual task, and even an account regarded by the violators as the correct account. The ability to perform correct probabilistic calculations seems not to be something that many people are not innately good at. But so what? The fact is that people are now deliberately trained to be good at it, and they are trained because it is increasingly widely recognized that probabilistic reasoning is sound reasoning—as indeed it is.

Bayesian Networks

I have stressed the fact that prior probabilities are exogenous parameters in the Bayesian model, and that they correspondingly take up the role of the sorts of synthetic premisses in inductive arguments that Hume correctly diagnosed must be present, however artfully concealed. But prior probabilities are not the only synthetic assumptions to play such a role. We saw earlier that de Finetti's exchangeability assumption (Chapter 4, p. 72) is just such another, able to generate the classic Humean inductive inference in which increasing data push the posterior probability of the next instance towards 1. Exchangeability is a weak independence assumption, and (probabilistic) independence judgements also themselves play a powerful supporting role. For example, we do not believe that the colour of an experimenter's eyes will in general be a factor influencing the outcome, and embody this in a corresponding likelihood assumption, $P(E|H) = P(E)$, where E is any outcome and H is the proposition describing eye-colour. All the useful applications of the theory are actually built on such assumptions.

They also play a crucial role in a recently developed and increasingly very important type of Bayesian modelling, so-called *Bayesian networks*. Since these are the subject of a great deal of study, particularly in view of the fact that they have great practical application as the basis of many successful expert systems, a brief description will not be out of place. A Bayesian network is a probabilistic model of a self-contained network of factors which influence each other in a hierarchical way, and is usually represented by, in the jargon, a directed acyclic graph in which nodes are the factors and the directed edges (connecting lines) display the possible dependencies between the factors. A common example is a diagnostic system, in which the nodes of the corresponding graph are a set of possible diseases and their symptoms, with the edges directed from the diseases to their respective, possibly joint, symptoms. The strength of the link in the network between parent and descendant nodes is represented by the conditional, or posterior, probabilities of the latter given the former.

If designed to be implemented on a computer, as it often is, the network is a type of expert system, and one reason why Bayesian networks have sprung into prominence is that a characteristic feature they embody makes the computation of the joint probability distribution over all the nodes more of a practical proposition than it otherwise would be. If the nodes constitute a set of n logically independent propositions, joint distributions over them require assignments to 2^n elements. Even to store that amount of information takes massive memory (2^{40} is around a million million, for example). More importantly, the sort of estimates that the average expert would be confident with will strongly underdetermine this distribution, even if their evaluations are probabilistically consistent. Generating a complete consistent distribution even for such applications therefore poses very severe problems. Representing the expert's knowledge (or beliefs, to be more accurate) as a Bayesian network goes some way towards a solution: consistency is automatically guaranteed, and the amount of storage required is usually dramatically reduced to the point where it becomes feasible. These properties flow directly from the central feature of such networks that they incorporate Markov-like assumptions of probabilistic independence whereby each node is conditionally independent of all other nodes in the hierarchy except its direct parents and its descendants.

The consistency problem is solved because such independence assumptions uniquely determine the joint distribution (Paris 1994: 135–6). Storing a Bayesian network in memory need not be an insurmountable task because the number of independent constraints the network represents is a function only of the number and sizes of the sets of factors directly influencing each node, and to orders of magnitude only the latter count. If these are not too large storage is feasible. Nor is this way of representing the expert's beliefs an arbitrary one. It is plausible precisely because the making of independence judgments is a ubiquitous and indispensable part of everyday life, and while probabilistic dependence is a broader category than causal dependence, a judgement of causal independence will usually translate into one of probabilistic independence. For this reason Bayesian networks seem the natural tool for modelling diagnostic and other systems intended to represent possible causal links and their strengths, at any rate as judged by the expert. For more information on this topic of growing importance in the field of artificial intelligence the reader should consult Pearl (1988), and for a more recent summary of results Paris (1994).

A Dynamic Equilibrium Model

This chapter started with a general discussion of what the Bayesian model was supposed to be a model of. I have presented it as a model of *reasoning from evidence* that I think represents, more or less, characteristic varieties of informal evidential reasoning that seem widely used in science. It has been fashionable for some time, however, to play down more or less traditional models of scientific inference, like this one, in which attempts to systematize and explain inductive reasoning as some species of sound reasoning are assigned a central role, as fundamentally misleading. In a celebrated discussion (1953), Quine proposed a holistic model in which science, indeed knowledge as a whole, is seen as a single entity like a confined field constantly striving to maintain an internal dynamic equilibrium. The effect of experience is initially felt as a shock at the periphery which is then propagated throughout the interior, rather than being embodied in discrete *local* inferences from data to hypotheses.[9] Later authors emphasize the undoubtedly considerable role played by often imperfectly understood technology, murky interfaces between experimental and theoretical procedures, 'trading zones', guesswork and hunches masquerading, and sometimes not even masquerading, as reasoned conclusions, the mechanical application of inappropriate statistical techniques, and much else that allegedly shows the inappropriateness of logic-driven models of inference from observation reports.

No doubt much of that is true. But the dangers of inference from noisy data are also well known. Too much attention to fitting the data results in overfitting, the using up of large numbers of adjustable parameters to result in a model that is almost completely unexplanatory, in the sense of concealing rather than revealing the underlying dynamics of the system. The fact is that there is evidence of an under-

---

[9] According to Quine (1953: 42), 'total science is like a field of force whose boundary conditions are experience'. It is interesting, if not ironical in view of the normal perception of it, that the Bayesian theory plus the principles of Bayesian and Jeffrey conditionalization is a quasi-Quinean theory of the influence of experience, since the acquisition of new information effects a global change in causing the passage to a new belief *function*.

lying logic to scientific inference, that it is not all merely a process of unreasoned movement to a state of lowest energy. Like any other activity the rational part of it will be bounded by all sorts of pragmatic factors. But there may still be underlying norms which exert an influence which may be quite powerful. I stressed that I do not (unlike many Bayesians, it is true) see the Bayesian model to be a model of even rational *behaviour*, let alone one of quotidian scientific behaviour. It is a model of a type of consistent reasoning, and those principles of consistent reasoning that it identifies do seem to find a respondent echo, more or less distant possibly, in some quite standard procedures of scientific inference. The degree to which those procedures can be represented within the model is sufficiently impressive, I believe, as to provide evidence—I now take off the Humean hat—that the logic of scientific discovery really is that of epistemic probability.

Chances

There remains some unfinished business. Increasingly, *chance* occupies a foundational role in modern science: in quantum mechanics, in statistical mechanics, in population biology, in genetics, in control theory, in communication theory, and more. Perhaps surprisingly in view of this, there is still some controversy about the nature of chance itself. Depending on the answer to the question of what chance is will be the answer to the subsidiary question of how hypotheses about chances are to be empirically evaluated. One thing seems agreed by everybody, however: these hypotheses do not make definite, categorical predictions however much detail about the usual sorts of initial conditions is supplied. And therein, of course, lies a rather large problem. If such hypotheses, *statistical hypotheses* as we called them in Chapter 5, simply do not make predictions in the ordinary sense, what does it mean—indeed, what could it possibly mean—to say that observable data confirm or disconfirm them? The Bayesian theory offers a promising line of attack in that the likelihood terms $P(E|H)$, the point at which the evidence itself enters the calculation of posterior probability via Bayes's theorem, do not demand there to be any deductive relation between H and E. One of the great merits of the Bayesian over other models of theory confirmation, particularly deductivist ones, is that it has this function inbuilt at the outset, an integral part of its 'inference engine'. Historically, the first great success of the Bayesian theory was Bayes's own calculation of the precise form of the posterior probability distribution for a chance. It is now thought that the calculation was possibly a little over-precise, depending as it did on a use of the principle of indifference that even Bayes was hesitant about. But the general procedure that Bayes introduced is not compromised, and in the next and final chapter we shall see what it is and why it works.

9

Chance and Probability

'Winwood Reade is good upon the subject,' said Holmes. 'He remarks that, while the individual man is an insoluble puzzle, in the aggregate he becomes a mathematical certainty. You can, for example, never foretell what any one man will do, but you can say with precision what an average number will be up to. Individuals vary, but percentages remain constant. So says the statistician.'

(Sir Arthur Conan Doyle, 'The Sign of Four')

Introduction

Since the beginnings of probability theory it has been broadly accepted that a knowledge of objective chances should determine one's epistemic probability; though not of course conversely. Though as I say it has been broadly accepted, the explanation of why and exactly how it should be so has been the subject of a good deal of discussion. Indeed, a diversity of explanations has been offered, including the 'null explanation' by Lewis and Levi that the dependence needs no explanation, but is somehow constitutive of the meaning of chance. The situation is further complicated by there being different *theories* of objective chance. I present one here, the only one that as far as I can see permits any explanation at all of the relation between a knowledge of objective chance and degree of belief. That explanation will also provide the means by which the Bayesian model is extended to the evaluation of chance hypotheses.

The literature on objective chance is a large one. It is also the arena for much controversy. I have added this final chapter after some heart-searching, because it is not likely to settle any of the issues currently debated, and nor is chance central to the topic of this book either. But some discussion is, I think, required, for chance is so fundamental to modern scientific theorizing that it is really incumbent on anyone proposing a model of inductive inference to show how chance hypotheses fit into it. The following account will be brief, but I hope to the point, even if it may strike those who have become (understandably) bound up with the ideas of David Lewis on the subject as devoting insufficient attention to them. In my opinion Lewis's theory disqualifies itself from the outset by implicitly defining chance, via what Lewis calls the 'Principal Principle' (below, p. 231), in terms of its relation to *beliefs*. It is like defining 'energy', or 'mass', in terms of how beliefs should be affected. Strangely, perhaps, in a work that is devoted to advancing the claims of a belief-based subjective notion of probability, I cannot regard a theory which in effect subjectivizes chance as adequate to explain its role as a foundation-stone of science. Most scientists who express an opinion on the nature of chance give chance an objective definition in terms of frequencies. The frequency approach has its problems—I shall mention them in what follows—but it does not subjectivise chance and it is, I believe, capable of withstanding the objections made to it. At any rate, it is this understanding of chance that I shall broadly support in the following pages.

Chance

The eighteenth and nineteenth centuries saw many experiments consisting of very large numbers of repetitions of a 'random' trial, like throwing dice or tossing coins. Bouffant and others tossed a coin many thousands of times and discovered that as the number of repetitions increased so the variation in the proportion of heads observed grew smaller and smaller, and that by the thousandth or so trial it was very small indeed. Similarly with dice: as the number of throws increased so again the variation in the observed proportions of each face diminished and grew very small. Meanwhile, during the nineteenth century, developments in the physical sciences and demography began to reveal that large enough aggregates of individually random events in a variety of contexts betrayed similar behaviour. For example, as Laplace had noticed, the proportions of male and female births were very nearly constant from department to department in France. Later in the same century the kinetic theory of gases provided evidence of virtually constant proportions of molecules in the same velocity-intervals, and the Scottish physicist James Clerk Maxwell famously discovered the functional form of the frequency-distribution to them.

These developments are the background to an identification that has had profound consequences in the mathematical sciences, at any rate in those mathematical sciences in which stochastic (i.e. randomly generated phenomena) of some sort or other are modelled: the identification is that of *chance* and *frequency*. The remarkable propensity of certain types of repeatedly instantiable conditions to generate apparently random outputs at the individual level but very uniform proportions for large enough aggregates of the individual outcomes was noted by Richard von Mises and made the empirical basis of his *Frequency theory* (the best informal exposition is still the classic account in von Mises 1957; a slightly more detailed one is given in von Mises 1964, ch. 1, or Howson and Urbach 1993, ch. 13). Today it is customary to regard the long-run stability of the observed proportions or frequencies, of each of the various possible outcomes, as evidence of a characteristic *tendency* in the experimental conditions to produce such outcomes, a tendency which is naturally measured by its visible effect, the long-run frequency with which the outcomes actually occur. Thus Pitowsky:

In the classical theory of probability [the chance interpretation], the observational counterparts of the theoretical concept 'probability distribution' are the relative frequencies. In other words, as far as repeatable . . . events are concerned, probability is manifested in frequency. (1994: 98)

Tendencies and chances are, in normal discourse, different sides of the same coin (no pun!): the inverse relation to 'the tendency of set-up S to deliver outcomes of type A' is 'the chance of getting As on S'. Thus von Mises's empirical law of large numbers suggests a model in which random event-generators determine *chance-distributions* over the class of possible outcomes, the numerical measure of the chances being the long-run proportions of the various outcomes.

It is very easy to show that $P(A)$, interpreted as 'the chance of getting As' (on a specified experimental set-up) and measured by the long-run frequency or proportion of As in repeated trials, satisfies the probability axioms I–III. We also obtain a new insight into the definition of conditional probability $P(A|B) = P(A\&B)/P(B)$ where $P(B) > 0$. $P(A|B)$ is (it is also easy to show) the proportion of As among the B-type outcomes. We can also note that the axioms continue to hold in the limit as the sample size m tends to infinity. This last fact is important, because it gives a precise mathematical sense to the otherwise vague 'long run'. Obviously, for any finite number k of trials the proportion pA of A-type events will necessarily be changed just by increasing k by one so long as pA is not zero or one, so we cannot consistently take 'the long run' as being any fixed number. This difficulty vanishes by going to the limit in an infinite sequence of trials, which is just what von Mises did, *defining* the (chance) probability of A to be the limiting value of the proportion of As in the sequence. The frequency definition did not originate with von Mises: there was a preceding line of thinkers who also thought of probability in these terms, starting it seems in the nineteenth century with John Venn, the author of Venn diagrams. Nor was von Mises by any means the last to adopt such a frequency definition of objective probability. But von Mises added something else of the first importance to the frequency idea, as we shall see.

Despite its widespread adoption by working physicists and statisticians, the frequency definition has been subjected to a good deal of criticism, some of it apparently well-founded. A principal objection is that since an infinite sequence of trials can never in principle be performed, any statement about limits of proportions in infinite sequences of trials is at best untestable, at worst meaningless (see e.g. Jeffrey 1992: ch. 11). Nobody can ever carry out an infinite sequence of trials, and even in a long enough finite one the equipment will distort and eventually wear out. The problem is exacerbated by the fact that a limiting value of the proportion of As in an infinite sequence of trials is consistent with any behaviour of the frequency in a finite initial segment, so that even if any sense could be given to sequences going on forever, we could never know what the limit of the frequency would be:

Quantum theory predicts only probabilities, and hence, in some strict sense, makes no physical predictions at all: every prediction refers in some strict sense only to an infinite-n limit that can never be physically realised. (Stapp 1989: 164)

To this extent the frequency definition appears to render chance hypotheses immune from empirical evaluation.

One way often suggested for getting round the problem is to appeal to a group of theorems of the mathematical theory, called 'laws of large numbers'. The first, historically, was proved by James

Bernoulli in his great work (1715), and is now known as the *weak law of large numbers*. Suppose that we are looking at a repeatable experiment and considering a particular outcome A of it. Suppose also (*a*) that the chance of A occurring at any given repetition is constant, equal to p, and (*b*) that the probability of any getting any specified sequence of As and non-As is simply the product of their probabilities p, 1 − p; in this case the repetitions are said to be *probabilistically independent*. Any sequence of trials satisfying (*a*) and (*b*) is called *i.i.d.*, standing for 'independent, identically distributed'. Bernoulli proved that if the sequence of repetitions is i.i.d., then as the number of repetitions tends to infinity the probability that the difference between the proportion of As and p is as small as one likes tends to 1. A stronger version of Bernoulli's theorem for i.i.d. trials, appropriately called the *strong law of large numbers*, states that if we consider the uncountably infinite set of all possible outcomes of infinite sequences of repetitions of the experiment, then with probability arbitrarily close to 1 there is a point at which thereafter the difference between the proportion of As is confined within an arbitrarily small interval around p. If a stronger additivity axiom (the axiom of countable additivity) is used, as it usually is by mathematical probabilists, then the strong law can be proved in a very simple form: it says that with probability 1 the limit of the proportion of As, as the number of repetitions tends to infinity, is equal to p.

Writing P(A) for p, probabilistic independence is easily shown to be equivalent to the condition that $P(A_i|X) = P(A_i) = P(A)$, and $P(-A_i|X) = P(-A_i) = 1 - P(A)$, where A_i says that A occurs at the ith trial, and X is any sequence of past outcomes before the ith trial (Howson and Urbach 1993: 41, 42). This is usually interpreted to mean that the chance of any given outcome is independent of previous outcomes, which seems to be a plausible assumption about classic repeatable random trials like coin-tossing, dice-throwing, etc. where there seems to be no causal connection between earlier and later outcomes (though the relation between probabilistic and causal independence cannot be pushed too far: it is not difficult to think of probabilistic dependencies with no direct causal connection). It also seems plausible that the other component of i.i.d., the constancy of the chance from trial to trial, is satisfied; at any rate over short enough historical periods before the apparatus wears out etc. So Bernoulli's theorem seems to make the prediction that in such trials there is a very high chance that we shall see the proportion of As fall within some small (and actually computable as a function of the number of trials) interval around P(A). Moreover, the strong law says that the chance is 1 that the limiting proportion of As will actually be equal to P(A). Doesn't all this make our earlier numerical definition unnecessary? And more than unnecessary, wrong? For the strong law also suggests that there is no necessity for the limiting proportion to be equal to P(A) if there is such a limiting proportion—since the convergence is merely something that is asserted to happen with a chance of 1; and indeed some have taken the law to implicitly suggest that there might not even be convergence to that or any limit.

On the other hand, it is not clear how without very strong additional assumptions such laws of large numbers explain the connection between chances and frequencies in repeated trials, or indeed explain any observed phenomenon at all. Bernoulli's law states that with a chance approaching 1 frequencies will be close to chances in i.i.d. trials. To take that as making a statement about actually observed frequencies presupposes that some sort of interpretative bridge between empirical fact and hypotheses about chance has already been established, which is just what the theorem is alleged to provide. The empirical character of law of large numbers explanations appears therefore to be just as questionable as that of von Mises's limiting frequency hypotheses. Not only that: von Mises's theory has if anything the explanatory advantage in being able to show that random trials which generate convergent relative frequencies *must* be i.i.d.

To show this requires going into some of the details of von Mises's theory. Because it is somewhat peripheral to the main concerns of this book I shall give only a sketch. Von Mises thought that a scientific theory of chance phenomena should satisfy two basic principles. The first we are already familiar with, that on repeated trials relative frequencies should converge to some characteristic value. This is the principle of *convergence*. The second is the one that makes the outcomes genuinely 'chancy': they must occur *randomly* within these sequences, or *Collectives* as von Mises called them. The intuitive idea underlying von Mises's technical definition is that outcomes occur randomly in a sequence if there is no computational method, which may if required also input reports of all the outcomes already observed, of picking out trials to bet on for which the odds of success differ from the average. Odds are functions of probabilities, and in a limiting-frequency theory of probability the randomness criterion becomes this: there should be no algorithm, which at any point can input information about past outcomes, for picking out an infinite subsequence in which the relative frequencies of the various types of outcome differ from those in the original Collective. It is now possible to show that this definition, together with the convergence principle, implies that the outcomes making up a Collective are i.i.d. (see von Mises 1967; a simpler discussion is in Howson and Urbach 1993: ch. 15). So what appears as a separate and not easily justifiable postulate in 'laws of large numbers' explanations actually emerges as a straightforward deductive consequence of the two basic principles of von Mises's theory.

There is a rather obvious problem none the less with the formal definition of randomness as it stands. According to it the two infinite sequences 1,1,1,1,1,1,1 . . . ; 1,2,3,4, . . . are random, since there is certainly no way of selecting an infinite subsequence of either sequence in which the relative frequencies of any of the characters tend to different limits; in the first sequence, the limiting relative frequency of 1s in any infinite subsequence will also be 1, and in any infinite subsequence of the second sequence the limiting relative frequency of any integer n will still be 0. But these sequences are highly *non-random* according to our intuition, and it would seem that von Mises's formal explication is at best incomplete. Fine (1973: 100) suggests a way of strengthening the randomness condition which would exclude this and other types of problematic sequence, but there is an obvious way of excluding the sequences above, which is to stipulate in addition that there should exist no method of actually predicting the outcome on the basis of some identifiable characteristic of any particular trial in the sequence.

There are other explications of randomness quite different from von Mises's. The best-known and most highly developed is that developed independently by Chaitin and Kolmogorov in which a (finite) sequence is said to be random if it cannot be reproduced by means of a program at least as short as the sequence itself. Such a sequence is random in the intuitive sense of there being no more simple rule for predicting, that is, reproducing, its members than the production of the sequence itself. This theory, sometimes called the 'incompressibility' and sometimes the complexity theory of randomness, was extended to infinite sequences by Martin-Löf and others. Unlike this account, von Mises's does not provide an account of the randomness of finite sequences, and intuitively we do often feel inclined to attribute randomness to these. On the other hand, it is something of an open question whether there is even a uniquely determined concept of randomness there to explicate; if anything, the evidence suggests otherwise. But in von Mises's account we do at least have something that underwrites the statistician's working definition of random samples as sequences of i.i.d. outcomes. Maybe that is not the last word, but it is good enough for most purposes.

Single-Case Chance

One thing von Mises's theory of probability does not do is ascribe chances to the outcomes of single trials, like the chance of this coin landing heads at this toss. This is held by some (though not by von Mises, for reasons of which we shall shortly be aware) to be a weakness of that theory, and alternative so-called single-case theories have been developed, principally by David Lewis and Popper (I am referring to his propensity theory). According to these accounts not only does it make perfectly good sense to speak of the chance of an event at any given single trial, but it is *necessary* to do so if theory is to be brought into contact with empirical data—because even a sample of n trials is a single trial of a new set of experiental conditions specified by repeating the original one n times. I shall briefly deal with these claims in turn (there is a longer discussion in Howson and Urbach 1993: ch. 15).

Consider the repeatable experiment of tossing a particular symmetrical and evenly balanced coin. In the account I have offered, 'the chance of heads is in a small interval around ½' relative to these conditions means nothing more than 'the apparatus would, repeated indefinitely in the same ambient circumstances, generate a collective in which the frequency of heads would converge to a value in a small interval around ½'. In Lewis's and Popper's (otherwise rather different) accounts, however, it is claimed in addition that the chance of a head approximately equal to ½ *is a property of each separate toss of the coin*. But there is a telling objection to that claim. The chance is allegedly ½ because the structure of the coin provides a symmetry of causal influence, and this is exhibited in the long run frequency of heads being close to ½. But that particular toss is one in which the upward force is applied to a particular point of the coin, at a particular point above the surface onto which the coin will fall, where the energy of the system after the impulse is rapidly dissipated in a particular way depending on the state of the gaseous medium at the time, etc. The coin plus tossing mechanism plus surrounding atmosphere is presumably a (large-scale) quantum system in which there is a certain amount of indeterminacy; nevertheless the more accurately the initial conditions are specified the more accurately the path of the coin is determined. A closer specification of the parameter-values at that toss will very likely give a chance of heads closer to 1 or 0.

This would seem to imply that the chance of a head at any given toss is almost never ½ or anywhere near it. A further consequence is that the usual coarse-grained statistics for such events, like sample frequencies, will at best only give correspondingly coarse-grained average values of the chances, and certainly not values that can be applied to individual cases. But this means that with nicely balanced and symmetrical coins which when tossed large numbers of times yield frequencies of close to ½ cannot be credited with generating chances of ½ at each toss. All we would appear able to say is that, depending on circumstances which we do not and probably cannot even in principle know in any detail, the chance, if it exists, is very close to 1 or 0. And this means in its turn that we have a theory which is almost never applicable in any interesting way to the vast majority of problems where we should want to apply it (quantum mechanics might be an exception).

Moreover, there also seems no reason to suppose that non-frequency chances should even satisfy the probability axioms. With frequency theories like von Mises we know that they do because the probability calculus is also a calculus of frequencies, including limiting frequencies, as can easily be checked. Lewis has an argument why they should: it is that where we have a knowledge of chance distributions, epistemic probabilities should be equal to those chances. This automatically guarantees that chances are formally probabilities, but Lewis's only argument for that principle appears to be that it is one everyone accepts more or less as an axiom. That is hardly an argument. As we shall see in the next few sections, a frequency theory of chance by contrast provides the basis for a very good argument for the principle, which in its turn shows how sample data can provide information about frequency-chances, sufficient in principle to devise empirical tests of hypotheses about chances in collectives.

Beliefs and Chances

It was pointed out earlier that there is a compelling intuition that there is some connection between chances and beliefs. In Chapter 7 we considered the view that beliefs should be equal to chances where the latter exist, but as we saw this apparently obvious answer faces serious difficulties.

A useful way to begin answering some of the objections is to observe that though we can't assume as yet, or indeed ever, that we know what the chance distribution over the set of possible outcomes of some particular experimental set-up is, we can consider how we should adjust our beliefs *conditional on information of that sort* (why this is a helpful way to start off will be apparent later). So consider the piece of information, call it B, that the chance of A is q on a particular experimental set-up S, and consider also what your degree of belief in the occurrence of A should be on the supposition simply that B is true. We are in effect trying to evaluate a conditional probability of the form P(A|B), where B = 'Chance(A) = p'. It is tempting to set this conditional probability equal to p: symbolically

$$P(A|\text{Chance}(A) = p) = p. \qquad (1)$$

This might not look well-formed, because of the double appearance of A; and with the second embedded in the functional expression Chance(A) which is itself a member of the domain of P. But there is no definitional regress here despite the appearance of one. The space of possibilities w is one which simultaneously confers truth-values on propositions like A not themselves referring to chances and assigns values between 0 and 1 inclusive to a class of random variables, *parametrized* by A,B,C, etc., which are misleadingly written 'Chance(A)', 'Chance(B)' etc., though they depend not on A but on w. It would be better possibly to write them explicitly in standard form as random variables depending on w, like $X_A(w)$, $X_B(w)$, etc., but I shall continue to use the informal expression 'Chance(A)' rather than the more forbidding X_A.

Rule (1) is an ancient one, ancient at any rate relative to the development of the mathematical theory of probability. Indeed, it is crucial to Bayes's own seminal paper, in which he set himself precisely the task of evaluating the posterior probability of a conjectured chance distribution. However, Bayes didn't, unusually for someone otherwise so careful to list all the postulates that he considered necessary to his argument, list this rule as a separate one. In fact, only well after Bayes wrote was the procedure identified and named: Jeffreys calls such conditional probabilities 'direct probabilities' (1961: 57), though it is often now called by the whimsical name, the 'Principal Principle', conferred on it by David Lewis (1980: 266–77). At any rate, (1), the principle of direct probabilities, the principal principle, or whatever the reader's favourite moniker for (1) is, is a fundamental Bayesian principle, crucial, as we shall see later, to its method of evaluating statistical hypotheses (recall that a statistical hypothesis is a hypothesis about a chance distribution).

Before that, we must see how (1) is justified—if it is. First—and an important point when introducing additional principles—it is easy to see that (1) will not lead to inconsistent probability assignments, because we know from Chapter 4 that chances themselves obey the probability axioms. So (1) is certainly a consistent way to relate probabilities to chances. Secondly, and more interestingly, it is the *only* consistent way of doing so. For suppose for some value, say s, other than q were assigned as the value of $P(A|\text{Chance}(A) = q)$. Also suppose 'Chance(A) = q' is true, and you were to bet k times with stake 1 at odds $s/(1 - s)$ on A, m of which you win (i.e. A occurs m of those k times). Then you would gain $m(1 - s)$ and lose $(k - m)s$, so your net gain would be $m - sk = k([m/k] - s)$. However, by the definition of chance, m/k tends to q since 'Chance(A) = q' is true. Hence in the limit your net gain would be $k(q - s)$, which is non-zero since by assumption $q \neq s$. So by betting at what are alleged to be fair odds you face the possibility of a guaranteed positive net gain or loss, contradicting the assumption that s was the value determining fair odds.

An interesting question is raised by this simple demonstration. Why, if it is a valid principle, is (1) not a probability axiom? And more seriously, how can we have a completeness result for the probability axioms excluding (1)? The answer is very simple. The axioms are provable complete relative to certain items in the vocabulary of the theory receiving suitably fixed interpretations, just as the usual axioms and rules of inference of deductive logic are provably complete relative to suitably fixed interpretation of the so-called logical constants which may or may not include identity, the connectives, quantifiers, and so forth. What is not regarded as fixed for the purpose of the completeness theorem in Chapter 7 is the interpretation of the propositions which are the arguments of the probability function, the As, Bs, Cs, etc. However, the validity of (1) clearly depends on interpreting one such argument, 'Chance(A) = r', in the usual way as a distribution of chances, understood as long-run frequencies, over some subset of the domain of P. When we do so, (F) generates the additional constraint (1).

Rule (1) expresses the general form of the way belief about chances interacts with belief in the occurrence of events in the outcome-spaces of chance-generating experiments, or, to use the terminology favoured in discussions of the chance-like 'reduction of the wave-packet' in quantum mechanics, of methods of preparation. That link expressed in (1) will turn out to be also the empirical link between finite observational data and the truth or falsity of hypotheses. Before we see how, there is a loose end to be tied involving once again the problem of countable versus finite additivity.

Countable Additivity Again

Rule (1) says that in suitable circumstances one's epistemic probability distribution over the outcomes of a chance-generating set-up should be identified extensionally with a chance distribution over those outcomes. Now epistemic, or Bayesian, probabilities are countably additive, and therefore, according to (1), so must chances be. But there is evidence which, prima facie, suggests that chances are not, at any rate when measured by long-run relative frequencies. Suppose we generate an infinite sequence in which every integer occurs with a determinate limiting relative frequency, namely 0, since $0 = \lim(1/n)$ as n tends to infinity. Also, the sequence is a *random* one in the sense of von Mises. However, the limiting relative frequency with which the infinite disjunction '1 or 2 or 3 or . . . or n or . . .' is satisfied in that sequence is 1 because that disjunction is exhaustive of all the possibilities, while the sum of the limiting relative frequencies of each disjunct is 0, since each of these is 0 and the sum of a countable number of 0's is 0. Hence the limiting frequency distribution for that Collective is not countably additive.

Later in his life von Mises did impose countable additivity as an additional constraint which relative frequency distributions had to satisfy in order to qualify as a Collective, but he did so in a way that seemed merely an *ad hoc* response to the objections of mathematical probabilists who were accustomed to the superior mathematical formalism its incorporation engenders (at any rate in what is called the measure-theoretic treatment due to Kolmogorov). There are, however, considerations that render it compelling. Consider all the subsets of the natural numbers of the form $\{n, n + 1, n + 2, \ldots\}$, open intervals in the usual order topology, and their intersections as n increases (the intersection of any family of sets is the set of members all have in common). It is not difficult to see that the intersection of all these open intervals as n tends to infinity is the empty set, extensionally speaking the impossible event which we know has probability 0. Now the probabilities of the sets $\{n, n + 1, n + 2, \ldots\}$ cannot increase as n increases (justify this observation by what you already know of axioms I–III and their consequences), and for infinitely many values of n must decrease. Intuitive continuity considerations would seem to require that the limit of the probabilities of that decreasing sequence of nested open intervals should tend to the probability of its limit, that is, of the empty set. *But it is not too difficult to prove that this continuity requirement is actually equivalent to countable additivity!* Indeed, it was in the form of exactly that continuity principle that Kolmogorov in his famous monograph (1956) introduced the constraint of countable additivity. For all these reasons, therefore, that axiom seems an independently natural one to impose on chance distributions.

Estimating Chances

Historically the first major scientific application of the Bayesian theory was in the area of evaluating a chance hypothesis, and it was made by none other than Bayes himself in his celebrated memoir (1763). It might seem at first blush that there is no special need of the Bayesian or any other sophisticated theory here: chances are measured by long-run frequencies, so to estimate any chance all one has to do is to examine the associated long-run frequency. But, as we noted earlier, matters are far from being so simple; on the contrary, on a closer examination they could hardly appear less promising. For 'long-run' actually means 'limiting', and not only is no mortal capable of examining what happens at infinity, but long before that point—infinitely long—not merely the mortal but the hardest bits of the hardware will all be long gone. And the sorts of finite data we can examine in repetitions of an observation conducted under similar conditions are very finite indeed, sometimes rather small. But however extended the data are, the brute mathematical fact remains that *the limiting value of any sequence imposes no constraints whatever on what happens in any initial segment.* The possibility of any empirical check on chance hypotheses seems hopeless.

That conclusion is premature. Recall the result mentioned a little earlier that inbuilt into von Mises's Collectives is the i.i.d. property, that the outcomes occur probabilistically independently of each other, and the same outcomes have the same chance of occurring at each point. This feature is represented in a derived Collective C_n obtained by partitioning the first one C into n-tuples, so that if C is an outcome of the original experiment repeated indefinitely often, C_n represents a sequence of indefinitely many repetitions of the experiment of repeating the original one n times. Remarkably, it is possible to show that C_n is a Collective if C is (see Howson and Urbach 1993: ch. 13, for a more extended discussion of these rather subtle points). The significance of that result for our discussion is that it tells us how to compute the chance of obtaining any particular outcome-sequence obtained by tossing the coin n times, relative to the derived collective C_n. A striking property of this chance is that it depends only on the number r of heads in the sequence, not on the order in which the heads and tails actually appear. Label such an outcome $e(r,n)$; then the chance is

$$\text{Chance}(e(r,n)) = p^r(1-p)^{n-r}, \tag{2}$$

where p is the original chance of heads. The proof is immediate from the independence and constant probability properties. The constant probability of heads is p, and of tails $1-p$, and independence implies that these multiply. Thus the chance of a sequence of r heads, occurring each with chance p, and $n-r$ tails, occurring each with chance $1-p$, is given by the right-hand side of (2).

The term 'constant probability' in this context should not be misunderstood. We know that von Mises's theory is emphatically not a single-case theory. In that case it might be asked how von Mises probabilities can be constant from trial to trial. But there is no contradiction: the answer is implicit in the observation that the Collective with respect to which these probabilities are referred is C_n.

For what we are talking about is the constancy of the probability of heads in the n-fold outcomes of repeating the first experiment n times in succession. So now we are dealing with a sample space S_n of all the possible 2^n n-tuples of heads and tails. On S_n these n 0,1-valued random variables X_i, $I = 1,2, \ldots ,n$, are defined such that $X_i(w) = 1$ if the ith member of the n-tuple w is a head, and 0 if it is a tail. '$X_i = 1$' says that the ith outcome in the particular sequence w of n tosses is a head. To say that heads and tails occur independently with constant probability means only that the X_i are independent random variables and $P_n(X_i = 1) = P_n(X_j = 1)$ for all distinct i,j, such that $1 \leq i,j \leq n$, where $P_n(X_i = 1)$ is the limiting relative frequency (in C_n now!) of n-tuples having a head at their ith place. In other words, constant probability from trial to trial does not refer to any specific tosses: it means only that the limiting relative frequency in C_n *of n-fold outcomes* having a head at the ith place is the same for all $i = 1,2, \ldots ,n$.

Note that (2) is derived from the sole hypothesis, call it H(p), that the coin tossing generated a Collective in which the chance of heads is p; (1) therefore tells us that $P(e(r,n)|H(p)) = p^r(1 - p)^{n-r}$. Our observational data from n tosses of the coin will of course be e(r,n) for some particular value of r. Bayes's theorem tells us that

$$P(H(p)|e(r,n)) = \frac{P(e(r,n)|H(p))P(H(p))}{P(e(r,n))} \tag{3}$$

and we can immediately substitute $p^r(1 - p)^{n-r}$ for $P(e(r,n)|H(p))$ in (3). Now suppose, as above, that we are interested in the relative odds on two different hypotheses, H(p) and H(p'), about the value of p based on the same data e(r,n) (since chances can take any values in the unit interval, which is a continuum, the prior and posterior probability distributions over chances will generally be continuous, in which case we should strictly regard P(H(p)) and P(H(p')) as probability-densities, and their ratios as odds-densities; but we shall ignore this complication). We correspondingly form the ratio P(H(p)|e(r,n))/P(H(p')|e(r,n)), obtaining

$$\frac{P(H(p)|e(r,n))}{P(H(p')|e(r,n))} = \frac{p^r(1 - p)^{n-r} P(H(p))}{p'^r(1 - p')^{n-r}P(H(p'))} \tag{4}$$

The picture will become clearer when it is seen that the function $p^r(1 - p)^{n-r}$, considered as a function f(p) of p with parameters r and n, has a single maximum at p = r/n, the relative frequency of heads in the sample e(r,n). This is suggestive, and even more suggestion is conveyed by the behaviour of f(p) as n is increased: the curve comes to resemble more and more closely a vertical spike at p = r/n, with the values of f(p) away from that point rapidly becoming negligible in relation to the maximum. Suitably normalized, the function $p^r(1 - p)^{n-r}$ (the *likelihood function* in the statistical terminology introduced by Fisher) is itself a probability-density distribution over the values of p, where of course these are located in the interval, called the closed unit interval, between 0 and 1 inclusive. In statistical theory the measure of the spread of values around the mean of this distribution (the mean is approximately equal to r/n for large n) is called the standard deviation. This is of the order of $1/n^3$, which tells us that as n increases practically the whole of the mass of the distribution becomes very quickly concentrated in a small neighbourhood around r/n.

We can now relate the behaviour of f(p) to (4). If p is sufficiently close to r/n, and p' is sufficiently distant from p, then (4) will become very large, to an extent that is increasingly insensitive to the magnitudes of either P(H(p)) or P(H(p')), assuming neither is 0. The same obviously remains true interchanging p and p'. This result is of the first importance. Given the priors P(H(p)) and P(H(p')), (4) allows us to compute exactly the posterior odds ratio for those hypotheses, and tells us that if p is sufficiently distant from p' and neither of the priors is too extreme this odds ratio will become very small or large for quite moderate values of n. In other words, far from not being able to use finite frequency data to discriminate between hypotheses about chance, we can assess exactly how much frequency data we need to make judgments of the relative credibility of chance hypotheses (but recall the remark earlier, that the priors H(p) and H(p') are likely to be prior densities, so we are talking really of finite prior *probabilities* only in small regions including p and p').

In fact, much more than this can be, and has been, done. Bayes himself, by dint of making suitably restrictive assumptions about the experiment he was describing—in effect he assumed that *only* chance could explain its outcomes, and he used the principle of indifference to justify a uniform prior probability distribution over the chances— gave an exact form for the posterior distribution of p conditional on e(r,n) (it is what is called a beta distribution). People have also been experimenting with other types of chance model than von Mises's (though it is fair to say that something like that model remains the one that scientists would acknowledge as the one they subscribe to if pressed on the matter). That model, as we saw, implicitly asserts that all chance phenomena must be fitted into a fundamental i.i.d. model. To a surprising extent this can be done: for example, chance systems exhibiting strong internal dependencies, like Markov chains, can be accommodated within such a model by regarding the attributes of the underlying Collective as entire stochastic processes. But a fundamentally i.i.d. model is still thought by many statisticians to be far too limited in scope to be applicable to the whole range of indeterminate phenomena that might be brought into the domain of systematic empirical theorizing, and often a very artificial theoretical environment for many of the systems which might be accommodated within it (for an excellent discussion of these issues, and the proposal of a quite different type of model, which he calls a *probability forecasting system*, see Dawid 1984). Still, in however temporary and transient state the sorts of statistical theorizing outlined above might be, it is still pretty much mainstream science, and its reconstruction within the Bayesian theory gives it a rationale that is otherwise wanting. Though other theories of statistical inference, like Fisher's and the Neyman–Pearson theory purport to be able to reach similar conclusions, we have seen in the earlier discussion that the way they do so is by the invocation of fallacious principles, in particular those underlying the No Miracles argument. It is not a historical accident that the Bayesian theory was developed to a very considerable extent by people, like Bayes and Laplace, and later Jeffreys, de Finetti, and Savage, trying to solve the fundamental problem of statistical inference, how finite observational data bear on hypotheses which do not make predictions, in any deductive way, about what can be observed in finite samples.

To those who are worried that such a conclusion might seem to conflict with the earlier denial that there is a positive solution to Hume's Problem, there are two things to be said. First, the posterior discriminations of the sort described above depend, if they are at all definite, on certain conditions on the prior probabilities being satisfied, as we have taken some care to note; and, if the earlier discussion is correct, it is in the priors that the question-begging that Hume declared present in all inductive argument is located. The object of the exercise above is to show that when these are fixed in the way people tend to fix them the Bayesian model—unlike any other that I am aware of—delivers a coherent and consistent reconstruction of the conclusions people do in fact draw from sample evidence.

Now let us change the example slightly and instead of considering the posterior probability, or more accurately probability-density, of a particular value or values of p, look instead at the posterior distribution F(p)—again, usually a density distribution—over the entire range of possible values of p, that is, over the closed unit interval. The fact that for large sample size n the likelihood function $p^r(1 - p)^{n-r}$ assumes the form of a sharp spike in the neighbourhood of p = r/n, taking negligible values over the remainder of the range of p, means that the prior distribution over p becomes increasingly unimportant in determining the posterior distribution, so long as it doesn't actually vanish anywhere near r/n. As is often remarked, this means that the precise form of the non-vanishing prior is fairly unimportant if the sample is sufficiently large; indeed, one might as well start off with a uniform prior as any other: in the long run the result will be the same to within the bounds of any assignable error. This property of the likelihood function also underlies the weak law of large numbers, and the convergence of the posterior distribution above is itself a type of law of large numbers (according to the eighteenth- and nineteenth-century writers it represented the successful 'inversion' of Bernoulli's law).

Finale

We have solved Hume's Problem in about the only way it could be solved, by divorcing the justification for inductive reasoning from a justification of its consequences. *Inductive reasoning is justified to the extent that it is sound, given appropriate premisses.* These consist of initial assignments of positive probability that cannot themselves be justified in any absolute sense. The 300-year-old programme for an inductive logic based on formal probability has arrived finally at maturity, ceasing at last to be merely a controversial and inconsistency-ridden bag of mathematical tricks; now, for the first time in its long history, it can display its own explanatory credentials as an authentic species of logic, kindred to deductive logic. We now know what it can do and what it cannot. Hume told us what it cannot do. What it can do is reconcile the correctness of his sceptical arguments with the entrenched belief that there are none the less sound inductive arguments. So there are, but like sound deductive arguments, they don't give you something for nothing: you must put synthetic judgements in to get synthetic judgements out. But get them out you do, and in a demonstrably consistent way that satisfies certainly the majority of those intuitive criteria of inductive reasoning which themselves stand up to critical examination.

Surely that can't be all there is to scientific rationality? Possibly not: I have scrupulously avoided discussing scientific rationality, partly because it is a highly contested area, but mainly because this is a book about *logic*, not about rationality. The rules, if there are any, determining what is rational and what is not to believe or do I am happy to leave to others to fight over. But what I do believe, and I believe that this extended footnote to Hume shows, is that no theory of rationality that is not entirely question-begging can tell us what it is rational to believe about the future, whether based on what the past has displayed or not. This is not to say that evidence tells us nothing. The trouble is that what it does tell us cannot be unmixed from what we are inclined to let it tell us. Increasing observational data certainly, *provably*, reinforces some hypotheses at the expense of others, but only if we let it by a suitable assignment of priors. We would like to think that an unbroken sequence of viewings of green emeralds reinforces the hypothesis that all emeralds are green. Unfortunately, it can equally be regarded as reinforcing the hypothesis that all emeralds are grue, which is inconsistent with the favoured hypothesis, unless we prevent it doing so by assigning appropriate prior weights. Without our assistance, the evidence cannot tell us that the course of Nature may not change, or for that matter remain the same in emeralds' continuing grueness. Nothing can. Hume was right.

Coda: 'Of Miracles'

Although Hume was not what today we would call a probabilist, remarks scattered about his philosophical writings show his probabilistic instincts to have been sounder than those of many a modern expert (we saw, for example, his penetrating, and wholly valid, criticism of the principle of indifference earlier in Chapter 4), and nowhere is this more true than in 'Of Miracles'. In this famous essay, a sustained polemic against the Christian and all faiths founded on alleged miracles, Hume proposed an explicitly probabilistic condition for regarding miracles as 'established' by testimony. At the time and subsequently there was a great deal of interest in how the new science of probability could be applied to the problem of the credibility of witnesses, and many results, not all equally respectable, were obtained. Hume's is actually one of the more respectable (though this has been contested). What is chiefly remarkable about it from the present point of view is that it provides a simple example of how an intuitive probability judgement is mirrored in the mathematics of probability.

Hume's own statement of his criterion in the *Enquiry* is clear enough:

That no testimony is sufficient to establish a miracle, unless the testimony be of such a kind, that its falsehood would be more miraculous, than the fact, which it endeavours to establish. (1748: X.1)

To see whether he is correct, however, we need to know exactly what Hume means by 'miracle'. In the same essay he explicitly defines a miracle as 'a violation of the laws of nature', a definition which has puzzled many commentators because it appears to contradict Hume's own sceptical philosophy. This is not really so. Hume is speaking in descriptive mode, in which a law of nature is a type of phenomenon that has so often been found to occur that, our innate expectations being of the kind they are, we cannot help but assign it a maximal or near-maximal probability of always being repeated in the same circumstances. There is, however, no implication that we are correct to do so. The point of Hume's criterion is to show that it is virtually a self-defeating strategy to argue for miracles, and hence indirectly for 'God', by appeal to the testimony of onlookers or others. For miracles have, by definition, a prior probability of close to zero. Hence, given what we know about the ability of people to be deceived easily, at their own behest or others', it can be virtually discounted that the probability of their being mistaken is actually *less* than that prior probability: it is bound to be much greater.

So everything turns on Hume's criterion. Is it right? Here I shall follow the account of Gillies (1991; my notation will differ slightly from his), who provides a Bayesian reconstruction of it in which it is a necessary condition for the credibility of a miracle given testimony. I shall then extend Gillies's account to show that the criterion is sufficient also—as Hume himself claimed it was. Let H stand for what the testimony claims, that is, 'the miracle [as described in the testimony] really occurred', and E for the testimony was supplied in the circumstances described by some general background information to which, as background, we can assume P assigns the value 1. Let $p = P(H)$, assumed to be very small, and let q be the probability that the testimony as given is false. How should we express this formally? Well, q can't just be the probability of M being false, because that does not involve the fact that it was testified to by people who may be unreliable, a possibility that is of course central to Hume's argument. Accordingly, q must be the probability that the testimony was supplied, in the given circumstances, *and* is false; i.e. $q = P(E\& - H)$.

This is Gillies's reading of 'the probability that the testimony is false', and I believe that it is the correct one. It is opposed by Earman on the ground that $P(E\&-H) = P(-H)P(E|-H) = P(E)P(-H|E)$; the last two products involve respectively $P(-H)$, the prior improbability of the miracle, and $P(E)$, the probability of the testimony having occurred as it did, and Earman claims that both these are irrelevant to the probability of the testimony being false (1998: 45). However, against that view, I maintain that both these quantities are highly relevant to the chance that the witness(es) would have testified falsely. First, the less the chance that the miracle occurred the less is the chance that the *content* of the testimony is true (these two propositions are clearly equivalent: the equivalence is an instance of Tarski's well-known T-schema), and secondly, the greater the probability that the witness(es) would testify anyway the greater, in the circumstances assumed, is the probability that they would testify as they did *had* the miracle not occurred, and this latter conditional probability is intuitively closely related to the chance of the witness(es) testifying falsely. In fact both assertions, that in the circumstances of very small $P(H)$, $P(E)$ is approximately equal to $P(E|-H)$, and that in those same circumstances $P(E|-H)$ is approximately equal to $P(E\&-H)$, are easily provable: the theorem of total probability,

$$P(E) = P(E|H)P(H) + P(E|-H)P(-H),$$

tells us, given the smallness of $P(H)$, that $P(E)$ is approximately equal to $P(E|-H)$, the probability of the testimony having been given on the supposition that the miracle did not actually occur, while Earman's first identity above tells us that if $P(H)$ is very small then $P(E|-H)$ is approximately equal to $P(E\&-H)$.

If all this is correct then we can express Hume's criterion formally as the condition that q, that is, $P(E\&-H)$, must be less than p, that is, $P(H)$, if the existence of the miracle is to be 'established' by the testimony. To evaluate Hume's claim we therefore need a precise formal rendering of what it means to 'establish' H through E. It might appear that, in explicitly probabilistic terminology, Hume means $P(H|E) = 1$. But this would be too strong. His text makes it clear that he intends something much more like a 'balance of probability' judgement in favour of one possibility and against the alternative to it:

When anyone tells me, that he saw a dead man restored to life, I immediately consider with myself, whether it be more probable, that this person should either deceive or be deceived, or that the fact, which he relates, should really have happened. I weigh the one miracle against the other; and according to the superiority, which I discover, I pronounce my decision, and always reject the greater miracle. (1748: X. 1)

A 'balance of probability' judgement in favour of some alternative is one which says that it is more probable than not, i.e. which has probability in excess of one half. So let us see what follows from assuming that there is a 'balance of probability' judgement in favour of H conditional on E, that is, that $P(H|E)$ exceeds ½. Well, we know that we can write

$$P(H|E) = \frac{P(E|H)P(H)}{P(E|H)P(H) + P(E|-H)P(-H)}$$

and we know that $P(E|-H)P(-H) = P(E\&-H)$. Hence

$$P(H|E) = \frac{P(E|H)P(H)}{P(E|H)P(H) + P(E\&-H)}$$

On the right hand side of the last identity we now have both the terms, $P(H)$, that is, p, and $P(E\&-H)$, that is, q, of Hume's criterion. On the other hand, we also have $P(E|H)$, which does not figure explicitly in it. However, Gillies shows that independently of the value of $P(E|H)$ it follows that if $P(H|E) > \frac{1}{2}$ then $q < p$ (1991: 256). This follows very quickly, in fact, for if we write $P(E|H)$ as a, then the last identity states that

$$P(H|E) = \frac{ap}{ap + q}$$

m and it follows immediately that $P(H|E) > \frac{1}{2}$ if and only if $q < ap$. Since $a \leq 1$, we infer that if $P(H|E) > \frac{1}{2}$ then $q < p$.

Thus Hume's criterion is a *necessary* condition for the miracle being more probable than not given the testimony. But Hume seems to have intended it also as a sufficient condition:

If the falsehood of his testimony would be more miraculous, than the event which he relates; then, and not till then, can he pretend to commend my belief or opinion. (1748: X. II)

Was Hume wrong in believing that his criterion was sufficient? Gillies does not address this question, but it is easily answered. If a < 1 it is not difficult to see that there are values of p and q such that we can simultaneously have $P(H|E) \leq \frac{1}{2}$ and $q < p$, but if $a = 1$ then for all values of q and p, $q < p$ implies that $ap/(ap + q)$, that is, $p/(p + q)$, $> \frac{1}{2}$, that is, $P(H|E) > \frac{1}{2}$. Thus a necessary and sufficient condition for Hume's criterion $q < p$ being itself a *sufficient* condition for $P(H|E) > \frac{1}{2}$ is that $P(E|H) = 1$. But I think we can reasonably assume this: that is to say, had the miracle occurred in the circumstances described then testimony to that effect would *certainly* have been forthcoming. It certainly is assumed in the continuing debate on Hume's discussion and I am certain that it was assumed by Hume himself. At any rate, grant it and we do indeed have P(E|H) = 1 and Hume's criterion as a necessary *and* sufficient condition for a balance of probability verdict in favour of miracles.

Hume undoubtedly had an ulterior motive in presenting his criterion, which is both a fairly commonplace piece of common sense and a novice's exercise in the probability calculus. His motive was to undermine the support for religious and particularly Christian faith that the various testimonies to the observation of miracles provided or were thought to provide. For, granted the exiguous independent probability of a miracle really having occurred, granted that the quality of the testimony, often at long temporal distance, often by primitive people, often at second or third—or greater—hand, and finally, granted Hume's criterion, it follows that the testimony provides no support at all. Unfortunately for Hume's purpose, however, his criterion turns out to be a double-edged sword. It encouraged the analytical investigation of the probability of testimony, a subject which accounted for a fairly substantial amount of the work of eighteenth- and nineteenth-century probabilists (Condorcet, Laplace, and Poisson are the great names), and in the course of the investigation the possibility became apparent that sufficiently much *independent* testimony would drive the improbability of it all being erroneous down to as small a number, in theory, as could be desired (Charles Babbage, the inventor of the 'analytical engine', seems to have been the first to see this; for a recent discussion and reinforcement of the point see Holder 1998 and Earman 1998). Thus Hume's own criterion can be turned on him. Those that live by the sword...

REFERENCES

Acton, Lord (1960), *Lectures on Modern History*, London: Fontana.

Adams, E. W. (1975), *The Logic of Conditionals*, Dordrecht: Reidel.

Albert, M. (1997), 'Bayesian Learning and Expectations Formation: Anything Goes', unpublished manuscript.

—— (1999), 'Bayesian Learning When Chaos Looms Large', *Economics Letters*, vol. 65, 1–7.

Anscombe, F. J., and Aumann, R. J. (1963), 'A Definition of Subjective Probability', *Annals of Mathematical Statistics*, 34: 199–205.

Armendt, B. (1980), 'Is there a Dutch Book Argument for Probability Kinematics?', *Philosophy of Science*, 47: 583–9.

Babbage, C. (1838), *Ninth Bridgewater Treatise*, 2nd Murray edition.

Bacon, Francis (1994), *Novum Organum*, translated and edited by P. Urbach and J. Gibson, La Salle/Chicago: Open Court.

Bailey, D. E. (1971), *Probability and Statistics: Models for Research*, New York: John Wiley.

Bayes, T. (1763), 'An Essay Towards Solving a Problem in the Doctrine of Chances', *Philosophical Transactions of the Royal Society of London*.

Bell, J. L., and Slomson, A. B. (1969), *Models and Ultraproducts*, Amsterdam: North Holland Publishing Company.

Bernoulli, D. (1738), 'Specimen theoriae novae de mensura sortis', *Comm. Acad. Sci. Imp. Petropolitanae*, 5: 175–92.

Bernoulli, J. (1715), *Ars Conjectandi*, Basle.

Blackwell, D., and Dubins, L. (1962), 'Merging of Opinions with Increasing Information', *Annals of Mathematical Statistics*, 32: 882–7.

Boyd, R. (1990), 'Realism, Approximate Truth and Philosophical Method', in C. Wade Savage (ed.), *Scientific Theories*, Minnesota Studies in the Philosophy of Science, 14. Reprinted in D. Papineau (ed.), *Philosophy of Science*, (Oxford, 1996), 215–56.

Broad, C. D. (1952), 'The Philosophy of Francis Bacon', in *Ethics and the History of Philosophy*, London: Routledge and Kegan Paul.

Bunge, M. (1963), *The Myth of Simplicity*, Englewood Cliffs, NJ: Prentice-Hall.

Carnap, R. (1950), *The Logical Foundations of Probability*, Chicago: University of Chicago Press.

—— (1952), *The Continuum of Inductive Methods*, Chicago: University of Chicago Press.

Carnap, R. (1971), 'A Basic System of Inductive Logic', in R. Carnap and R. C. Jeffrey (eds.), *Studies in Inductive Logic and Probability,* i, Berkeley: University of California Press, 33–167.

—— and Jeffrey R. C. (1970, 1982), *Studies in Inductive Logic and Probability*, 2 vols, Berkeley: University of California Press.

Carroll, L. (1895), 'What the Tortoise Said to Achilles', *Mind*, 4: 278–80.

Casscells, W., Schoenberger, A., and Grayboys, T. (1978), 'Interpretation by Physicians of Clinical Laboratory Results', *New England Journal of Medicine*, 299: 999–1000.

Cussens, J. (1996), 'Deduction, Induction and Probabilistic Support', *Synthese*, 108: 1–10.

Dawid, A. P. (1982), 'The Well-Calibrated Bayesian', *Journal of the American Statistical Association*, 77: 605–13.

—— (1984), 'Statistical Theory: The Prequential Approach', *Journal of the Royal Statistical Society*, A, 147: 279–92.

de Finetti, B. (1964), 'Foresight: Its Logical Laws, its Subjective Sources', in H. Kyburg and H. Smokler (eds.), *Studies in Subjective Probability*, New York: Wiley, 93–159 (de Finetti's paper was published originally in 1937 in French).

—— (1972), *Probability, Induction and Statistics*, New York: Wiley.

Deutsch, D. (1997), *The Fabric of Reality*, Harmondsworth: Penguin Books.

Dirac, P. A. M. (1958), *The Principles of Quantum Mechanics*, Oxford: Oxford University Press.

Dorling, J. (1992), 'Bayesian Conditionalization Resolves Positivist/Realist Disputes', *Journal of Philosophy*, 89/7: 362–82.

Dubois, D., and Prade, H. (1988), 'Modelling Uncertainty and Inductive Inference: A Survey of Recent Non-Additive Probability Systems', *Acta Psychologica*, 68: 53–78.

Duhem, P. (1906), *The Aim and Structure of Physical Theory*, Princeton: Princeton University Press, 1991.

Earman, J. (1992), *Bayes or Bust? A Critical Examination of Bayesian Confirmation Theory*, Cambridge, Mass.: MIT Press.

—— (1998), *Hume's Abject Failure: The Argument against Miracles*, Oxford: Oxford University Press (forthcoming; page references are to the manuscript).

—— *et al.* (1992), *Introduction to the Philosophy of Science*, Englewood Cliffs, NJ: Prentice-Hall.

Edwards, A. W. F. (1972), *Likelihood*, Cambridge: Cambridge University Press.

Evans, B. St. J., and Over, D. (1996), *Rationality and Reasoning*, Hove: Psychology Press.

Field, H. (1980), *Science without Numbers: A Defence of Nominalism*, Oxford: Basil Blackwell.

Fine, T. (1973), *Theories of Probability*, New York: Academic Press.

Fisher, R. A. (1925), *Statistical Methods for Research Workers*, 12th edn., London: Oliver and Boyd.

—— (1935), *The Design of Experiments*, London: Oliver and Boyd.

—— (1956), *Statistical Methods and Statistical Inference*, Edinburgh: Oliver and Boyd.

Forster, M., and Sober, E. (1994), 'How to Tell when Simpler, More Unified, or Less Ad Hoc Theories Will Provide More Accurate Predictions', *British Journal for the Philosophy of Science*, 45: 1–36.

Galison, P. (1987), *How Experiments End*, Chicago: University of Chicago Press.

Garber, D. (1983), 'Old Evidence and Logical Omniscience in Bayesian Confirmation Theory', in J. Earman (ed.), *Testing Scientific Theories*, Minnesota Studies in the Philosophy of Science, 10, Minneapolis: University of Minnesota Press.

Gärdenfors, P., and Sahlin, N.-E. (1988), *Decision, Probability and Utility*, Cambridge: Cambridge University Press.

Giere, R. N. (1984), *Understanding Scientific Reasoning*, 2nd edn., New York: Holt, Rinehart and Winston.

Gillies, D. A. (1991), 'A Bayesian Proof of a Humean Principle', *British Journal for the Philosophy of Science*, 42: 255–7.

—— (1998), 'Confirmation Theory', in P. Smets (ed.), *Handbook of Defeasible Reasoning and Uncertainty Management Systems*, i. *Quantified Representation of Uncertainty and Imprecision*, Dordrecht: Kluwer Academic Publishers, 135–69.

Glymour, C. (1980), *Theory and Evidence*, Princeton: Princeton University Press.

—— (1992), 'Realism and the Nature of Theories', in J. Earman *et al.*, *Introduction to the Philosophy of Science*, Englewood Cliffs, NJ: Prentice-Hall, 104–32.

Goldman, A. I. (1986), *Epistemology and Cognition*, Cambridge, Mass.: Harvard University Press.

Good, I. J. (1950), *Probability and the Weighing of Evidence*, London: Griffin.

—— (1968), 'Corroboration, Explanation, Evolving Probability, Simplicity, and a Sharpened Razor', *British Journal for the Philosophy of Science*, 19: 123–43.

—— (1983), *Good Thinking*, Minneapolis: University of Minnesota Press.

Goodman, N. (1946), 'The New Riddle of Induction', in *Fact, Fiction and Forecast*, Indianapolis: Bobbs-Merrill.

Hacking, I. (1984), 'Experimentation and Scientific Realism', in J. Leplin (ed.), *Scientific Realism*, Berkeley: University of California Press.

Haldane, J. B. S. (1939), *Science and Everyday Life*, Harmondsworth: Penguin Books.

Halmos, P. (1950), *Measure Theory*, New York: Van Nostrand, Reinhold.

Hauptli, B. W. (1994), 'Rescher's Unsuccessful Evolutionary Argument', *British Journal for the Philosophy of Science*, 45: 295–302.

Hellman, G. (1997), 'Bayes and Beyond', *Philosophy of Science*, 64: 190–210.

Hempel, C. (1945), 'Studies in the Logic of Confirmation', *Mind*, 54: 1–26, 97–121.

Hintikka, J. (1992), 'The Concept of Induction in the Light of the Interrogative Approach to Inquiry', in J. Earman (ed.), *Inference, Method and Other Frustrations: Essays in the Philosophy of Science*, Berkeley: University of California Press, 23–43.

Hodges, W. (1974), *Logic*, Harmondsworth: Penguin Books.

Hoel, P. (1971), *Introduction to Mathematical Statistics*, 4th edn., New York: John Wiley.

Holder, R. D. (1998), 'Hume on Miracles: Bayesian Interpetation, Multiple Testimony, and the Existence of God', *British Journal for the Philosophy of Science*, 49: 49–65.

Horn, A., and Tarski, A. (1948), 'Measures in Boolean Algebras', *Transactions of the American Mathematical Society*, 64: 467–97.

Horwich, P. (1982), *Probability and Evidence*, Cambridge: Cambridge University Press.

Howson, C. (1973), 'Must the Logical Probability of Laws be Zero?', *British Journal for the Philosophy of Science*, 24: 153–82.

—— (1983), 'Statistical Explanation and Statistical Support', *Erkenntnis*, 20: 61–78.

—— (1988), 'On the Consistency of Jeffreys's Simplicity Postulate, and its Role in Bayesian Inference', *Philosophical Quarterly*, 38: 68–83.

—— (1997a), 'Bayesian Rules of Updating', *Erkenntnis*, 45: 195–208.

—— (1997b), 'Logic and Probability', *British Journal for the Philosophy of Science*, 48: 517–31.

—— (1997c), *Logic with Trees*, London: Routledge.

—— and Franklin, A. (1985), 'A Bayesian Analysis of Excess Content and the Localisation of Support', *British Journal for the Philosophy of Science*, 36: 425–36.

—— —— (1986), 'A Bayesian Analysis of Content and the Localisation of Support', *British Journal for the Philosophy of Science*, 36: 425–31.

—— and Oddie, G. (1979), 'Miller's So-Called Paradox of Information', *British Journal for the Philosophy of Science*, 30: 253–61.

—— and Urbach, P. (1993), *Scientific Reasoning: The Bayesian Approach*, 2nd edn., La Salle/Chicago: Open Court.

Hughes, R. I. G. (1989), *The Structure and Interpretation of Quantum Mechanics*, Cambridge, Mass.: Harvard University Press.

Hume, D. (1739), *A Treatise of Human Nature*, ed. D. G. C. Macnabb, London/Glasgow: Collins, 1962.

—— (1740), *An Abstract of a Book lately published entitled A Treatise of Human Nature*, ed. J. M. Keynes and P. Sraffa, Cambridge: Cambridge University Press, 1938.

—— (1748), 'An Enquiry Concerning Human Understanding', in *Hume's Enquiries*, ed. L. A. Selby-Bigge, Oxford: Clarendon Press, 1963.

Jeffrey, R. C. (1965), *The Logic of Decision*, Chicago: University of Chicago Press, 2nd edn.

—— (1992), 'Mises Redux', *Probability and the Art of Judgment*, Cambridge: Cambridge University Press.

Jeffreys, H. (1939), *Theory of Probability*, Oxford: Oxford University Press.

—— (1961), *Theory of Probability*, 2nd edn., Oxford: Oxford University Press.

Kac, M., and Ulam, S. M. (1968), *Mathematics and Logic*, New York: Dover Publications.

Kahneman, D., and Tversky, A. (1972), 'Subjective Probability: A Judgement of Representativeness', *Cognitive Psychology*, 3: 430–54.

Kelly, K. (1996), *The Logic of Reliable Enquiry*, Oxford: Oxford University Press.

Keynes, J. M. (1973), *A Treatise on Probability*, London: Macmillan (1st edn., 1921).

Khinchin, A. I. (1949), *Mathematical Foundations of Statistical Mechanics*, New York: Dover Publications.

Kneale, W. M., and Kneale, M. (1962), *The Development of Logic*, Oxford: Clarendon Press.

Kolmogorov, A. N. (1956), *Foundations of the Theory of Probability*, New York: Chelsea Publishing Co.

Korb, K. (1991), 'Explaining Science', *British Journal for the Philosophy of Science*, 42: 239–53.

Kreisel, G. (1969), 'Informal Rigour and Completeness Proofs, in J. Hintikka (ed.), *The Philosophy of Mathematics*, Oxford: Oxford University Press, 78–95.

Kuhn, T. S. (1962), *The Structure of Scientific Revolutions*, Chicago: University of Chicago Press.

Kyburg, H. E. (1983), 'Conjunctivitis', *Epistemology and Inference*, Minneapolis: University of Minnesota Press, 232–55.

Ladyman, J. (1999), 'Review of J. Leplin: *A Novel Defence of Scientific Realism*', *British Journal for the Philosophy of Science*, 50: 181–8.

Landau, L. D., and Lifschitz, E. M. (1958), *Quantum Mechanics*, Massachusetts: Addison-Wesley.

Langley, P., Simon, H. A., Bradshaw, G. L., and Zytkow, J. M. (1987), *Scientific Discovery*, Cambridge: MIT Press.

Laplace, Marquis de (1951), *Philosophical Essay on Probabilities* (first published, in French, 1820), New York: Dover Publications.

Latour, B., and Woolgar, S. (1986), *Laboratory Life: the Construction of Scientific Facts*, Princeton: Princeton University Press.

Leplin, J. (1997), *A Novel Defence of Scientific Realism*, Oxford: Oxford University Press.

Leslie, J. (1989), *Universes*, London: Routledge.

Lewis, D. (1973), 'Probabilities of Conditionals and Conditional Probabilities', *Philosophical Review*, 85, 297–315.

—— (1980), 'A Subjectivist's Guide to Objective Chance', in Carnap and Jeffrey, 1982.

Lipton, P. (1991), *Inference to the Best Explanation*, London: Routledge.

—— (1993), 'Is the Best Good Enough?', in D. Papineau (ed.), *Philosophy of Science*, Oxford: Oxford University Press, 93–107.

McGee, V. (1988), *Truth, Vagueness and Paradox*, Indianapolis: Hackett.

Machover, M. (1996), *Set Theory, Logic and their Limitations*, Cambridge: Cambridge University Press.

Mackie, J. L. (1980), *The Cement of the Universe*, Oxford: Clarendon Press.

Mackinnon, E. (1980), 'The Rise and Fall of the Schrödinger Interpretation', in P. Suppes (ed.), *Studies in the Foundations of Quantum Mechanics*, Philosophy of Science Association, 1–59.

Macnamara, J. (1991), 'Understanding Induction', *British Journal for the Philosophy of Science*, 42: 21–49.

Maher, P. (1993), *Betting on Theories*, Cambridge: Cambridge University Press.

Martin-Löf, P. (1985), 'A Limit Theorem which Clarifies the "Petersburg Paradox" ', *Journal of Applied Probability*, 22: 634–43.

Matthews, R. A. J. (1998), 'Facts versus Factions: The Use and Abuse of Subjectivity in Scientific Research', *Working paper, European Science and Environment Forum*.

Maxwell, N. (1998), *The Comprehensibility of the Universe*, Oxford: Oxford University Press.

Mayo, D. (1996), *Error and the Growth of Experimental Knowledge*, Chicago: University of Chicago Press.

—— (1997), 'Error Statistics and Learning from Error', *Philosophy of Science*, 64: 195–212.

Mill, J. S. (1891), *A System of Logic, Ratiocinative and Inductive*, London: Longman's, Green.

Miller, D. (1994), *Critical Rationalism: A Restatement and Defence*, La Salle/Chicago: Open Court.

Milne, P. M. (1997), 'Bruno de Finetti and the Logic of Conditional Events', *British Journal for the Philosophy of Science*, 48: 195–233.

Milton, J. R. (1987), 'Induction before Hume', *British Journal for the Philosophy of Science*, 38, 49–74.

Montuschi, E. (2001), 'The "Inquisition" of Nature: Francis Bacon's View of Scientific Inquiry', unpublished ms.

Musgrave, A. (1993), *Common Sense, Science and Scepticism*, Cambridge: Cambridge University Press.

Niiniluoto, I. (1998), 'Truthlikeness: The Third Phase', *British Journal for the Philosophy of Science*, 49: 1–31.

Nowell-Smith, P. H. (1961), *Ethics*, Harmondsworth: Penguin Books.

O'Hear, A. (1977), *Beyond Evolution: Human Nature and the Limits of Evolutionary Explanation*, Oxford: Clarendon Press.

Pais, A. (1982), *Subtle is the Lord*, Oxford: Clarendon Press.

Papineau, D. (1993), *Philosophical Naturalism*, Oxford: Basil Blackwell.

—— (1995), 'Methodology: the Elements of the Philosophy of Science', in A. C. Grayling (ed.), *Philosophy: A Guide through the Subject*, Oxford: Oxford University Press.

—— (ed.) (1996), *The Philosophy of Science*, Oxford: Oxford University Press.

Paris, J. (1994), *The Uncertain Reasoner's Companion*, Cambridge: Cambridge University Press.

Pearl, J. (1988), *Probabilistic Reasoning in Intelligent Systems: Networks of Plausible Inference*, San Mateo, Calif.: Morgan Kaufmann.

—— (1991), 'Probabilistic Semantics for Nonmonotonic Reasoning', *Philosophy and AI: Essays at the Interface*, Cambridge, Mass.: MIT Press.

Peirce, C. S. (1960), 'Pragmatism and Abduction', *Collected Papers of Charles Sanders Peirce*, ed. C. Hartshorne and P. Weiss, Cambridge, Mass.: Harvard University Press, 112–31.

—— (1961), 'Pragmatism and Induction', *Collected Papers of Charles Sanders Peirce*, vi, Cambridge, Mass.: Harvard University Press.

Pitowsky, I. (1994), 'George Boole's Conditions of Possible Experience and the Quantum Puzzle', *British Journal for the Philosophy of Science*, 45: 95–127.

Poincaré, H. (1952, *Science and Hypothesis*, New York: Dover Publications.

Poisson, S.-D. (1823), *Recherches sur la probabilité des jugements en matière civile et en matière criminelle*, Paris.

Popper, K. R. (1959), *The Logic of Scientific Discovery*, London: Hutchinson; New York: Basic Books.

—— (1960), 'The Propensity Interpretation of Probability', *British Journal for the Philosophy of Science*, 10: 25–42.

—— (1962), *Conjectures and Refutations*, New York: Basic Books.

—— (1968), Comments on Carnap: 'Inductive Logic and Inductive Intuition', in I. Lakatos (ed.), *The Problem of Inductive Logic*, Amsterdam: North Holland, 285–303.

Popper, K. R. (1970), *Objective Knowledge*, Oxford: Oxford University Press.

Popper, K. R. (1983), *Realism and the Aim of Science*, London: Rowman and Littlefield.

—— and Miller, D. (1983), 'A Proof of the Impossibility of Inductive Probability', *Nature*, 302: 687–88.

—— —— (1987), 'Why Probabilistic Support is not Inductive', *Philosophical Transactions of the Royal Society of London*, A 321: 569–91.

Putnam, H. (1965), 'A Philosopher Looks at Quantum Mechanics', in R. Colodny (ed.), *Beyond the Edge of Certainty: Essays in Contemporary Science and Philosophy*, New York: Prentice-Hall.

—— (1975), *Mathematics, Matter and Method*, Collected Papers, ii, Cambridge: Cambridge University Press.

Quine, W. V. (1953), 'Two Dogmas of Empiricism', in *From a Logical Point of View*, Cambridge, Mass.: MIT Press.

—— (1969), 'Epistemology Naturalized', *Ontological Relativity and Other Essays*, New York: Columbia University Press.

Ramsey, F. P. (1931), 'Truth and Probability', in R. B. Braithwaite (ed.), *The Foundations of Mathematics*, London: Kegan Paul.

Rescher, N. (1990), *A Useful Inheritance*, Savage, Md.: Rowman and Littlefield.

Rissanen, J. (1982), 'A Universal Prior for Integers and Estimation by Minimum Description Length', *Annals of Statistics*, 11: 416–31.

Rosenkrantz, R. D. (1977), *Inference, Method and Decision: Towards a Bayesian Philosophy of Science*, Dordrecht: Reidel.

Russell, B. A. W. (1971), 'Induction', in *The Problems of Philosophy*, Oxford: Oxford University Press (first published 1912).

Savage, L. J. (1954), *The Foundations of Statistics*, New York: Wiley.

Scott, D. and Krauss, P. (1966), 'Assigning Probabilities to Logical Formulas', *Aspects of Inductive Logic*, eds. J. Hintikka and P. Suppes, Amsterdam: North Holland Publishing Company, 219–64.

Shafer, G. (1976), *A Mathematical Theory of Evidence*, Princeton: Princeton University Press.

Shannon, C. E. (1948), 'A Mathematical Theory of Communication', *Bell System Technical Journal*, 27: 379–423, 623–56.

Shapin, S., and Shaffer, S. (1985), *Leviathan and the Air-Pump: Hobbes, Boyle and the Experimental Life*, Princeton: Princeton University Press.

Shimony, A. (1955), 'Coherence and the Axioms of Confirmation', *Journal of Symbolic Logic*, 20: 1–28.

—— (1993), *Search for a Naturalistic World View*, i. *Scientific Method and Epistemology*, Cambridge: Cambridge University Press.

Smith, C. A. B. (1961), 'Consistency in Statistical Inference and Decision', *Journal of the Royal Statistical Society*, B 23: 1–25.

Stapp, H. P. (1989), 'Quantum Nonlocality and the Description of Nature', in J. T. Cushing and E. McMullin (eds.), *Philosophical Consequences of*

Quantum Theory, Notre Dame, Ind.: University of Notre Dame Press, 154–72.

Stove, D. (1984), *Popper and After: A Study of Four Modern Irrationalists*, Oxford: Oxford University Press.

Strawson, P. F. (1952), *An Introduction to Logical Theory*, Oxford: Oxford University Press.

Suppe, F. (1989), *The Semantic Conception of Theories and Scientific Realism*. Urbana: University of Illinois Press.

Swinburne, R. (1979), *The Existence of God*, Oxford: Clarendon Press.

Teller, P. (1973), 'Conditionalisation and Observation', *Synthese*, 26, pp. 218–58.

Urbach, P. (1987), *Francis Bacon's Philosophy of Science*, La Salle/Chicago: Open Court.

van Cleve, J. (1984), 'Reliability, Justification and Induction', in P. A. French, T. E. Uehling, and H. K. Wettstein (eds.), *Causation and Causal Theories*, Midwest Studies in Philosophy, 4: 555–67.

van Fraassen, B. C. (1980), *The Scientific Image*. Oxford: Clarendon Press.

—— (1984), 'Belief and the Will', *Journal of Philosophy*, 86: 236–56.

—— (1989), *Laws and Symmetry*, Oxford: Clarendon Press.

von Mises, R. (1957), *Probability, Statistics and Truth*, London: George Allen and Unwin.

—— (1964), *The Mathematical Theory of Probability and Statistics*, New York: Academic Press.

Walley, P. (1991), *Statistical Reasoning with Imprecise Probabilities*, London: Chapman and Hall.

Ward, K. (1996), *God, Chance and Necessity*, Oxford: One World.

Worrall, J. (1996), 'Structural Realism: The Best of Both Worlds', in D. Papineau (ed.), *Philosophy of Science*, Oxford: Oxford University Press.

INDEX

DATE DUE			
NOV 0 2 2004			